HOW TO RECTIFY

An Introduction to the l   .... of Life

Also in this series

ASTROLOGER'S COMPANION   John & Peter Filbey

ASTROLOGICAL COUNSELLING   Christina Rose

ASTROLOGY OF KARMA   Pauline Stone

ASTRONOMY FOR ASTROLOGERS   John & Peter Filbey

BOOK OF WORLD HOROSCOPES   Nicholas Campion

CHART SYNTHESIS   Roy Alexander

CHINESE ASTROLOGY   Derek Walters

DARK STARS   Bernard Fitzwalter & Raymond Henry

DRACONIC ASTROLOGY   Pamela A.F. Crane

FORECASTING BY ASTROLOGY   Martin Freeman

HARMONIC CHARTS   David Hamblin

HORARY ASTROLOGY   Derek Appleby

HOW TO INTERPRET A BIRTH CHART   Martin Freeman

MUNDANE ASTROLOGY   Michael Baigent, Nicholas Campion & Charles Harvey

NATAL CHARTING   John Filbey

SOLAR AND LUNAR RETURNS   John Filbey

SYNASTRY   Penny Thornton

TWELVE HOUSES   Howard Sasportas

HOW TO RECTIFY
A BIRTH CHART

by

Laurie Efrein

THE AQUARIAN PRESS

First published 1987

© LAURIE EFREIN 1987

British Library Cataloguing in Publication Data

Efrein, Laurie
How to rectify a birth chart: an
introduction to the mathematics of life.
1. Horoscopes
I. Title
133.5'42   BF1728.A2

ISBN 0-85030-528-4

*The Aquarian Press is part of the Thorsons Publishing Group,
Wellingborough, Northamptonshire, NN8 2RQ, England*

Printed in Great Britain by Billings & Sons Limited, Worcester

3   5   7   9   10   8   6   4   2

CONTENTS

ILLUSTRATIONS

ACKNOWLEDGEMENTS

Special thanks to: Elizabeth C. Marshall for her encouragement and assistance in formulating ideas; Al H. Morrison for his patient and skilled mechanical assistance in assembling the diagrams; and to the scores of clients and friends whose charts and lives taught me the contents of this book.

PREFACE

The modern student of astrology has been seriously hindered in relating to astrology's ancient roots in that in those days traditional usages and the world view supporting them were rarely written down, and when they were, the wording was usually terse, so terse as to risk loss of intended meaning. Young men learned astrology directly from master astrologers, to whom they were apprenticed to serve, in daily personal contact and participation. In the absence of sophisticated instruments, all observations had to be confined to readily recognizable phenomena, verified by *direct observation*, with methods imparted from master to student orally.

Astrology is, and always has been, a language of references to time and space. Current thinking in the physics of subatomic particles returns us to the most ancient astrological view that time and space are incidental to kinetic energy, serving as the context in which such energy is considered. In a sense, the latest speculations of cosmology and astrophysics have returned to our oldest astrological model of reality: 'As above, so below' implies simultaneity and symmetry, such as can be *observed and verified* in tangible material reality.

Yet in the absence of explicit written instructions from ancient astrological practitioners, and lack of modern emphasis upon immediate observation as the grounding for astrological work, the specific time/space references inherent in astrology have over a long time drifted into being taken as symbols, and now the symbols have become installed in place of the reality. It is time we discarded the word 'symbol' when considering space and time which is measurable in exacting ways, rather than reducing such to abstract, vague, or non-quantifiable terms. Thus the intent here is to identify the manifestations of cosmic energy in the individual in a space/time context which the astrologer has criteria to identify and assess with exactitude.

One vehicle through which the astrological craft was passed down from the ancients (albeit not in textbook form) was biblically, woven through the book of Ecclesiastes in The Holy Bible (King James version); in a sense, this book by Laurie Efrein is nothing more than the careful spelling-out of the instructions contained in Ecclesiastes, of which some of the technology has been lost in successive translations by scholars unfamiliar with the original practice of astrology, perhaps unaware that what they translated was technical astrological procedures. We do not pursue today all the injunctions found in this biblical book; we have added nothing to the basic concepts, while adapting to using precise published data instead of direct observations of astronomical phenomena.

How to Rectify a Birth Chart: An Introduction to the Mathematics of Life, while not using terminology from the world of physics, nevertheless brings the observational basis of astrological tradition into a modern time/space framework. The key factor here is the care and discipline of the astrologer, actually looking at and recognizing the correspondence between the living individual and the horoscope and, conversely, recognizing when failure of that correspondence indicates that the birth data is in error.

The usages spelled out herein work just as well with the newly-discovered planets as with those observed by the bare eyes of the ancient astrologers. Also, in a somewhat more modern context, this book is a restatement of the procedures used by the great English astrologers of the past three centuries, in adherence to the basic concepts of their tradition.

In the absence of opportunity to participate daily in the practice of a master astrologer, this book is one of the most useful ways to learn to do traditional astrology in modern times.

Al H. Morrison

FOREWORD

Astrological literature is replete with books about how to cast charts, how to delineate charts, how to dissect them and compare them and analyse their symbolism and cycles, as well as how to view them from varying perspectives, such as psychologically, philosophically, and metaphysically. Many methods are offered to judge what will happen in the native's lifetime based upon examination of the birth chart alone.

It is almost as if astrology is something you just sit down and do, with all the guidebooks laid out in front of you, for if you only follow the instructions, it is bound to work.

Astrologers know how often this isn't the case. Some charts do not appear to 'work' (i.e. suggest appropriate delineations) as well as others. Other charts, although they seem to describe the native fairly well natally, do not seem to respond adequately to 'timing' indicators, such as progressions and transits.

Indeed, tracing planetary movements through *time* is a characteristically tricky pursuit. Given the peculiar nature of our 'raw materials'—at root, the many concentric circles of planetary orbits each proceeding at respectively different rates of speed—as soon as we depart from the fixed point of origin, the birth chart, to any succeeding point in the native's life (such as what happened when the native was three?, eleven?, twenty-five?), the chart is thrown into a state of flux. Transiting Venus proceeds at one rate, the progressed Sun at another, the progressed Moon at another, and so forth. To judge what is *dominant* in the multi-orbited picture, the astrologer either juggles his/her attention across shifting focal points, or analyses indicators one by one, and the parts do not necessarily add up to a whole.

With multiple options of focus (the many simultaneous planetary orbits), so intent can the astrologer become upon identifying what 'works', that what is often neglected is what *doesn't*: the discerning of an inappropriate indicator (such as an experience of the character of Mars marked by the advent of Saturn); or recognition that a judgement about the native's life is vaguely-defined because there is little in the astrology to support it. More commonly, an astrologer simply takes the zodiacal positions at hand and tries to make it 'fit' the native's life.

Even when we recognize that the astrology at hand does not seem to describe what is happening in the life, it can be an exasperating task to spot which points in the chart are mathematically out of synchronization, by how great an interval, and to assess what adjustments will enable us to read the chart accurately. Such challenges may approach insurmountability when the starting point of the astrological evaluation, the birth chart, is uncertain, because a birth time is approximate or—real trouble!—unknown. If we are not able to *begin* at some exact, correct birth time, the mathematics of any time *later on* in the life appears a hopeless jumble!

It is no wonder that the astrological field is flooded with so many books about how to delineate the *birth* chart, and so few about what happens astrologically for the *rest* of the native's life! The mathematical complexities can seem prohibitive.

This book is designed to clarify the astrologer's perceptions of those complexities, and to introduce tools which make astrological mathematics manageable: graphic aids, step-by-step thinking, succinct units of measures, mathematical short-cuts; in short, ways of co-ordinating the vast merry-go-round of astrological time into a readable context and clearly-defined focus.

We are also about to venture onto new ground. We will travel not only the world of numbers but into the very dimensions of space and time: our perceptions of both, and how astrology, through its numerical language, links the world of time/space with actual life experience—point-by-point, pattern-by-pattern correspondences between shifting astrological indicators and life itself.

This is astrology's great gift to us: not dry, dull calculations, but the power to translate the patterning, directions, and energies of the lives we live from a graphic, numerical form. How and why the many magical equivalencies between mathematics, time, space, and life itself came into being may be as inscrutable as the act of creation. Whatever their origin, however, they are there not as a burden but as a guide, a way of directing our attention to where our efforts will be the most effective. We are not blind men with canes; mathematics is our way of focusing clear vision from the bewildering mass of objects circulating through the skies, and translating their presence into the realities of human experience.

Now let us clear our minds of distractions, settle down, and imagine a world less complex than the one we have come to know. We are about to depart for a quiet place, far from the cities, pollution and noise, to witness a hallowed, age-old mystery: the moment of birth. Within *it* lies the means to bring astrology down from the skies, off the printed page, out of theories and abstractions, and into the wonderfully exact synchronization coming into view on the pathway ahead: *the mathematics of life.*

PART ONE:
THE LIVING NATIVE
IN TIME AND SPACE

1.
HOW A LIFETIME OF ASTROLOGY IS BUILT IN AT BIRTH

The 'Governing' Influence of the Birth Chart

For the astronomer in his observatory, measuring time as well as space, the spatial location of a planet, taken alone, is insignificant. Every position, however, is accompanied by the *time* of its movement through a specific area of the heavens. It is not relevant to the astronomer that the Sun is in 0 Libra, its zodiacal position; it *is* relevant that the Sun is at autumnal equinox, which is a time/space *relationship*—where the Earth is in space in relation to the Sun at that time of the solar year.

Nor, to the astronomer, is any particular passing moment more significant than another for any human or creative reason. When he has perfectly co-ordinated space with time, his job—from the standpoint of performing the calculations—is done.

The natal astrologer generally takes the astronomical time/space calculations of whatever appears to be the native's birth minute (or birth *hour*, as the case may be!) as is, at face value, in their astrologically-converted form (zodiacal positions); and this is where his/her job *begins:* the job of interpretation. Space and time are now impregnated with *meaning*.

But are we not leaving something out? Yes, of course: the native! We can pose the old, nostalgic question: 'Where were you when. . .' For all the astrologer knows, were he/she to pose that question to any particular native in relation to his presumed birth minute, the answer might come back, 'I was still in my mother's womb', or 'I was already alive and kicking for an hour and twenty-five minutes!' Our chart as calculated is in one space and time; but what if our native was in quite another?!

Let us backtrack a moment. The astronomer, the scientist, has performed the calculations. We, the interpreter, the artist, took those numerical figures and assigned them meaning. Now we discover that at the (presumed) 'moment of birth', the native was nowhere to be found!

Will our interpretations of the 'birth chart' still be valid? Can they be, if they are not interpretations of the *actual* astronomical positions at birth? Logic suggests that there would be something invalid about the interpretation of a birth chart cast for a wrong birth time, whether the astrologer is aware of the time discrepancy or not.

However, this liability appears to be *built into* astrological practice, in that the act of interpretation is once removed from the actual experience of birth. In other words, we don't have to have been personally present at the birth, looking at the clock to time the first breath. We can simply be handed an already-calculated chart (such as, let's say, one cast for 19 July 1969 at 4.30 a.m. in Liverpool), and start right in interpreting it. It matters little whether anyone was actually *in* Liverpool drawing his first breath at 4.30 a.m., the time for which the chart was cast.

Or *does* it matter? If we don't have to experience the birth moment at first hand in order to produce the (presumed) 'birth chart,' don't we nevertheless encounter some 'essence' of the birth moment when we *read* that chart?

Let us relate to that question by imagining an opposite 'birth moment scenario'. This time it is the astrologer who knows nothing of the birth and never interprets that particular birth chart. Will the chart still be operative from the instant of birth onwards? (Note: here is where the very validity of astrology comes into play.) If astrology is valid, *of course it will!* Whether the chart is ever calculated or not, the birth moment was real and experienced by the native. He has his birth chart *within him*—so says the astrologer—whether he understands astrology, believes in it, or curses it to the demons. He can no more divorce himself from the pervasive ramifications of his birth chart than he can step out of his own skin. He is a walking compass, with subtle energies and directional impulses, innate drives and aversions arising from his own characteristic modes of functioning, the reality of which is represented in the chart. He experiences his birth chart more intimately in his everyday functioning throughout the course of his life than any of we astrologers ever will!

To return to the Liverpool chart, if someone was actually born at 4.30 a.m., 19 July 1969 in Liverpool, a chart cast for 4.30 a.m. will presumably be functional throughout the life whether an astrologer ever casts that chart or not. However, if the native was actually born at 3.57 (i.e. an astrologer, a relative, or even some birth document was in error about the actual, exact birth time), will it not be the chart cast for 3.57 that the native will be 'living', notwithstanding that the astrologer is looking at and interpreting a chart cast for 4.30?!

In other words, is it not the astronomy of the *actual birth time* that (we would expect) 'governs' the native's life?

Now let's take this inference and see if it reflects usual assumptions about astrology. The time and space of birth is somehow (we don't know how) internalized within the native from birth, as indelibly as is, let's say, his genetic pattern, which is present in every cell of the native's body throughout his life. At least we assume some type of internalization (whether we can describe it scientifically or not) when we say that the birth chart is 'within' the native. If that birth chart is indeed within, there and doing its work for life, then the birth moment is, in effect, continually reiterated throughout the life as a kind of permanent 'birth moment experience'. This is what we encounter when we read the native's chart *now*.

This much astrologers do agree upon, if tacitly, or no-one could presume to give a natal reading. In other words, we don't say, 'This was your chart at the moment of birth'. We say, 'This is your chart'. For life. Period.

Expanding the Governing Influence to Transits and Progressions

But do the progressions and transits 'govern' the native's life as well? Past points of common agreement about the ubiquitous *natal* chart, concepts about the chart 'governing the native's life' characteristically diverge into a pot-pourri of philosophy (such as the fate/free will issue), psychology (such as 'awareness' of planetary influences determining their effects upon us), abstractions (such as 'synchronicity') and—alas, only occasionally!—pragmatic demonstrations of a limited scope.

Why is there such relatively uniform conviction about the pervasive influence of the *natal* chart, and such diverse opinion about the transits and progressions governing the native's life span in both their overall sweep (a governing *principle*) and at each marking point along the way (life's so-called 'events')?

First, it would seem as though the natal chart is completely out of the realm of personal choice, whereas once a person is living, breathing, changes and grows, and develops faculties of judgement and decision, his fate rests more in his own hands, something which—we rationalize—is the *opposite* of being 'governed'. We say it is 'fate *versus* free will,' and naturally, it is desirable for free will to triumph. We say that 'the stars *im*pel, but they do not *com*pel. We say we always have 'choice', and that nothing need 'govern' us but ourselves, who create our lives on our own terms.

This all sounds humanistic. However, since accuracy of a chart precedes its application to living (i.e. the native born at 3.57 a.m. cannot 'choose' to live the 4.30 a.m. chart, however adept the astrological interpretation), we need enquire if this philosophical viewpoint has emerged because of, despite, or simply in ignorance of astrological reality.

Astrology is very explicit in this regard. The stark reality is that planetary movements (astrology's basis) all the way through the life are completely out of the realm of choice! For example, if your natal ascendant is 5 Sagittarius, Pluto will be transiting 5 Sagittarius in March 1997, again in November 1997 and finally in the summer of 1988. So from the moment of your birth on, you have no choice whatsoever that that transit will arrive on your ascendant at those specific times in the future.

Note here that astrological pedagogy generally separates calculations from delineation (e.g., a major computer service slogan, 'We calculate—You delineate'), so this interrelated unity of astronomical/astrological life has been artifically schismed. Here, in an initial reintegration of that separation, we recognize that planetary movements—the basis of astrological mathematics—are the very basis of astrology itself, without which we would have no zodiacal positions, no houses, no aspects, no way to determine the location of the planets—in other words, nothing to 'delineate' at all!

Moreover, the example of transiting Pluto is only a tiny, microcosmic view of the whole. Every transit, every progression or other type of direction is predetermined and unalterable from the moment of birth on. Just produce a birth chart and an astrologer can map out an entire continuous lifetime of progressions and transits, hard-and-fast figures entirely out of the native's choice!

The birth chart may indeed be 'within you'; but be that the case, your progressions and transits are 'within you', too! What we have, effectively, is an interdependent whole: the birth chart, but also the transits, progressions and other directions are all given, 'predetermined' from the moment of birth, *no less than* the natal chart.

How Much is Predetermined

At this point, some readers might be thinking ahead and wondering how this apparently deterministic situation affects *delineation*? In other words, if the planetary positions are predetermined, are interpretations predetermined as well? (This issue has undoubtedly been astrology's chief bugaboo from the time of the casting of the very first astrological chart.)

This question becomes doubly important in rectification work. Why? Because rather than focusing upon traits, tendencies and predispositions—the usual fare of natal readings—it considers *what has concretely happened* in the life. Actual life experience either *has* corresponded definitively with those predetermined astrological indicators, or it has not. If it has, we call the chart accurate; if it has not, we say the chart is in need of mathematical adjustment.

In one sense, of course, the 'calculations' side of the 'calculations/delineation' unity is necessarily moot, in that we cannot alter the movements of the heavens, so we are obviously encountering an *astronomical* determinism of a rather absolute character. This in itself, note, is no cause for dismay, since every *science* is built upon some form of determinism in the natural universe (obviously so, or scientific experimentation would not produce consistent results), without of itself postulating that it limits human will as we generally understand it.

However, is astrological *delineation* also deterministic? The answer is a qualified yes. It is deterministic, but relatively so. Note, this is not a statement of personal opinion, but necessarily underlies virtually all astrological practice.

For example, when a chart is subjected to numerous Saturn aspects, what happens in the native's life at that time is *Saturnine*, general qualities which are grounded into specific reference by the natal and progressed chart. It *has to* operate in a 'Saturnine' way, not a Jupiterian way nor a Venusian way; and that '*has to*' is a form of determinism. If what happens in the life experience at the time of multiple Saturn aspects is *not* Saturnine, the accuracy of the chart itself might be questioned.

Moreover, if astrological interpretation did not engage in such relative determinism, it would a priori have no validity at all as an interpretive tool.

Now, lest we consider our astronomical, quite absolute determinism limiting of our interpretive purview, a closer look reveals the reverse. If we consider the full complement of planetary and cuspal positions for a natal and progressed chart, along with the transits, as some type of 'road-map for life', then at any particular life juncture, would not relating to a larger overall context—i.e. where *all* the transits are, where *all* the progressions are, and where they are *in relation to the natal chart*—suggest both a greater range of life options (since we are viewing life's 'larger road-map') and a clearer focus upon their specifics (since more details of the road-map will be filled in)?

Indeed, we have a paradox in the making, because ironically, the best way to transcend rigid, limiting, or 'predetermined' delineation, is to take into account a more comprehensive, genuinely absolute determinism in astrology's concrete basis, astronomy. Conversely, the more the astrologer rejects the 'total determinism' of astronomy, the more limited are astrology's 'relatively deterministic' judgements!

A simple, common-sense approach works just as well as intellectual arguments. Since we cannot *alter* any of the millions of separate planets and cuspal positions automatically set into place from the moment of birth, why not view them simply as natural law, an object of knowledge rather than avoidance, since avoiding the inevitable is, at best, scarcely likely to result in 'free choice'. (As a seasoned colleague of mine, Al H. Morrison wittily remarked, 'If you can't see it coming, you don't have the chance to duck!')

Be that as it may, probably many astrologers have eschewed a more incorporative approach to astrological indicators for the simple lack of examples of how such a 'whole picture' *works*. Indeed, with more demonstrations of the incorporative, multi-orbited functioning of the natal chart, progressions and transits all-at-once, perhaps many a reservation would not have developed at all. (Is it not human nature to justify not doing what one has not personally mastered?) In any case, our surest route of correction is a *technical* one. We need charts that are technically accurate prior to debating how the meaning of life might be reflected in them.

Can We Work with the Whole Picture?
The foregoing isn't difficult to follow—basically, that the primary guide for astrological work is the ephemeris and Table of Houses (rather than our philosophical outlook or our psyche), whose 'predetermined' patterns give the basis for *both* calculation and delineation of the unlimited number of possible charts they might generate. From them come the vast array of 'givens' for astrological work, such as the continuous patterning of all the transits and progressions throughout any given life span.

This 'whole picture' is familiar in abstract and general terms. But where is any individual road-map to be found? There seem to be too many positions to plot out—all the changing positions for transiting Venus throughout the life, for example, and all the aspects it successively forms. Moreover, each is fleeting and ephemeral.

The natal chart, in contrast to transits and progressions, is comparatively problem-free. It is simpler to work with, in that it 'holds still', so no-one even quibbles whether or not it is 'deterministic'—even though logic suggests that for each 'predetermined' but fleeting transit, there is a predetermined *permanent* position of that same planet natally, a much more formidable version of 'determinism' indeed!

Our next built-in aid for natal delineation is that we can *see the natal chart visually*. Thus we can isolate and cite its specifics, such as Saturn in the third house, or Venus square Pluto. By contrast, with progressions and transits, even if we bring the parade of planets to a halt at some key moment in life, which planets and cusps demand our focus, and what kinds of relationships give interpretive keys?

Moreover, the characteristics of the natal chart (such as Moon trine Mars or Saturn square Uranus) are a self-contained system which is not substantially altered by a relatively small birth time discrepancy. With the progressions and transits, however, their effect depends upon their *relationship* to the natal chart, and the same small birth time discrepancy (such as five minutes) which might not hinder a natal reading, takes on major significance for a progression or transit. As we will see, that five minutes could easily signify a whole year or more in the native's life!

Given a birth time discrepancy of only minutes, the astrologer could well calculate a full complement of transits and progressions for some key date, only to discover no 'expected' relationship to the natal chart. Given a lack of meaningful correspondences and with no systematic means of chart adjustment, there is neither incentive to plot out an entire *lifetime* of planetary motions, nor—even when plausible aspecting is detected—have there been means to create a readable 'whole picture' across longer timed spans in the native's life (i.e. many years).

We have seen through simple reasoning that not only the natal chart, but a lifetime of planetary motions are 'within us'. If it were not for the natal chart's positioning at birth, those progressions in those exact positions later on would not be; nor would some transiting Saturn or Uranus seem so harsh in its effect were not the natal chart cast as it was, with the ascendant exactly here, Venus exactly there and so on. But how can we be selective, given such a mass of continuous figures for any native's life? How can we see the zodiacal positions in a continuous context, spot which are the most prominent and why and, especially, how can we recognize their effects upon the native?

Well, there is a flip side of this astrological coin that might hold the key. Astrological reality may appear complex, but the key lies in *seeing* it in its simplest, most condensed terms. The better we can see multi-orbited time as a whole unit, the more manageable it will become. Since natal chart, progressions and transits are necessarily interrelated, *why not see them in terms of each other?* Use progressions to *adjust* the natal chart, rather than to confound it. Use the natal chart to assess if the progressions it generates describe the native's actual life experience.

Perhaps instead of plotting out transits and progressions *against* the natal chart, the key lies in viewing them all together as a unified whole.

Sample Models Incorporating Natal, Progressed and Transiting Positions

We are going to begin by constructing some simple visual models of natal, progressed and transiting positions across spans of time. For the moment, we simply want to demonstrate that the three are necessarily interrelated and can be viewed as a unit. By interlinking the three as a continuity with patterns and interrelatedness, rather than a hit-and-miss selection of planets and cusps in an isolated form, the mystery of the chart so-called 'governing' the human life span may seem a bit less mysterious, which will open the door to many of the timing skills that are so vital to rectification work.

An analogy to a familiar means of telling time, the ordinary clock, can serve as a springboard. If we think of the birth chart as a clock, with the planets and cusps as the clock's 'hands', then if it is set to the wrong time to begin with, it will always read the wrong time—earlier or later depending upon in which direction the original mistake was made. If you just said, 'the birth happened *now*, 4.30 a.m.', and never had to look at the chart/clock again, you would never catch the error. But now that we know that the natal chart is not isolated, but part of a 'package' which includes transits, progressions and other directions, we can take those astrological indicators from any *later* point in the life and—should the aspecting between natal and progressed or transiting positions not make sense—develop means to adjust the original (apparently wrong) birth time.

Now, every so-called 'major event' that happens in the life will involve many astrological factors, not just one. But frequently, one special indicator—usually a progressed major aspect involving a chart's *angle*—will set the tone for specific types of changes in the native's life for the period of time it is in orb. The following examples will cite some of the types of single major indicators that are instrumental in major life changes, based upon actual examples from chart rectifications.

First, we will take a hypothetical chart showing only the chart's tentatively-set angles and the natal Mars (Figure 1, A, B & C). Note that for all three charts, the signs on the angles are the same, but they are set at different degree numbers.

A difference of one degree on the midheaven signifies about four minutes' difference in the time of birth, so we are going to postulate that the first chart (A) with 5 Scorpio on the midheaven is cast for 3.12 p.m. on some specific date, the second chart (B) with a 4 Scorpio on the midheaven for 3.08 p.m. (i.e. one degree earlier equals four minutes earlier), and the third chart (C) for 9 Scorpio on the midheaven at 3.28 p.m. (5 Scorpio at 3.12 + 4 degrees at 4 minutes per degree = 4 × 4 [16] minutes later = 3.28). Let's say that the native could have been born at any of these three times.

Now, the position of the natal Mars, shown in each chart, were the native born at 3.08, 3.28 or any time in between will not vary greatly, barely 1' at the most on a day when Mars is moving rapidly; so we are rounding off the natal Mars for each of these charts to exactly the same zodiacal position: 6 Aries.

Each respective chart shows the distance Mars will be travelling to reach the IC of the chart. Let's say it is progressing by solar arc (the same progression rate as the Sun of the chart in question), which moves at approximately one degree per year, rounded off to exactly one degree for this example. Chart A shows a difference of 29° between Mars and the IC; chart B 28°, and chart C 33°. Translated into the native's *age* at each of these respective arcs, it would be twenty-nine years old for chart A, twenty-eight for chart B and thirty-three for chart C.

Certain types of events will characterize the year in which this particular Mars/IC direction becomes partile (i.e. exact). It might have been great stress (Mars) in the home (fourth cusp), let's say a family illness which disrupts (Mars) the home life (fourth cusp)

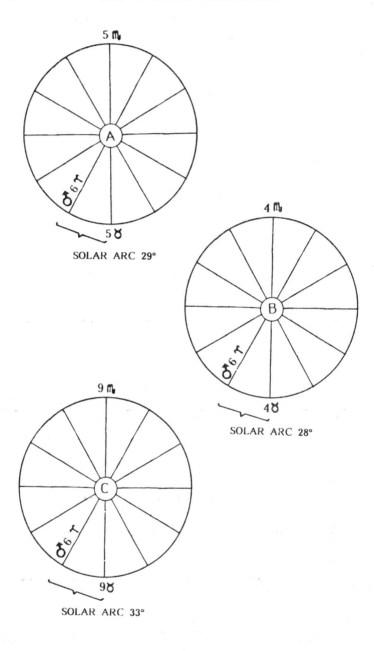

Figure 1.   Solar Arcs

and also interferes with (Mars opposition) the life course and/or career (tenth cusp).

Or perhaps this was the year that the native left home (fourth cusp), but if so, it was stormy, willful or under stress (Mars). Or perhaps the native made a clean break (Mars) from his job (opposition tenth cusp) either by way of 'You're fired!' or 'I quit!' (Mars dissension and/or independence).

Any of these major life changes could be signalled by such a direction, given a supporting context.

Let's say that the native states that such an event took place when he was twenty-eight years old. Assuming that the astrology as a whole confirms such a change at that time, chart B might be the most likely choice. Or let's say he was thirty-three at the time. Then chart C, with 9 Scorpio on the midheaven, might be the true chart.

The key point here is that the natal chart taken alone will not confirm itself. We need to know the *timing* of this particular event (and others), translate the native's age at the time into progressed planetary motion and match up the timing of that moving indicator (in this case, the Mars/solar arc direction) with the original, permanent natal chart. Thus the solar arc direction and the natal chart have become inextricably related to one another.

Now we are going to take the same Mars/solar arc direction to the IC and enlarge its context in two different ways.

First, let's say that for this particular native, the direction coincided with his family's relocation away from his homeland (fourth cusp family/home) under great stress (Mars), as things were politically unstable and volatile. The Mars direction to the fourth cusp shows the major change in circumstances but, in this case, let's say that what actually provoked the move was militiamen firing at the native's home. Gunfire, drama, danger—it would come as no surprise to find *Uranus* transiting the midheaven (and opposition fourth cusp), would it. Uranus opposition fourth shows the home subjected to gunfire, the home environment being suddenly shattered, being forced to move immediately, under crisis.

Let's say that the solar arc at the event was exactly 28°, giving a fourth cusp of 4 Taurus (chart B). Now, when we look at the date on which the native's family was forcibly evacuated, transiting Uranus is found at 4 Scorpio, in exact opposition to that cusp (Figure 2).

This tells us two things: one, that the natal chart is more likely to be correct given *two* major indicators (the Mars/solar arc direction

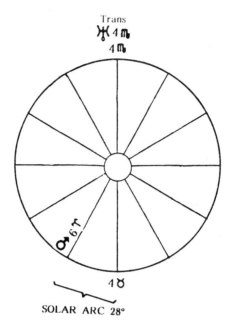

Figure 2.   Solar Arc Plus Transit

and now the Uranus transit as well) than it was with just one. It also shows that natal chart, solar arc direction and now also transit are inextricably related.

In other words, even though we have done a minimal amount of work on this native's chart, the systematic approach has begun to make 'the whole picture' accessible to us. Both solar arc direction and transit were dependent upon the correct positioning of the *natal* chart to spell out what happened in the native's life at that time. Conversely, the natal chart of itself did not spell out this exact event nor, certainly, its *timing*. The moving indicators—solar arc direction and transit—did.

We have begun to view the natal chart, progressions and transits as an indivisible whole.

Next is a second way in which we can enlarge the context of the Mars/solar arc direction. Instead of considering different 'orders' of aspects (natal, progressed and transits are different 'orders'), we will limit ourselves to just progressions of an angle to natal planets; but we will view these aspects across a span of many years.

Let's first fill in a few more planets in the native's chart, preparatory for further work with the chart's timing. We'll put in Jupiter at 3 Gemini, the Sun at 5 Virgo, Mars of course remains at 6 Aries, and then the Moon at 8 Aquarius (Figure 3A).

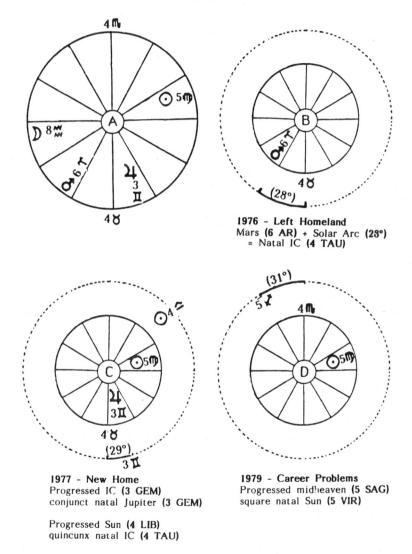

1976 - Left Homeland
Mars (6 AR) + Solar Arc (28°)
= Natal IC (4 TAU)

1977 - New Home
Progressed IC (3 GEM)
conjunct natal Jupiter (3 GEM)

Progressed Sun (4 LIB)
quincunx natal IC (4 TAU)

1979 - Career Problems
Progressed midheaven (5 SAG)
square natal Sun (5 VIR)

Figure 3A-D. Sequence of Progressed Midheaven Aspects

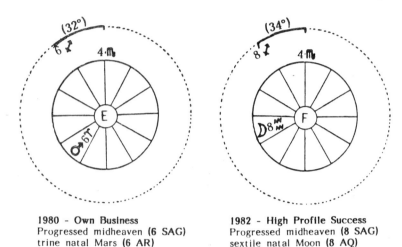

1980 - Own Business
Progressed midheaven (6 SAG)
trine natal Mars (6 AR)

1982 - High Profile Success
Progressed midheaven (8 SAG)
sextile natal Moon (8 AQ)

Figure 3E & F.   Sequence of Progressed Midheaven Aspects

We have already established that when Mars came to conjunction the IC by solar arc direction, at age *twenty-eight*, the native left his homeland. Let's say that was in *1976*. Notice now that at age *twenty-nine* (29° solar arc), in *1977*, the IC by progression will come to conjunction the natal Jupiter at 3 Gemini (4 Taurus + 29° = 3 Gemini). Note that the same year, the Sun by progression is at 4 Libra, quincunx the natal IC. (The meridian and the Sun progress at the same rate, since the meridian's rate of progression is *based* on the rate of progression of the Sun.)

Two years later, *1979*, the progressed midheaven at age *thirty-one* reaches 5 Sagittarius, square the natal Sun at 5 Virgo. In *1980* at age *thirty-two*, at 6 Sagittarius the progressed MC is trine the natal Mars at 6 Aries. In *1982* at age *thirty-four*, it has reached 8 Sagittarius, sextile the natal Moon at 8 Aquarius.

What would the course of the native's life be apt to look like during such a sequence of progressions? Figure 3, B-F illustrates how the sequence looks mathematically. Regarding the contents of the life experiences this sequence of progressions signifies, we go to the principle of relative determinism to see what makes sense. (In actual practice, such sequences are each mathematically distinctive, and that, combined with supporting indicators aids in minimizing guesswork.)

We already know that the native left his homeland at age *twenty-eight* in 1976, at the Mars/solar arc direction to the IC. The next year, 1977, the progressed IC came to conjunction natal Jupiter at 3 Gemini, so let's say the native was received with welcome arms elsewhere (i.e. it *had* to be easier and have Jupiterian characteristics) and was sheltered in a comfortable environment. Of course, this was also the year when the progressed Sun was at 4 Libra quincunx the natal IC at 4 Taurus. The Sun is still a benefic, but the quincunx shows dissatisfaction, decisions with mixed motivating factors and mixed circumstantial benefits. Since the Sun is closely connected with the career, this native might be experiencing difficulty in grounding himself professionally.

Two years later, 1979 at age *thirty-one*, the progressed midheaven at 5 Sagittarius is square the natal Sun at 5 Virgo. If the native was, let's say, trying to re-establish professional credentials at this time, he discovered obstacles in his path. The very fact that the Sun is involved in major aspect with the midheaven will make it an *issue*. Perhaps he was denied some equivalent credential, or cannot arrange necessary schooling or other opportunities. It could even be a turning point in his assessment of his identity in his new environment, or he may be unwillingly redirected through force of circumstances.

Let's say that in 1980, at age thirty-two, with the progressed midheaven at 6 Sagittarius trine natal Mars at 6 Aries, he has a spurt of enterprising spirit—a likely time for it!—and he goes into business for himself. This is plausible, because Mars signifies independence, aggressive energy and new beginnings, and one can function successfully as a loner under such aspecting. The trine from the midheaven to the Mars frees (trine) that Mars energy for this new, spirited initiative.

Two years later, 1982 at age thirty-four, with the progressed midheaven at 8 Sagittarius, sextile the natal Moon at 8 Aquarius, the native's life and career went high profile (midheaven and Moon in combination oft-times do this), and let's say the native's success is publicized, and there is a wave of public sentiment (the Moon) supporting the native's achievement (midheaven) as a new emigrant.

Remember now that the original Mars/solar arc direction was first given support by the Uranus transit opposing the IC, which made it more plausible that the timing of this direction gave a natal IC of 4 Taurus.

Now we have a second way to confirm the meridian of the natal chart. Since the timing of the *surrounding* events seems to work as well, the correctness of the Mars direction to the IC as the true timer of the move seems yet more likely, since it was part of this important new facet of 'the whole picture', the longer timed sequence of events.

Returning to the Moment of Birth
We have just looked at a few rudimentary demonstrations that there are ways to organize the 'whole picture' of astrological timing in manageable ways. Yet our preliminary venture into time has also looped right back into our common starting point: the agreement that in some sense we encounter the birth moment itself *whenever* in the native's life we read his chart. It now appears that to relate to the native's life astrologically, we must establish the birth moment with exactitude or *the entire life span* is askew, astrologically speaking. If your chart as cast, shows you beginning life at 'the wrong time and space', you are out-of-step from then on in, a bit like you participating in the choreography of life one beat later or sooner than the rest of the troupe. They're on the downbeat when you're on the upbeat. They're busy twirling while you're stamping your foot in place. An embarrassing scenario that your astrologer should by all means attempt to straighten out!

We need to 'return' to the moment of birth and verify it with certainty. But how can this be done? Time-travel backwards? Stand there with a telescope and make the planetary sightings? Can't we only reconstruct the birth moment indirectly? How can we *know*?

Our answer has already been inferred. If the birth moment experience is continually reiterated throughout the native's life, throughout all of his life experiences, *is there not a trail of evidence in its wake?* In the Foreword, we touched upon the apparent confusion of numerous concentric planetary orbits moving at respectively different rates of speed, our dazzling encounter with astrology as experienced in time. Here, with the birth chart, is a pillar of constancy! Its centrality, its dominance must surely be apparent in many ways.

We will see in chapters to come that we do not have to have been personally present at the native's birth to deduce quite precisely when he/she was born as a verifiable reality. Mathematics are indeed intimately involved with that deduction, but now, an additional, essential and integral parameter is confirmed: the native's life experience through the course of time. We are never simply deducing mathematical positions when we bring a birth chart to exactitude; we are recreating experience or, in a term familiar to many, we are *synchronizing* our astrology with the native's own life experience to date.

Conversely, if we have dissynchronized the native from his actual time/space of birth by representing that moment wrongly by a certain interval (e.g. saying the birth occurred at 4.30 a.m. when it was actually 3.57), we have, to that particular degree of inaccuracy, *disassembled the very basis upon which astrology functions.*

'Where were you when . . .?' 'Squawling my very first breath', we hope!

Returning now to that squawling new-born infant (whose life has just been theoretically plotted out for him), at least 'we astrologers know' that the birth moment is central. But it is central in reference to *him*. Our next area of discovery is to see how the centrality of the birth chart is apparent from *relating directly to the native*. He won't give us the correct birth time directly in astrological terms, so if it is not obvious *somehow*, then we will have a schism between the native and his birth chart rather than an identification and correspondence between the two.

We need the native's direct assistance. There is nothing about the birth chart, understand, that is right or wrong *per se*. Its accuracy is only revealed through its correspondence to the living native. We cannot simply take the birth chart, proclaim that it 'works', and tell the native how. If it is in error, it is not centred on that internal compass the native has within him, thus the information we offer will not concur with his actual life history. Only he, possessor of that compass, can confirm if his chart is accurately cast.

If only he knew a little astrology! Wouldn't that help?

The answer to this, ironically, is *no*. The native's knowledge of astrology has nothing to do with how vividly he conveys his true birth chart to the astrologer. He will convey it anyway—even a sceptical native, or a protesting one, or one who knows nothing of astrology at all.

We will again join the new-born to demonstrate that this is so. But now not even an astronomer will be in sight, much less an astrologer. Only our native treading the fine edge of time and space, like a high-wire acrobat. We are guaranteeing in advance that his steps will be secure on that thin wire, that the laws of nature will do it for us, that he needs no astrologer for him to reveal his actual positioning in the universe. He is about to do that just by being his own distinctly non-astrological self.

2.
THE NATIVE AS LIVING
EVIDENCE OF HIS BIRTH CHART

Time, Space and the Common Man

Most babies do not enter into life accompanied by their newly-cast astrological charts. Most parents do not measure their gradual ascent to maturity by the transits of Saturn, or their achievements through the harmonious advents of Jupiter or the Sun. Most children, and most adults as well, simply live their lives as is, with no awareness of how the planets might have altered their course for good or ill or, for that matter, at all.

Yet in each case a birth chart *could* have been cast, and presumably the astrological outlook for a child with a chart would be neither more nor less accurately ascertained than what would be the 'astrological outlook' for a child without a chart had that chart been cast.

In other words, there are presumably properties within *life itself* which translate into astrological terms whether the native is ever self-consciously aware that this is the case, much as everyone has a heartbeat whether or not he/she has ever been given an ECG.

By this way of thinking, astrology is not something we *superimpose* upon a life, but is a means of defining and deciphering that particular life's natural patternings. Much as an ECG isn't the heartbeat itself but its graphic representation, nor is the astrological chart the actual living person it merely represents. The chart can work only the way the native's life 'works'. As the life changes, so change the planetary positions within and against the chart. Likewise, planetary movements are not separate from, but simply define in a graphic, spatial language, changes in the native's life as lived.

In fact, there is nothing at all to support the erection of a natal chart except the literal, physical native and the life he is living/has lived/is about to live.

This thrusts the astrologer into the role of translator between life itself and its astrological representations. It also prescribes that the living native is our starting point, rather than the position of the Sun and Moon, the wheel of houses or any other purely astrological focus, for the obvious reason that without him there would be no birth chart at all.

This seems logical, though it does not reflect much of common practice. More often, the astrologer is trained to examine the chart first, to assume its independent reality, and then to attempt to convey its 'relevance' to the person sitting across the work table. No matter that if it weren't for the native's person and his life experience, there would be no basis for his chart to be 'relevant' at all. Whatever the astrologer may wish to tell him about his Sun or Moon, the native is already *living* it!

Moreover, if the chart is cast for an uncertain birth time, the chart's very validity—much less its 'relevance'—is seriously in doubt. This suggests that the only secure starting point is not delineation, but observation of the native personally and consideration of his life history and patterns. The basis for delineation is within *him*; the astrological chart only represents that in graphic form. If we can verify that the chart in our hands is true-to-life, in that it faithfully describes both the native's person and the course of his life, *then* we can use that chart as a basis for continuing delineation. Otherwise we have to use whatever means we can to adjust the natal chart to some exact birth time which *does* faithfully describe the native and his life, a process called 'rectification'.

Putting the living native into central focus is too seldom done. Consideration of the birth chart alone—irrespective of the native, who may be alive, deceased, or ten thousand miles away—seems work enough, requiring many different types of delineation. What sign is each planet in? In what house? What are its aspects and to what planets? How many planets are in each element, in each mode? Scores of books and decades of pedagogy have encouraged us to this very task: to break the chart down into tiny bite-sized pieces and consider each of them singly one by one, something like dumping the contents of one's purse onto the table and then picking through the assemblage object by object.

Then we dare ourselves to put the pieces back together again. After all the tedious cataloguing, we still face the task of *combining* the many diverse strands of delineation skillfully enough to produce a so-called 'synthesis'.

No wonder the great challenge of astrology is considered to be chart integration! Perhaps the chart might have worked if we had simply left it alone. Yet there is characteristically little chance to find out. In our eagerness for *information*, we routinely disassemble the chart's *structure*. Then we fret about how difficult it is to 'see the chart as a whole'.

Added to such self-defeating methods is more than we can reasonably cope with anyway—three trines and four squares, five Water planets and none in Earth, a heavily-tenanted ninth house and so on. Our mental concentration is at capacity just trying to piece it all back to where it was originally. To consider the native *'also'* in the midst of such cosmic clutter may be perceived as both an overload and difficult to integrate into the delineation process. Why even bother? The native is, after all, just sitting there, conspicuously the most non-astrological entity in sight. He may consider our reading benignly irrelevant at best, and he is certainly not plastered with signs directing us to his Venus in Scorpio or his Mars-Saturn square! Probably, to boot, he knows no astrology; so of what use could *he* possibly be before we, the experts have sorted out the technicalities?

Let's find out. In one brash move, the spotlight comes off astrology entirely and will shine on the average person, who can presumably provide us astrologers with not just some collection of details about himself, but the very *basis* upon which we can proceed.

Now, we hardly expect the average person, perhaps a banker or an engineer, a shopkeeper or a housewife to see life through an abstract reality of odd-looking glyphs, intersections of space, or chaotic-appearing patterns splashed across the page. That's for us unconventional folk! But truth to tell, it is the native who characteristically goes much further, into the very mysteries of cosmic time and space every time he/she begins to tell us about 'my life'.

There we have it, our starting point: 'my life'. Yes, even the most coarse, materialistic type who thinks life is little more than flesh and bone (and perhaps money!) *naturally* thinks of life in terms of time and space with no prodding from us. We simply take 'my' as the possessive form of 'me', and that is the physical person occupying *space*, while the 'life' component of 'my life' is a panorama of personal experience spanning *time*.

Now we can allow the person who was just so kind as to verify astrology for us—undoubtedly an unwilling draftee!—to recede into the background. We have the crux of it in a nutshell: time/space/life.

Time and Space: The Structure of Life

This gives us pause. Time? Space? Has our common man actually mouthed abstractions?

No, not really. He has simply identified something which supersedes his Venus in Scorpio or his Mars-Saturn square, the road-map to which—we despaired—was not plastered across his chest. Our native is telling us that his life has a framework, a structure, a continuity. That it is not just a collection of diverse contents, but it is structured and ordered in space and time.

The structure of life *always* precedes its content. Content only precedes structure in the local mental wards, where people babble disconnected things with no reference, no orientation, no grounding within the continuity of life.

So taking the native's own assertion, he is saying that he relates to 'my life' in terms of *structure*. This is our lead. Now how can we translate this into its astrological representations?

First space. The 'me' of 'my life' is a spatial entity (i.e. physical, occupying space) irrespective of time. Our bodies continually occupy space whether today, yesterday, or a year from now. 'Me' is also constant, unchanging, continuous. Many things *happen* to 'me', but I remain intact. The body may age but every cell of it is still 'me' throughout the entirety of life.

We find the 'me' of life represented in the natal chart, as a constant, unchanging pattern in space. Whatever are the native's constant physical traits (such as facial shape, colouring, bone structure and so on) or characteristic expressive traits (such as intensity, reserve, buoyancy), their analogues register within *the space of the natal chart*.

What of the 'life' part of 'my life'? This is the *time* component of astrology. It includes all changing factors within and against the chart. From within the chart come the secondary progressions (day-for-a-year), progressed angles and other cusps, and solar arc directions, which are all derived from factors specific to any natal chart. Against the chart are the transits.

Reflecting for a moment, something remarkable has happened in the translation process between life and its astrological analogues. The 'me' of 'my life' is a constant; I am the same person as at birth and for so long as I am alive. 'Life' changes, progresses, moves through periods and phases, exists within the flow of *time*. However, since we cannot see any visible separation between 'me' and 'my life', and since me and my life experience all happen within the same physical body, the apparently subtle distinction between the two is left implicit and submerged in ordinary language. It is astrology which, remarkably, makes this distinction explicit: 'me', the natal chart, our constant throughout the years; and 'life', those astrological factors that change throughout the lifespan.

Something else is implied by 'my life', unexpressed in ordinary language, but which astrology represents in concrete, graphic form. Since 'me', represented by the natal chart is always the same, notwithstanding the onward flow of living, the natal chart necessarily has a *continuing relationship* with the many changing astrological indicators which show the passage of time.

To use an analogy with air travel, we haven't just hopped a plane from 'here' (the starting point, the natal chart) to 'there' (moving astrological indicators for some later point in life). We may have moved to 'there', but we are still always 'here' with the natal chart. So all changing astrological indicators are always viewed *relative to* that unchanging point of departure into life.

This seems to prescribe two basic ways to ascertain whether the original time/space of the chart is accurate. We can look at the natal chart alone, which is a lifelong reflection of the *physical* native, since it is a constant, not dependent upon any other astrological positions but its own. We can also look at 'the chart in motion' (progressions, transits, progressed angles and so forth) *in relation to* the natal chart, since the natal chart and the chart in motion, in effect, run parallel to one another for the duration of the life.

Since the 'me' component of 'my life' appears to be rooted in the spatial component of the natal chart, whereas the 'life' component is rooted in time, our two basic means of chart rectification will be tailored to the character of each respective component, spatial (the native's person) and temporal (the native's life).

How Space Registers in the Chart
Space is the starting point, as it is easier to work with what remains stationary (space) than it is to work with relationships that change (time).

Space, 'me', the natal chart, is what corresponds to the native himself, the physical person, so this part of the rectification process, in a nutshell, involves looking at the native, looking at the natal chart and discovering whether the chart as cast faithfully describes the native's person (notably by the rising sign, though that is by no means the only factor).

This is space that we see visually at a glance, through the divisions and glyphs of the chart, and through the bodily lines, shapes, colours, patterns of movement and other physical qualities characterizing the native. This is the artist's version of 'space', rather than the strictly mathematical 'space' (i.e. units of measures) which will be of greater importance in other contexts.

Time is, in effect, built into the space we are looking at, in that it is the birth time which determines the spatial locations of the planets and cusps of the natal chart. But since the birth time is a fixed, single moment only, we don't see the time element visually, leaving us free to consider space alone. This 'fixed' time (the birth time, as contrasted with life-experience time, which *moves*) gives 'fixed space', and it does so literally, i.e. the native's appearance develops only in accordance with the space of the natal chart which is, in turn, based upon the single, fixed moment of birth. It is only because the native 'looks like' *only this one specific, fixed time and space* that we can draw direct correspondences between the native's person and the spatial layout of the chart.

Let's see this in tangible form. Let's say that a native is born with the middle of Taurus rising. That person is apt to look quite Taurean physically, let's say a square jaw with a thick neck, large brown eyes that fix upon you with steady gaze, a well-developed chest, short torso and a measured, deliberate gait.

By the age of fifteen, let's say, the native's natal ascendant has progressed onwards through the latter part of Taurus and is now entering Gemini. The native's head and neck do *not* suddenly become elongated, his eyes do *not* suddenly become dart-like, he does *not* suddenly sprout a long waist and tapering fingers, he does *not* suddenly walk with a sprightly gait or start producing terse, clipped or nervous speech patterns. All of the preceding are Gemini characteristics, but progression of the ascendant from Taurus to Gemini does not alter the native physically or, as we might say colloquially, it 'doesn't change his space'. Physically, he will always be Taurean.

It may be that on another planet, the native's space would keep pace with his time, and how interesting it would be to go through two or three completely different physical bodies and corresponding personality types in a single lifetime, such as Taurus, then Gemini, then Cancer. Every thirty years or so—when the progressing ascendant was entering the next successive sign—everyone would comment, 'My, how you've changed in the past year!' *Indeed!!*

For better or worse, here on Earth we cannot undergo such startling transformations. Once Taurus rising, always Taurus rising. Once Sagittarius rising, Sagittarius rising for life.

Thus do we literally *see* the native as we look at his natal chart.

How Time Registers in the Chart

By contrast time—as we generally understand it—is fluid and changing. We can trace the chronology of life experience such as, 'We moved house on such-and-such date, I got a wonderful job on such-and-such later date, and then still later on, my mother took ill on such-and-such date', and so on. But unlike the solid physical reality of the human form, the chronology of life moves through time without any tangible physical structure that we can see or touch. When time is past, it no longer has any reality in the gross physical sense of the word. All we can produce about time that is 'tangible'— and we do need something tangible to verify *anything!*—is fixed mathematical units of measure, such as hours (all sixty minutes) and days (all twenty-four hours). We recognize these graphic representations of time as 'tangible' in their own terms.

Now, when we translate these clock-time measures into various forms of astrological measures (such as one degree's progression on the midheaven 'equals' one year of life, for example), we arrive at measures a little more complex than the ordinary clock's, but the principle of time measurement is the same. We can show the units of time *visually*, and these units serve as representations of time— something we cannot see directly—in a tangible, measured form.

Any unit of measure is a division of space, so it is now clear why we were distinguishing between 'artist's space' (the appearance of the physical native) and 'mathematical space' (units of measure timing his life). We can also distinguish visually between so-called 'fixed time and space', which shows the whole person as is, as a permanent imprint of form; and 'moving time and space', which moves from 'here' to 'there' via spatial measurements, usually some unit of time in relation to units in later or earlier positions, such as 5 May in relation to 1 May, or the progressed midheaven at 11 Scorpio in relation to the natal midheaven at 17 Libra.

We can relate to fixed and moving time and space as a marvel of what is still unknown in physics, or as some kind of metaphysical marvel. The 'why' of it matters little so long as we clearly recognize what facet of reality we are examining, and what is that reality's representations in astrological form. Spatial reality, the native's physical form, is represented in the space of the natal chart. Temporal reality, the native's life experience, is represented in mathematical units of measures as they apply to natal (stationary) and moving factors within and against the chart.

Space versus Time

Space and time alone are shown respectively through the natal and progressed/transiting positions. But 'What if', the reader might ponder, 'I have done all the work matching up the native's physical person with the chart's space, plus all the work matching up his life with the chart's timing, and I come up with *two completely different results?*'

Horrible prospect! Could it happen?

It is important to clarify this point early on, since it seems likely we are about to develop two complementary but different sets of skills, one as an observer and artist (to gauge space) and one as a mathematician and scientist (to gauge timing). One might also be tempted to specialize in one area rather than another, thinking that this might be sufficient.

Skills in both areas are essential. In fact, one cannot be a skilled chart rectifier without fluency in both types of skills and the ability to cross-check each against the other.

A simple analogy clarifies one main reason why this is so. Let's picture the birth time you are looking for as an imaginary object, perhaps most suitably, the proverbial 'needle in the haystack'. No birth time is given at all, and you have all twenty-four hours of the birth date within which to search. That's sixty minutes per hour, so we are talking about 1,440 minutes (60 minutes × 24 hours), of which only *one* is the actual minute of the native's birth.

Now think of the birth *date* as a large house with many rooms, let's say twelve, a parallel to the twelve signs of the zodiac. Now, if you use mathematical means and timing indicators *only* to arrive at the true time of birth, that is like looking through all the rooms of that huge, twelve-room house for this one tiny needle. You could spend days, even weeks with tedious calculations, only to arrive at the wrong spot! Mathematics alone is really not an efficient way to rectify a chart, especially if the birth time is very uncertain.

However, if you work with space *first*, then let's say you've narrowed the search down to two out of the twelve rooms, let's say the ones that mean 'Gemini rising' and 'Aquarius rising'. (They are both Air signs, and signs of the same element can 'resemble' one another via the native's physical person.) Assuming that your judgement is sound, you have narrowed down the search from twelve rooms to two! Great step forward.

Then you might see that if Gemini is rising, the planet Saturn would also be rising (i.e. in the first house), and that would bring Saturnine characteristics to the fore; whereas if Aquarius were the true rising sign, the native would have Venus rising, a very different model indeed. Maybe the search can be narrowed down to a single room from out of the twelve *before you do any mathematics at all.*

In other words, space shows the outer form of that room where the 'needle' is hidden, so you will always want to work with space *first.*

However, after you have narrowed down the birth time to a range worth testing, only astrological mathematics will land you right on the mark. Why? Mathematical measures used in rectification work are peculiarly tiny; you will be using one degree orb *maximum* for aspects, unlike natal delineation, which allows for wider orbs. Only exact mathematics will usher you through that relatively tiny passageway of time to where the imaginary needle is located.

There are also numerous ways in which time and space *verify each other* in rectification work. For example, you may have 'seen' Saturn rising in a natal chart (space), some undetermined number of degrees into the first house. Let's say Cancer is rising and Saturn is at 10 Cancer. Since Saturnine characteristics are 'visible' in the native, we've placed Saturn in the first house, one of our imaginary rooms—but *where* in that room? This could give a range of a full sign or more.

Now let's say we think Cancer is rising in the chart. Is the ascendant at 2 Cancer, giving a distance of 8 degrees between ascendant and Saturn? 5 Cancer, giving a distance of only 5 degrees?, and so on.

What happened in the life (time) when the progressing ascendant in early Cancer contacted the natal Saturn at 10 Cancer? The number of degrees between the ascendant and the Saturn (which in turn translates to the native's approximate age at the progressed ascendant/natal Saturn conjunction) will mark an ascendant/Saturn period in the life. If the true ascendant is 2 Cancer, that will have come at approximately age eight (2 Cancer + 8° = natal Saturn at 10 Cancer). If the true ascendant is at 5 Cancer, that will have to have come at approximately age five (5 Cancer + 5° = natal Saturn at 10 Cancer). *Thus the space of the birth chart and the timing of the native's life verify each other.*

Conversely, you may encounter the timing element before the spatial one. Let's say the native describes to you what seems like a

Saturnine train of events at a very young age—a chronic illness draining the energy, a serious fall, father left home and family depressed and impoverished, unusual restrictions imposed, or some such. *Then*, perhaps, you notice that the native looks Saturnine physically—flat cheeks, pale skin, goat eyes, short legs, and so on. If, indeed, the early Saturnine period was truly marked by progressed ascendant conjunct Saturn, then you have just discovered its verification in *space*, by observation of the native's appearance.

There are undoubtedly underlying principles of physics and/or metaphysics (as yet undiscovered) to explain *why* it is not possible to be born into one space with non-corresponding astrological time clocks or vice versa. Experience does consistently confirm that such is not possible, whatever its reason, so only the pragmatic results need concern us here. In effect, it works like the warp and woof of a fabric: it is the strength of the interweaving which holds the fabric together securely. In like manner, only space-based and time-based methods interwoven with one another will produce reliable rectification work.

3.
ADJUSTING THE CHART'S TIME AND SPACE TO FIT THE NATIVE

The Skill-Based Approach to Adjustments

Now let's get down to brass tacks. We say we look at the native and 'see his space'. We listen to the chronology of his life events and we say he is 'telling us about his time'. This gives our general orientation. But now the native has actually arrived for his reading, and we have a mass of planetary glyphs and a jumble of figures before us. Is the chart correctly positioned or not? If not, what alerted us to the error? How shall we adjust the chart to exactitude?

Bear in mind that it is easier to demonstrate the accuracy of a correct chart than it is to take an incorrect chart and know how to adjust it. I could demonstrate methods that will work with a correct chart and then, if they fail with the chart at hand, tell you to 'try another birth time'. That will create a lot of extra work (since you have performed some complete methodology or another on a wrong chart), and still not train you in rapid recognition of a chart's probable accuracy or not *before* attempting lengthy and complicated calculations.

This is why learning set methodologies might seem quick and easy, but will not be adequate in the context of actual astrological practice. What is required is the development of *skills*—training to be observant, flexible, and to notice prominent clues rapidly. Sample delineations are needed and will be given; but that will give you a list, not a skill.

Now, to begin mastering the skills needed for rectification work you, the reader, are about to get into the driver's seat, and begin adjusting the chart of the native (whom we picture sitting right here) to exactitude.

SPACE

Seeing the Chart True-to-Life

First we want to look at the chart and see how much of a difference and how obvious a difference a discrepancy in birth time will make in the chart's *space*. Remember, work with space precedes work with time, so as to narrow down the birth time to a workable *range* before working with exact mathematics.

To adjust the space of the natal chart, we need observe the native physically. Now, if you consider yourself an artist (as do many astrologers), think of a portrait-painting artist who is sketching a portrait from life. Have you noticed how an artist will look back and forth between canvas and living person and perhaps shorten the nose or make the jaw-line more pronounced or add some other touch that makes the portrait more true-to-life? If the artist has a preconceived notion of how the person 'should' look, instead of how he *does* look, or is painting from the description of a third party instead of looking at the person himself, the portrait will be unlikely to resemble the painter's subject.

It is much the same with astrological charts. Your first consideration is that the chart in front of you might not be graven in stone. Its accuracy rests upon how accurately it describes the native.

Astrologers are used to considering the natal chart as a static, stationary entity. This is 'given', not up for question, and it is the basis for delineation of the planets, aspects, signs and house locations. It is often simply accepted as accurate, and astrologers focus their attention directly upon interpretation.

For rectification work, however, the astrologer needs to immediately view the chart as a more fluid entity. The native *could* have been born a little earlier, or a little later. What difference would that make? Are there features of a chart cast for an earlier or a later time that seem to *better describe the native?*

Adjusting the Chart's Angles to Reflect the Native's Appearance

If the chart does *not* reflect the native's appearance, you don't have a paintbrush to alter the chart, but you do have a way to adjust the birth time structurally. The chart's structural basis is its *angles*, the ascendant and midheaven. It is the ascendant (i.e. the rising degree) which defines the native's physical form as he projects out into the world, though planets near the seventh cusp (the other end of the ascendant axis) may also affect the physical appearance. The meridian (tenth and fourth cusps) defines his rootedness in the world (fourth cusp) and his worldly position (tenth cusp), but planets near either of these cusps are also likely to affect the physical appearance. It is also both angles, specifically, that define the exact *time* of the birth.

Now, if we imagine for a moment that the angles of the natal chart, the ascendant axis (first/seventh cusps) and the meridian (tenth/fourth cusps) are levers we can manipulate manually, we can practice making rudimentary adjustments in the chart's space.

Let's say that for a given birth time, the native has a Scorpio rising chart. If the same native was actually born two hours *later*, think of those 'levers' (the angular axes of the chart) being manipulated *forwards*, into the sign that follows Scorpio, Sagittarius. Now return to the original Scorpio rising position. Now imagine that the native was actually born two hours *earlier* than this chart cast for Scorpio rising. In your mind, manipulate that lever *backwards* in space, and the native's true ascendant would fall in the sign preceding Scorpio, Libra.

Figure 4 illustrates. (Note that the birth time discrepancy of two hours was chosen for maximum plausibility, since that is the average length of time it takes for a sign to rise.)

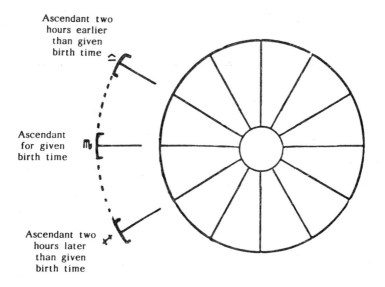

Ascendant two
hours earlier
than given
birth time

Ascendant
for given
birth time

Ascendant two
hours later
than given
birth time

Figure 4.   Adjusting the Ascendant Backwards and Forwards

Now let's try a second exercise. This time, disregard which sign is rising and have a *planet* rising (i.e. in the first house). Let's say it is Uranus, which tends to give severe-looking body lines—high, rectangular-shaped shoulders, high prominent cheekbones, a stiffened gait, a steely look across the eyes. You look at the native and cannot see any of these Uranian characteristics. So you take the

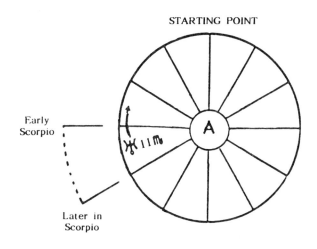

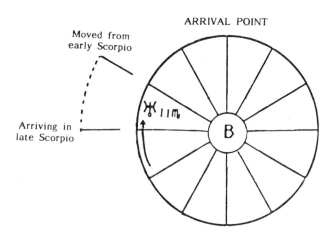

Figure 5. Using a Rising Planet to Adjust the Ascendant

imaginary lever attached to the ascendant and move it *forwards* (i.e. a later birth time), because the best way to get that Uranus out of the 'rising' position is to push it back into the twelfth house, where you will not see it in the native visually (Figure 5A & B). In other words, from what you can see visually, the native was probably not born at the given time, but more likely at a *later* time.

The reverse works, too. If the native has obvious Uranian characteristics, and the Uranus for the given birth time is in the twelfth house, you can move it ahead to the first (i.e. an *earlier* birth time).

The two illustrations we have just used—identification of the rising sign and identification of rising planets—are two of the most critical considerations in adjusting the space of the chart to exactitude.

We will not be delineating what each rising sign or prominently-positioned planet 'looks like' until we are used to this rudimentary manipulation of the chart's space. Obviously, we each have all the signs and all the planets in our charts. But to know which signs and planets are the most 'visible' we first need to know *where to look* in the chart.

The Many Types of Spatial Differences

We now have some idea why we might want to adjust the space of a birth chart (the native doesn't resemble the rising sign for the given birth time, for example) and how to do it (move the ascendant backwards or forwards in space to give a rising sign that might better describe the appearance). Now for demonstration purposes, we will examine a pair of birth charts, especially constructed with planetary positions that maximize the number of visible differences (visible in the *native*, that is) that can occur with a discrepancy of only one hour in the birth time (Figure 6A & B).

First note that the hour's difference between charts A and B has crossed over from one rising sign to the next: chart A has Scorpio rising and chart B has Sagittarius rising. (This may or may not happen within an hour's time, but in about half of all instances, it would.)

The hour's shift has also altered the rising and culminating planets: chart A has Jupiter rising and Uranus culminating; chart B has Saturn rising and Mercury culminating.

Other factors bearing upon the native's appearance are listed underneath the charts, in a format designed for ready comparison. Also listed are those chart factors which will *not* enter into assessment of the native's appearance, so nothing is left ambiguous. (Note, for

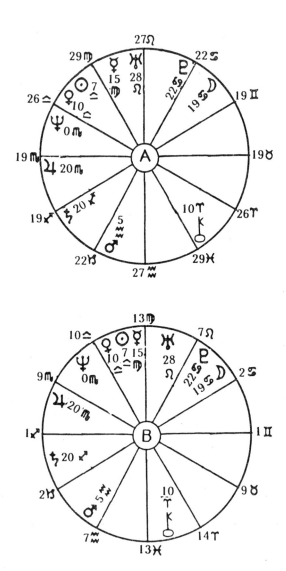

Figure 6A   Two Birth Charts Cast One Hour Apart

VISIBLE AND POTENTIALLY VISIBLE
CHART FACTORS

Chart A   Chart B

RISING SIGN

Scorpio   Sagittarius
Water sign   Fire sign
Fixed sign   Mutable sign

RULER OF RISING SIGN
(chart ruler)

Mars (co-ruler Pluto)   Jupiter

ASPECTS TO CHART RULER

Mars trine Sun, Venus   Jupiter trine Moon,
Pluto conjunct Moon   Pluto

RISING PLANET(S)

Jupiter in Scorpio   Saturn in Sagittarius

CULMINATING PLANET(S)

Uranus in Leo   Mercury in Virgo

EXACT ASPECTS TO ASCENDANT

Moon trine   None

NON-VISIBLE CHART FACTORS

Chart A   Chart B

SIGN ON MIDHEAVEN

Leo   Virgo

LOCATION OF RULER
OF MIDHEAVEN

Sun eleventh house   Mercury tenth house
                         (this Mercury will be
                         visible, but because
                         it is culminating, not
                         because it rules the
                         midheaven)

Figure 6B.   How One Hour's Time Difference Registers in the
Chart's Space

example, that the sign on the ascendant will always be visible in the native, whereas the sign on the midheaven will not. Only a *planet* near the midheaven will be.)

Not all the listed 'visible' characteristics are equally important for every chart; much depends upon the individual chart layout. For the moment, simply imagine using 'the artist's eye' to assess the differences between the charts. Imagine, if you will, that the different types of visible differences are colours on a canvas. In a chart where there are no rising or culminating planets and no planets near the chart's angles, you may find a very 'pure' example of a rising sign, much like a canvas being coloured blue in its entirety.

Now imagine that other planets or signs enter in 'visibly', such as we find in charts A and B. Chart A features Jupiter rising; chart B features Saturn rising. These are influences which contrast with each other (Jupiter large, expansive and free; Saturn constrained, measured and restricted) and each will have a strong modifying influence upon the respective rising signs of the two charts.

Now the chart's 'blue' rising sign is modified by a different colour—let's say red, most suitable if you find a rising Mars! In other words, the native will show a mixture of rising sign influence and rising planet influence.

Or the chart's canvas might become all that much more intense a 'blue', because some consonant factor is prominent—such as Scorpio rising native with rising Mars (the *ruler* of Scorpio) or a Cancer rising native with a culminating Moon (the *ruler* of Cancer) which, in both cases, would intensify the apparent influence of the rising sign.

In actual practice, you will encounter somewhat more 'composites' than you will 'pure' types (perhaps a key reason why this area of astrology has rarely been clarified), giving another reason why skills in discerning differences and making adjustments bear emphasis rather than simply flat delineations, such as 'everyone with Gemini rising will look like this: . . .' You will encounter relatively 'pure' Gemini rising natives who do look like that, but also many 'hybrids'.

This pair of hypothetical charts are definitely instances of 'hybrids', designed to highlight various types of differences. For the moment we are only training our eye *where to look*. For every key area cited, you will be looking at the chart and then to the native to see if he faithfully reflects that prominently-placed planetary or sign influence. Conversely, whatever prominent physical characteristic you find in the native (be it large, liquid eyes or short legs or an oval-shaped head, all will be accorded their astrological analogues), you will be looking for its astrological analogue in some prominent location of the natal chart.

Your key tool for chart adjustment will be those imaginary levers attached to the ascendant of the chart and to its midheaven. It's that simple. (For a detailed analysis of what the natives corresponding to chart A and chart B would be likely to look like in real life, see 'Working With Composites', pp. 259-264.)

If our 'artist's eye' has been astute, and the adjusted chart now 'looks like' the physical native, this puts us way ahead in our quest for the true time of birth.

Next we will consider the types of skills needed to work with the chart's *time*. Off with the artist's hat, on with the mathematician's!

TIME

Seeing Time in Terms of Space

When we originally spoke of 'fixed time and space' and 'moving time and space', we identified 'fixed space' as artist's space, the space of the natal chart, and 'moving space' as mathematical space, the chart's *timing*. As the latter implies, the optimum way of working with time *is* through seeing it in terms of space!

This goes way back to our earliest time/space orientation: learning how to tell time. Presumably we do not have a sensory faculty which is 'pure time perception'. How did we learn to tell time? By sitting for several hours until we could gauge by some mysterious inner faculty what time 'is', or what it 'feels' like? Of course not. We were taught how to read a clock, and shown how its hands changing their relative positions in *space* would tell us the *time*! Even the ancient sundial with its interplay of light and shadows told time through changing relationships of space.

Fundamentally, we see time in terms of space when we look at a clock. Conversely, we also see space in terms of time. For example, we know that the space between '12' and '1' on the clock represents five seconds, five minutes or one hour depending upon which hand is crossing that spatial segment of the whole circle—the second hand, the minute hand or the hour hand.

The natal chart is, in a sense, 'where the clock stopped' at the moment of birth. It also has 'hands', but more than an ordinary clock—the eleven planets in their respective orbits may be seen as such 'hands'. This is more than the clock's simple three, nor do these planetary hands move at constant speeds, as do the clock's. They even move retrograde at times!

Moreover, not only do the 'hands' of the astrological chart/clock move, but so do the 'numbers on the dial', i.e. the house cusps. From the moment following birth and every moment thereafter, the ascendant, the midheaven and all the cusps in between have moved on to new positions.

Still, mightn't we nevertheless see the chart as a giant, multi-handed clock, simply a little more complex than the clock on the wall? Not quite. The real obstacle to seeing the spatial measures of the chart (i.e. its exact zodiacal positions) in terms of *time* measures, is that with an ordinary clock, simple though it be, we can see the hands changing their positions as we watch.

With the natal chart, by contrast, so far as we can tell visually, the planetary and cuspal positions are frozen in space. If we want to view the astrology of some later time in the life, we calculate the progressions, look up the transits, and then *superimpose* them upon the natal chart. We have no ready way to recognize that astrological space and astrological time are interdependent, which would be obvious if we could watch the planets and cusps gradually arriving at their new (spatial) positions from their original ones as a natural, continuous process of passing time.

If, however, we can represent the continuity of time in a spatial format, then we can work with it tangibly. Although we cannot do that completely (as in plotting new planetary positions for every day of the life), what we can do is to learn to *think in time spans* rather than in isolated zodiacal positions.

Our many efforts to represent time as a continuous flow through space may take various forms, but with the same overall function of seeing time in terms of space. We will also view space in terms of its time equivalencies, e.g. the space of one zodiacal degree 'equals' a certain measure of time, or a measure of time 'equals' some division of space that we can see visually.

How can this be done?

Time Scales and Time Frames

Planets and cusps do not move at constant rates, like the hands of a clock. Mercury may transit 2° one day, and only 37′ on a day a few weeks later. It may even come to a complete halt at station. Simultaneously, all the other planets move at respectively different rates of speed.

However, although astrological time-telling is more complex than the ordinary kind, we still make our observations in terms of constants, in that the planetary positions are given for midnight each day, not 12.15 a.m. one day and 11.57 p.m. the next. The Table of Houses provides new cuspal positions at four-minute intervals in the birth time.

In other words, even though the rates of planetary movement are variable, the *time scales* we use to measure them are constants. A time scale is its rate of motion—how far a planet or cusp moves in a certain integer of time measurement, such as '1°48′ *per day*'. Here the fixed, constant unit is the '*per day*'. Naturally, with this time scale (relatively rapid-moving), we would be referring to transits, which are recorded in the ephemeris one midnight position *per day*.

For a secondary progression (day-for-a-year), that same day would signify a whole year in the life, so we can also see that daily measurement of 1°48′ *per year* as the time scale for a certain progression (undoubtedly, at that rate, Mercury) or as 9′ *per month* (1°48′ per year ÷ 12).

We need to think in terms of time scales to calculate exact planetary positions, or even to make approximations, as is often useful in rectification work.

Time scales are always our starting point of time measurement. However, we want to consider not only where, exactly, a planet is zodiacally at a certain time, but its *effective period* of transit or progression against the natal chart. For this, we need convert our thinking to time *frames*. A time frame, for rectification work, is the length of time during which a planetary movement will be in close enough orb to be an instrumental part of change in the life.

There is also a constant involved here, and that is that only an aspect within *a single degree's orb* will be effective in the materialization of some 'event' in the life. (See 'The Seven Rules', Rule 3, 'Tightness of Orb', p. 123.) So the time frame of effectiveness is the period of time during which some planet or cusp will fall within that single degree of some exact aspect.

To capsulize, we use time scales to make our calculations. We use time frames to determine their effective period of application. (Note: 'application' means the period during which the aspect is effectively applicable, not 'application versus separation' of an aspect.)

Figure 7, A and B exemplifies. In example A, transiting Jupiter is moving along at a rate of 12′ per day, its *time scale*. It is effectively conjunct the natal midheaven within one degree of application and one degree of separation. Since the aspect takes five days to apply at a scale of 12′ per day, and five days to separate, the *time frame*

A

Aspect: Trans Jupiter conjunct natal MC

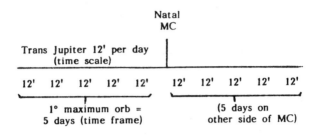

TIME FRAME FOR THIS ASPECT = 10 DAYS

B

Aspect: Prog Sun trine natal ascendant

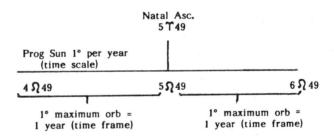

TIME FRAME FOR THIS ASPECT = 2 YEARS

Figure 7.   Time Frames

for the effectiveness of this particular aspect is ten days.

With example B, we find the natal ascendant at 5 AR 49, and the progressed Sun beginning to apply into a trine at 4 LEO 49, with the aspect one degree shy of partile for an exact trine. The *time scale* for the progressed Sun is about 58′ per year, which, for this example, we have rounded off to one degree per year. The effective period of this aspect—its *time frame*—is one year applying plus one year separating, equals two years.

Multiple Convergence

How can we use these means of measurement to ascertain when something of significance happens in the life?

Again, since planetary motions are irregular and multi-orbited, let's cut back to the simpler model of an ordinary clock to demonstrate a principle. We can readily see that the most 'significant' times of the day are the change-over points from one hour into the next. Now we look at a clock and tell time automatically, but originally, we had to learn skills in translating each hand's position into the time component it signifies, such as the minute hand on digit '8' means forty minutes after the hour, on a time *scale* of five minutes per integer on the dial, and within the time *frame* of whichever hour it occurs, such as between six and seven o'clock (equals 6.40).

But the marking point itself which closes one hour and opens the next is not simply a conglomeration of measurements, but is *a synchronization of all the hands*. It's not 2 (hours): 60 (minutes): 60 (seconds). It's *exactly three o'clock*. When does the hour change *exactly*? It is when (1) the minute hand exactly reaches '12' on the dial; *and* (2) the second hand exactly reaches '12' on the dial; *and* (3) when the hour hand reaches the integer on the dial that it has spent a whole hour approaching. One hand alone doesn't do it. We look to the second hand on 'the last stretch' of the hour, because it is moving the most rapidly, but were it not for the hour hand also approaching some exact number from '1' to '12', we wouldn't know what time it was at all!

The most significant times of life, registered through astrology, work on the same principle as the most significant times of day are registered on the clock. We have already likened the planetary and cuspal motions to the motion of hands on the clock; and the aspects becoming partile may be likened to the clock's hands reaching exact integers on the clockface. The significant times of life are marked by many aspects becoming partile *simultaneously*, especially when they involve the most central positions of the chart, the angles, which are much like '12', '3', '6', and '9' on the face of a clock.

Nor are only transiting planets forming aspects sufficient—that would be like multiple second hands alone—nor many progressions forming exact aspects alone, which would be analogous to multiple minute hands alone. None alone will mark off an important event date, for that would be like the second hand or minute hand alone telling us when we were about to enter the new hour.

Multiple Orders of Aspects

It is also significant not just that several types of 'hands' are jointly telling us the time, but also the natural priority in which they are organized because of their varying rates of speed. The hour hand marks off the longest period on a clock, so we look to that first for the time to the nearest hour. Within that longest period is subsumed shorter periods of minutes within which is subsumed still shorter periods of seconds.

Analogously, with astrology we want to consider the longest timing indicators *first*. The easiest way to organize our thinking about astrological time is by the fixed and permanent positions, which is of course the natal planets and cusps; the longer timers, which are the secondary progressions and progressed cusps, and the shorter timers, which are the (more rapidly-moving) transits. (The slower-moving transits, especially Uranus, Neptune and Pluto, tend to be a special case, but for the moment we will include them in the shorter timer category.)

The natal chart is a permanent, 'clockface' type matrix for the life. The slower-moving progressions 'set the tone' for an entire period, a year or sometimes more, during which things of a certain character are prone to happen; but then it is the transits—the equivalent of the 'bingo!' of our spunky little second hand marking off the new hour—which spark off an event in the life specifically *because* they are embedded in slower-moving indicators which predispose towards certain types of events happening.

So we have expanded the concept of multiple convergence to not just convergence of several 'hands' simultaneously, but specifically of hands taken from the different 'orders' of aspecting: natal, progressed and transiting.

In an actual example, what we might see is, for example, progressed Venus trine natal midheaven *while* transiting Mars is conjunct the progressed midheaven *while* transiting Uranus is sextile the progressed ascendant *while* the progressed Sun is square the natal Jupiter and so on.

It's a bit like an orchestra. With music, at a point of climax (the 'significant time'), there is fuller orchestration, in fact the whole orchestra is incorporated into one unit. All the choirs are represented—strings, winds, brass and percussion—with the rhythms synchronized for greater impact!

Applying it to Life

We now have a basic model of expectable structural components for an accurate chart at a time of important change in the life. Now let's focus upon the all-important counterpart to whatever happens in the chart: the native's life as lived.

The native's physical person is reflected in the *space* of the natal chart. For its *timing*, the criterion is that the aspecting at the event date has to exactly time, as well as describe the native's actual life experience. If the aspects suggest some 'important' time and the native relates that nothing much was happening at that time or, conversely, if the native relates a very significant juncture for which we find little support in the aspecting, we have a serious problem with the chart's accuracy.

Usually the astrologer will have to watch a chart's timing more closely than its space, because the native's space is expressed in the physical constants of his own form, whereas his life experience will be related from memory. Yet at the time of the event itself, it was literally happening to him, so the astrology would have to have been literally descriptive.

Although we cannot 'see time' in the same way that we could literally 'see space' in the physical native, the native's direct input is of equal and central importance in deciphering the chart's timing as it was for its space. Remember that the timing of the chart has *no reference point but his experience.* The native will be telling you when various things happened to him over the course of his life, important events such as marriage or an accident or a large financial venture, a move to another country, a great career breakthrough or a death in the family. And that '*when*' is every bit as literal and tangible as the nose on his face or the jaunt in his walk or the literal sound of his voice.

To illustrate the chart's timing mechanisms tangibly, we will use models that parallel those we used to highlight differences in the chart's space: a discrepancy of a single hour's birth time. Let's examine some specific event in some hypothetical native's life to familiarize ourselves with what types of differences to look for, how much difference that single hour's time makes, and why.

Our hypothetical child was born at 2 p.m. The astrologer's 'version' of the chart, however, is cast for 3 p.m., an hour later than the true time of birth.

How much difference does an hour's discrepancy make? In regard to the transits, not very much—approximately a half-degree for the Moon and considerably less for the other planets. Where we do find a relatively huge difference, however, is in the chart *angles* (the ascendant and midheaven). One hour is fifteen whole degrees of midheaven motion on a time scale of four minutes per degree (1 hour = 60 minutes ÷ 4 = 15 degrees). The difference on the ascendant is between ten and *thirty* degrees of motion, depending upon whether the rising sign is long ascension or short ascension and the latitude of birth.

Even for natal delineation (i.e. prior to any consideration of timing factors), a fifteen-degree discrepancy on the angles is so wide that it can make for a patently unacceptable chart. The signs on one or both angles are likely to be shifted from one sign into the next adjacent one, planets fall into different houses, prominent planetary influences become subsidiary and vice versa. (Figure 6, pp. 50-51, was a good example of all these considerations.)

Now we come to the fifteen-degree discrepancy in the chart's *timing*. Since the *natal* chart—the permanent matrix of the life—is askew, this translates into differences in timing *throughout* the life, since all really major changes register against the chart's angles, which would be fifteen degrees off consistently from the moment of birth on. (Note: all the *progressed* angles will be thrown off accordingly as well.)

Let's look at specifics. Let's say that transiting Mercury is moving at a rate of 1½° per day on the date of some major event in the native's life. Any relevant aspects to an angle will be *ten days* off (15° ÷ 1½° = 10). The rate for Mars might be 40' per day, giving a Mars transit off by 15° ÷ 40' = 22½ days; and for Uranus, at perhaps only 2' per day, the discrepancy becomes very marked indeed.

If transits seem problematical, progressions magnify the problem. Let's say that transiting Venus at exactly one degree per day, gives a fifteen-day discrepancy for some expected exact aspect to the natal midheaven. *Progressed* Venus is, let's say, moving along at the same scale of one degree per year, giving a discrepancy of not fifteen days, but *fifteen years*!

The result: not only does that single hour's discrepancy in the birth time throw the timing of all the various astrological measures off, but it throws them off in different time scales!

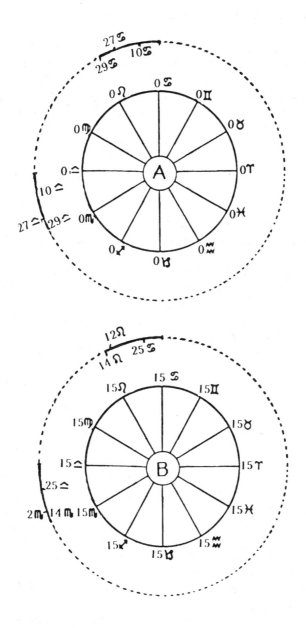

Figure 8A & B. Differences in Progressed Angles for Two Birth Charts
Cast One Hour Apart

Let's see this now in a visual model. We want to work with something simple and manageable, so we do not want to get side-tracked into mathematical complications; thus our hypothetical example will feature equal house charts and perfectly even rates of progression—something, I must emphasize emphatically, will *not* do for an actual chart rectification. It will, however, serve to provide a suitable format for training the eye to spot key timing differences.

The wheel shown in Figure 8A is cast for 2 p.m., the native's correct birth time. Chart B is (wrongly) cast for 3 p.m., on the strength of the child's uncle (or next-door neighbour, or yes, mother!) being 'positive' that this was when the child was born.

We are noting several changes in this hypothetical life. To simplify, these changes each happened at exact-to-the-day ages in the native's life—this native apparently had exceptionally active birthdays!

Let's say that the family moved far away to another city when he was ten; he became a doctor when he was twenty-seven; he married at twenty-nine.

For chart A, with the natal midheaven at 0 Cancer, progressing at the rate of one degree per year by solar arc, the native's family moved when the midheaven had progressed to *10* Cancer. He became a doctor when the midheaven came to *27* Cancer. He married when the midheaven came to *29* Cancer.

We use the same series for the ascendant at 0 Libra. His family moved when the progressed ascendant came to *10* Libra; he became a doctor when the ascendant came to *27* Libra; he married when the ascendant came to *29* Libra.

'Not by *my* chart!' protests our contesting astrologer. 'His family moved when the midheaven progressed to *25* Cancer (15 Cancer + 10°)' he became a doctor with the midheaven at 12 Leo (15 Cancer + 27°); he married with the midheaven at 14 Leo (15 Cancer + 27°). The ascendant was at 25 Libra at the family move, 12 Scorpio when he become a doctor, and 14 Scorpio at the native's marriage. Prove me wrong!'

Let's focus upon one event, the native's marriage. That's a *seventh house* matter. Chart A puts the natal ascendant at 0 Libra, and the natal seventh cusp at 0 Aries; the progressed ascendant at the time of the marriage was 29 Libra and the progressed seventh cusp, 29 Aries. Chart B puts the natal ascendant at 15 Libra, and the natal seventh cusp at 15 Aries; the progressed ascendant at the time of the marriage was 14 Scorpio and the progressed seventh, 14 Taurus.

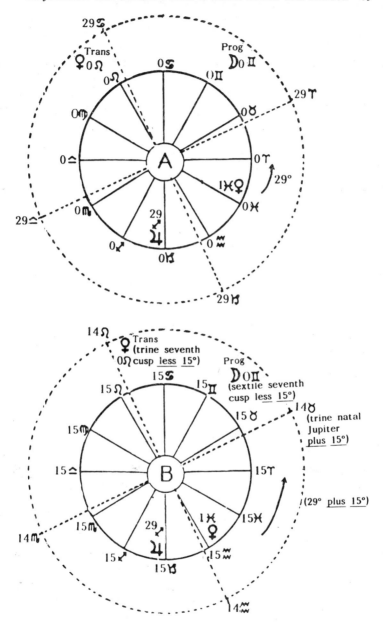

Figure 9A & B.   Differences in Angular and Planetary Directions for
Two Birth Charts Cast One Hour Apart

The native described his marriage as a lovely, harmonious match, marked by happiness at the time and continuing with love and harmony. Chart A in Figure 9 shows progressed and transiting aspects that commonly occur at such times: Solar arc Venus has reached conjunction natal seventh cusp (natal Venus 1 Pisces + 29° solar arc = 0 Aries conjunct natal seventh cusp). The progressed Moon at 0 Gemini is sextile the natal seventh cusp at 0 Aries. Transiting Venus at 0 Leo is trine the same cusp. The progressed seventh cusp at 29 Libra is sextile the natal Jupiter at 29 Sagittarius.

With Chart A, these aspects all 'fit' perfectly against the chart as cast. Chart B shows the same indicators, to highlight the discrepancies—and what discrepancies they are!

Venus by transit, co-operating by moving exactly one degree per day for our example, is exactly trine the natal seventh cusp in Chart A. In chart B, with the Venus still at 0 Leo, but the natal seventh at 15 Aries, the Venus is fifteen days shy of the trine.

The progressed Moon at 0 Gemini, which with the true chart, chart A, is sextile the natal seventh, is, again, fifteen degrees shy of coming to sextile chart B's seventh cusp at 15 Aries. However, since the progressed Moon is moving at a rate of approximately one degree per *month*, instead of 15 days' discrepancy as with the transiting Venus, the progressed Moon indicator is off by *fifteen months*.

Meanwhile, solar arc Venus, reaching only 0 Aries with a solar arc of 29°, is fifteen degrees shy of the natal seventh cusp; but since the solar arc is moving at a rate of one degree per *year*, that represents *fifteen years*! No better for the 'aspect' between progressed seventh at 14 Scorpio and the natal Jupiter 29 Sagittarius; fifteen degrees equals *fifteen years* past the sextile.

Just a single hour in birth time discrepancy, an infinitesmal integer of cosmic time, and the native's chart explodes in a massive confusion of fifteen days, fifteen months . . . fifteen *years* off!

A birth time in error by a single hour? Disaster!

Indeed, we sincerely hope that our hypothetical native will survive into the next section of this book. First he did not attend his own birth. Next he had to verify astrology without the slightest notion of its relevance to his life. Now, but for an hour's grace, he would neither physically resemble himself nor would any of the prize events of his life have happened to him. An uncertain birth time appears to have its own range of odd perils!

However, as we will explore in the section to come, not only small, single differences, but overall patterning, structure and focus within the context of the whole astrological chart can all serve as pointers to the true spatial positioning and the true timing of the native's astrology.

PART TWO:
THE BIRTH CHART—
MODELS FOR LIFE

4.
YOUR SIGNATURE IN SPACE:
THE BIRTH CHART AS A MIRROR

The Matching Process

Every living thing, whatever its species or genus, differs from all others, however minor or insignificant the differences may seem. Even relatively simple life forms, like two leaves on the same tree, have all their *characteristics* in common—they are of the same 'model', so to speak—but are never exact duplicates.

Human life, the most advanced life form, is characterized by the greatest degree of sophistication and differentiation. Parallel to the advanced mental, emotional, and spiritual functions of human beings are the great range and subtlety of physical differentiations which register as significant, recognizable physical traits which differ from one person to another.

Every astrological chart, with its specific planetary placements and layout of house cusps is no less differentiated. Because of the great number of concurrent planetary cycles each moving at respectively different rates of speed, as well as the rapid movement of house cusps at varying latitudes, non-duplicability of any one chart is ensured for aeons to come.

We have been briefly introduced to the correspondence between the space of the birth chart and the appearance of the physical native. Since every chart, as well as every native, is demonstrably unique, each chart should provide ample correspondences to confirm or nullify that it faithfully describes the native's person.

This is a 'matching' process—we will be matching chart against person. To ground our orientation, let's take a matching process which is relatively straightforward: fingerprint identification.

The fingerprint, like the chart, is non-duplicatable from person to person all across the world, providing a means of proof-positive identification. This matching process is based purely upon divisions of space on a two-dimensional surface on a comparative basis: the comparison of a known print of an individual with a newly-taken print of the same individual.

This is matching like against like. If one print were etched on a transparency, a simple superimposition could accomplish a proof-positive match, if all the lines and swirls of both prints would exactly coincide.

Like the fingerprint, the natal chart is a two-dimensional surface (notwithstanding that it represents a three-dimensional reality). But its counterpart 'match' is hardly either two-dimensional or stationary —a living human being! Matching one against the other entails a *translation* process, from the living native to the graphic representation of his traits within the chart and vice versa.

We can view the chart, metaphorically, as a 'mirror', which is not the actual person, but 'looks like' the person in equivalent astrological representations.

Whole Form Correspondence

Nor do chart and human being exactly correspond on a piece-by-piece duplication basis (as with the fingerprint), which might have produced odd guidelines like, 'Look at the midheaven of the chart while you look at the native's head and the fourth cusp while you look at his feet'. *No.* The whole of the human form has the whole of the chart 'within him', which we trace in ways which are certainly specific and graphic but in a whole, integrated way.

Our 'artist's eye' will look across the whole frame of the physical native, and gauge patterns of 'whole frame correspondence', not just isolated characteristics corresponding to single specific astrological components of the chart.

A rudimentary example will serve as a model. Let's say native A has late Aries rising. Taken alone, a late Aries rising native will tend to be tall and large-boned but with a spare frame and an evenly-proportioned body (i.e. the length of the legs and arms and the length of different parts of the torso fall into a balanced picture, none appearing long or short in relation to each other).

Now let's say that native B also has Saturn rising (in the first house), either in later Aries or Taurus. Saturn rising tends to *shorten* the person, but not the whole person proportionately; it specifically tends to shorten the *legs*.

Thus we are looking at a person whom we can see would be quite tall *if not for* shortness in the legs. Let's say that that gives—as a *composite*—a person of average height. In other words, this person is tall from the head to the hips and short in the legs, which gives a whole-body length of 'average'.

Native C, let's say, has a mid-Virgo ascendant and is of average height, common for this sign. But Virgo, with its *Mercury* rulership, will give limbs of at least average length or longer. The arms and legs will also tend to be the same proportional length in relation to each other. Native B has long enough arms but it is the legs that are short.

For native C with Virgo rising, average height is simply a whole-body characteristic. However, for native B with late Aries rising but Saturn rising in the first house, *his* 'average height' is a superimposition of tall Aries and short-legged Saturn, i.e. the astrologer needs to look at *all* of the native and the complete layout of the natal chart to see exactly what type of astrological composite (here the Aries ascendant *plus* the rising Saturn) describes the native in his whole form. Figure 10 illustrates this.

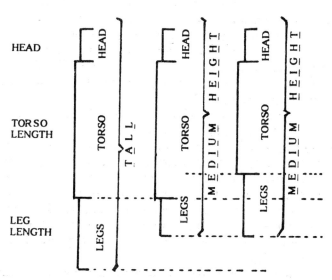

Figure 10.   Differences in Proportioning

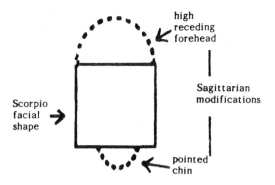

Figure 11.   Modifications in Facial Shape

Figure 11 illustrates another example of superimposition. Let's say this is a native with a square-shaped compact body, with a large, notably square-shaped head, very dark hair, large, dark, wide-set eyes with arching eyebrows ('Mephistopheles style') and the mouth turned downwards in a sort of permanent grimace. It sounds very Scorpionic, doesn't it?

Figure 11 homes in on the facial shape. Be the native's true ascendant Scorpio, you then notice that he also has a high receding forehead and a pointed chin, modifying the basically square-shaped face. Those characteristics sound Sagittarian.

This is something that comes up frequently—two sets of characteristics typical of two successive signs, such as Gemini modified by Cancer, or—in the above example—Scorpio modified by Sagittarius. Frequently, what it means is that the first sign is rising, but that there is a planet of the succeeding sign rising in the first house. The native described above sounds like a candidate for Scorpio rising with some planet rising in Sagittarius, because what has been described sounds like a Scorpio-Sagittarius *composite*. Visually, it works something like a photographic superimposition, as Figure 11 illustrates using solid and broken lines.

Back in the sub-chapter 'The Many Types of Spatial Differences', pp. 49-53, Figure 6 showed which single factors in the natal chart will be reflected in the appearance and demeanour. Now we are going to approach that from a whole-chart, whole-person perspective, so we can learn to look at what is more important or overriding *first*, and let that set the tone for the 'mirroring' process between person and chart.

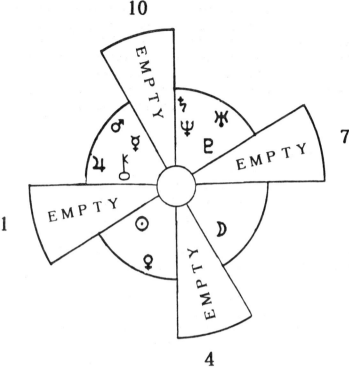

Figure 12. Lack of Angular Planets

Special Prominence of the Rising Degree

Usually it is easiest to match person and birth chart when there is only the ascendant to consider. Wherever the planets may fall in a chart, the one factor, the *only* factor that you will always be sure is 'visible' in the native for *any* chart is the rising degree. It may or may not be modified by other factors superimposed upon it, but there will always be several concrete ways of identifying the true ascendant in the chart.

Since all charts have all the planets within them, it is their *placement* within the context of the whole chart that will determine whether their influence will be superimposed upon that of the ascendant, or whether they will be, in effect, 'invisible'. Figure 12 shows the most common case of virtually *no* interference with the expression of the rising sign. Note the absence of any planets in the angular locations of the chart, namely the first, tenth, seventh, and fourth houses, including a cusp of three to five degrees. There are other ways in which locations of planets within the chart will produce 'visible' influences in the native, but normally, the most prominent influences will show in the angular houses, so these are the locations to check for *first*. If these houses and their cusps are empty, generally the ascendant will be relatively clear-cut in its manifestation (such as the late Aries rising native *without* a rising Saturn or any other rising, culminating, or setting planet. Pure Aries).

The Visibility of Angular Planets

How visible are angular planets? Often very much so, though our 'chart/mirror' is not even and flat in its reflections, but graded in intensities. If a planet is *exactly* on the midheaven, for example, it will exert a dominant influence, as though a camera lens had brought it into exact focus. A planet in the tenth house, but close to the eleventh, still may manifest in the native visibly if there are no planets above it or rising in the first house, but it will be much less likely to take on the same prominence as a midheaven planet.

The prominence of each of the respective angles are also graded as to their visible influence. Rising planets, even well into the first house will register in some way. If there are several, the first rising will tend to take precedence, but will not block out the other rising planets. Occasionally, a planet rising early in the second house will be visible, but generally only in the absence of more prominently-placed planets.

With the tenth house, a planet well into the tenth may not be as visible as a planet well into the first house, especially if there are planets close to either the ascendant or the seventh cusp. But if you find that planetary influence *dominating* the appearance, it is likely that it is within three degrees of the midheaven or just five or so degrees into the tenth.

Planets in the seventh house, especially very close to the angle, may have the same relative strength visibly as rising planets. With planets in the fourth house, their influence may be muted visually (being in 'darkness') unless the other angles of the chart are untenanted; but again, if the planet is very nearly *on* the fourth cusp, you find exceptions.

The general rule of thumb is that the closer a planet is to an angle, the more visible it is in the physical native. Exceptions are that any rising planet (i.e. anywhere in the first house) will tend to be visible and fourth house influences are the most easily masked by more prominently-placed planets.

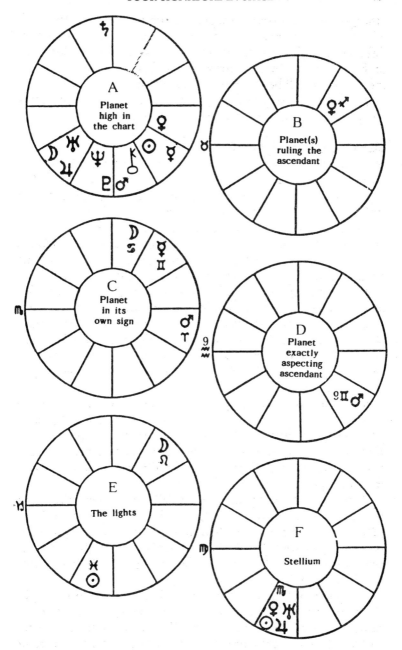

Figure 13. Visible Factors in the Chart

I would allow a five-degree cusp for an angle at the maximum for visibility, and would prefer to be more conservative at three.

Other Factors Giving Visibility
Angular planets, though important, are not the exclusive visible factors in the chart. Other factors are listed below, with examples of how each looks in the chart shown in Figure 13, A–F.

A. *Planet high in the chart:* The most elevated planet in the chart (i.e. closest to the midheaven from either side, even if from the eleventh or the eighth house) will tend to be visible, especially if it is isolated, and most especially, if it is a hemisphere singleton (i.e. the only planet above the horizon).

B. *Planet ruling the ascendant*: The planet that rules the ascendant (Mars for Aries, Venus for Taurus and so on) is often visible by the sign in which that planet is placed. If it is *very* visible, this often means that it is also angular.

If the ruling planet is conjunct another planet, that planet will often be visible. In one instance, the native had Cancer rising with Cancer's ruler, the Moon, in Gemini in the twelfth house but *conjunct Saturn*. The person looked identifiably Cancer rising, but also had a characteristically flat-cheeked face found so often with Saturn influence, even though Saturn fell in a cadent house, the twelfth. (Note: the chart lacked planets in Saturn-ruled signs.) Because there were no angular planets in this chart, the chart ruler and its aspecting assumed special prominence.

C. *Planet in its own sign:* Venus in Taurus, the Moon in Cancer, Jupiter in Sagittarius, and so on will tend to show visibly in planetary/sign characteristics, even if in a cadent house, such as Saturn in Capricorn in the third house. However, strongly angular planets may mask their visibility.

D. *Planet exactly aspecting the ascendant*: A planet in exact aspect to the ascendant will be visible, if not as strongly as a rising planet, so long as the aspect is major (including the quincunx) and *exact* (I would give two degrees' orb maximum if applying, one degree if separating, meaning that the *ascendant* is applying into or separating from the aspect, since the ascendant moves more rapidly than the planet).

E. *The lights*: The Sun sign or the Moon sign may be visible in the native, but not as often as you might expect. If it is cadent, even succedent, and other planets are more prominently placed, you might be hard-pressed to find it in the appearance. (The Moon, notably, will give the native's emotional 'tone', without necessarily being visible in the physiology.) In any event, the rising sign, on the whole, has unquestionable predominance over the Sun sign in matters of physical appearance, which cannot be overemphasized.

F. *Stellium*: A stellium (four or more planets in the same sign) may be quite visible, especially if it includes the Sun or the Moon. Even if the stellium is in a cadent house (third, sixth, ninth, or twelfth), four planets or more in the same sign will register traits of that sign in the appearance. An interesting case in point occurred when I was asked to do the charts of two unrelated infants, each of whom had Scorpio stelliums in the third, and were each born of parents with no Scorpio in their charts at all. The first child did not seem to look like either parent. Then I met the second child and noted that he, with his square little head, and look-right-through-you eyes didn't resemble either of *his* parents, either—but that he looked like 'someone' I had met. It was the first child! They looked enough alike to be brother and sister, since the Scorpio stellium (along with the same rising sign) was so 'visible' in both. A remarkable object lesson.

Using Visibility to Narrow the Range of Birth time
Visibility of planetary influences can give very precise tools for narrowing down the range of an uncertain birth time. Any rising sign is a full thirty degrees, a very wide range of space indeed, and if the rising sign were all we could 'look at' in the native to make our assessment, it would make the succeeding step of working with finely-tuned mathematics (the chart's timing) unwieldy indeed. But the chart as a whole, with its four key angles, can assist in homing in on the mark. As the planets each rise, culminate, set, and come to the IC, they 'duck in and out of view', as it were, approaching and separating from the angles, coming into visibility on the approach of a few degrees to the angle and through the angular house, moving into non-visibility through the cadent and succedent houses. (The planets move counter-clockwise through the zodiac in direct motion, but *appear* to be moving clockwise through the course of the day in relation to the much faster counter-clockwise motion of the chart wheel. It's a bit like a fast-moving train passing a slower-moving train, which momentarily appears to be moving 'backwards'.)

Figure 14 (cast for 42N latitude) illustrates how to apply 'visibility

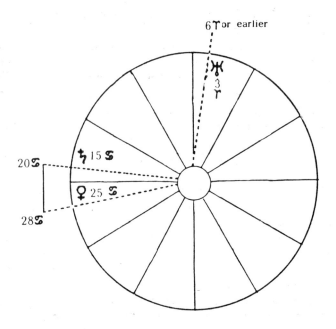

Figure 14. Using Visibility to Narrow the Range of Birth Time

skills', which we might also term 'recognition skills', since we are training in how to recognize what a visible planet 'looks like' in the native. Let's say you have already ascertained that given a birth time range of many hours, the rising sign is almost surely Cancer: the native has pale, fleshy skin, rounded body lines, a 'slushy-sounding soft-spoken voice, has large liquid eyes that observe and follow you with vivid emotional involvement, and so on through many of the more typical Cancerian traits.

Note that two planets in the rising area of the chart are posited in Cancer: Saturn at 15 Cancer and Venus at 25 Cancer. Let's say that the native seems to be devoid of any Saturnine characteristics outwardly: his bodily motions are not reserved, rigid or measured; his eyes do not have a flat gaze; there is no 'boniness' in the physique; his jaw-line is not keenly defined, and so on.

However, the native does have some obvious Venusian characteristics: instead of the sensuous, rounded lips of many a Cancerian, it is modified into a 'bow mouth'; the eyeline comes halfway down the face; the features are evenly-spaced with the eyebrows gently curved, and so on.

Venus could be rising anywhere in the first house and be apparent visibly. However, we cannot go back *too* far in Cancer for the ascendant, because that would bring the Saturn into visibility. To be on the safe side, we want to find Saturn at least five degrees risen into the twelfth house, meaning that the natal ascendant cannot fall earlier than 20 Cancer (20 – 5° = 15 Cancer, location of the natal Saturn). Nor can the ascendant fall past 28 Cancer, three degrees past the natal Venus, or the Venus will no longer be prominently 'visible'.

The dotted area in Figure 14 shows the range in the sign of Cancer within which the ascendant would fall to correspond with the visible evidence of the native's physical person.

Meanwhile, with this particular chart, we can narrow it down still further, since Uranus is apparently near the midheaven of the chart, and we can make the determination of whether it is in 'visible' range or not by observing the native.

Let's say that for this particular native, Uranus is *very* visible: the shoulders are high and bony-looking with an elongated upper back; the cheekbones are very prominent, with a steely look across the eyes; the voice is high, harsh, and definitive, and so on.

With Uranus this prominent, the midheaven of the chart cannot fall more than three degrees past the natal Uranus, which is placed at 3 Aries, making the true midheaven of the chart 6 Aries or *earlier* (since an earlier midheaven will bring Uranus into the tenth, where it will still be visible). Note that a 6 Aries midheaven, the *latest* the midheaven can be, will give (for the birth latitude of 42°N) 24 Cancer on the ascendant. This means we have lopped four more degrees off the possible ascendant, the degrees from 24 to 28 Cancer, because those later degrees would indicate a later midheaven, which would push the Uranus out of visible range.

Our final range has been narrowed down from all 30 degrees of Cancer to just *four* degrees of Cancer, from 20 to 24! In fact, with this particular chart, given a very visible Venus and an 'invisible' Saturn, I would definitely prefer to place the ascendant as close as possible to the last degree of the range, 24 Cancer, where the visibility/invisibility contrast would be maximized. We have now narrowed a birth time down to a workable range. We have also 'cut across' the chart in several ways, much like examining and confirming the dimensions of a many-sided sculpture. We can cut away a planet rising in the first house and relocate it into the twelfth. We can adjust the angles of the chart (our imaginary 'levers') to bring a planet onto an angle from a cadent house, or to knock it off the angle. The chart is still a 'mirror' of the native, but as we can see, it reflects the native's form from many views: the ascendant, the whole rising area of the chart, the four angles seen as a unit, planets elevated and set apart, and so on. The 'art of the living native' becomes the art of an accurately-cast chart!

Influence of Sign versus Influence of Planet

Each planet, of course, is posited in some sign, but whether it is the influence of a planet or of its sign which emerges the most visibly is not completely consistent from chart to chart for reasons which vary. It is a relative subtlety at this early stage; one or the other will give the needed clues, though I do think primary visibility will generally register through the planet (i.e. Mercury on the ascendant will look Mercurial whether the Mercury is in Taurus, Capricorn, Libra and so on).

I rectified one chart where it turned out that Mars in Virgo was right on the midheaven. This person had a fairly uncommon facial characteristic that the shapes of the cheeks and jaw looked much like a chipmunk or someone with a case of mumps. I couldn't say *why*, but that characteristically odd shape is specific to mid-Virgo. On looking closer I also discovered Martial characteristics, but it happened to be the Virgo that was immediately obvious. Putting Mars in mid-Virgo on the MC brought the chart to exactitude, as mathematical timing indicators confirmed.

Note here as well that we are concerned with relative judgements with many charts—not surprisingly, as in this part of rectification work we are functioning as artists in our discernments. The lines and shapes of the body are indeed objective and identifiable, but the trained 'artist's eye' will more readily see the main lines and forms within the 'composite' picture that characterizes so many of us. What is a pure colour in one painting may be muted or blended in another, yet still be clearly discernible. A person with Capricorn rising and no rising planets may look very Capricornian. Another person with the same degree of Capricorn rising, but with (let's say) Venus, Mercury and the Moon rising will present a composite of four—the rising degree plus each of the three planetary influences.

Ironically, in the context of actual practice, composites can be a great aid. You may not be sure at first whether you are looking at a dominant Mercury or Gemini rising, but within the structured layout of the entire chart, within some exact chart wheel, you can adjust the angles and relocate planets to account for visibility to a degree of sophistication that would not be possible without the phenomena of composite influences: sign influence versus planetary influence, angular versus non-angular planets, whole-body identification versus modification of components of the bodily frame, features that 'aren't quite characteristic' of one sign, but incorporate the influence of others.

Probably the trickiest thing to sort out, short of having the whole chart in front of you to look at, is discerning whether you are looking at someone's rising sign, or at a very prominently-placed planet which *rules* that sign, such as: Taurus rising or a prominent Venus? Sagittarius rising or a prominent Jupiter? Cancer rising or a prominent Moon?

It is helpful to realize that a rising sign and a prominent planet do not carry the same weight. The rising sign is more pervasive. This is what gives whole-body build, and the framework within which one approaches life. Planetary influences, although they can modify many specifics of the form, and can pour their own characteristic energy into the personal functioning, still function within the more comprehensive grounding of the rising degree.

For example, one native had a very prominent Mars. It was in the eleventh house, but a hemisphere singleton above the horizon. She had a very piercing direct energy, and eyes that arched upwards as surely as Scorpio, though there was no Scorpio in the chart (nor Aries).

However, the rising sign was Taurus, with a sturdy Taurean build, a deliberate gait, a sure and steady manner and strong, magnetic ('earthy') energies.

It is as though the rising degree is the 'shell', and the planetary influences are the 'filling'. Once you become used to recognizing what is pervasive (the rising sign) and what is modifying, activating, or specifying (the planets), it will become an easier process.

The distinctive imprint of form and expression that is the living human being is now reflected as a distinctive imprint of form which is the natal chart. This is the native's 'physiological signature'. We might also call it the native's 'signature in space'.

Our next exploration is into the native's 'signature in time', 'The Birth Chart as a Blueprint'. We are about to take the same fixed layout of space that we could 'see' in the native, and now it will become the road-map for the native's lifelong journey through time. We are taking our chart/mirror off the wall and laying it down on the ground ahead of us, like an architect's blueprint beneath our feet.

5.
YOUR SIGNATURE IN TIME: THE BIRTH CHART AS A BLUEPRINT

How Patterns Unravel from Birth

The chart laid out flat on the drawing board is the same chart we just held upright as on an artist's easel. That very condensed view of space was the many imprints of form superimposed upon the fixed physical mass of the native. Our new kind of 'space', the architect's space, is fluid and changing, unravelling through the vivid if intangible pathways of time.

We might say that whereas we have just *looked* at the native, it is now time to *listen*. Stories are woven into the timing of the native's life much as lines and forms and shapes were woven through the native's physical self.

Now, the space of the chart is not only an enduring constant but it is also a starting point, immediately set into motion from the moment of birth on. We now view the planets and house cusps in terms of the *direction* in which they are moving and the *speed*. The ephemeris and Table of Houses will reveal the course of these timed directional impulses—the transits, progressions and other directions that are 'within us' from birth.

Whatever we can do about our lives—though essential and considerable—we cannot alter the time patterning the chart/blueprint sets into place from the birth moment on. The chart's timing blueprints are a 'given'. If you were born in 1974 with 17 Sagittarius rising, for example, with transiting Uranus due to pass over the ascendant in 1985, it is inevitable from the time of birth that that transit will be effective then; and that the progressed ascendant at age 18 (2 Capricorn, let's say, for a 39°N latitude of birth) will be sextile your natal Jupiter at 2 Pisces.

Now, past understanding that these positions are 'given' from the time of birth on, we will need to begin making correspondences between those directions in the chart and the actual life experience of the native at those corresponding times in his life. *What happened* at age eleven (at the Uranus/ascendant transit)?; *what happened* at age eighteen (the progressed ascendant sextile natal Jupiter)?

Note we are considering not transits nor progressions alone, but always in relation to the natal chart. The directions within and against a chart do not alter the chart's original space; rather they highlight it. All the directions, though zodiacally exact in and of themselves, are grounded in to specific reference because they *rebound against the natal positions*. With the above example, it was the transiting Uranus that was conjunct the *natal* ascendant, and the progressed ascendant that was sextile the *natal* Jupiter.

The concept of 'blueprint' becomes clear when we see that all the parts of the natal chart are successively realized as they are successively aspected, meaning that they come to the fore and take the central spotlight for the duration of the transit or progression that is aspecting them.

Blueprint 1: Development of Natal Qualities

There are four different but interrelated ways in which the birth chart works effectively as a blueprint, all of which will be confirmed when a chart is rectified to exactitude. Note this does not mean that every chart need be systematically viewed each way to be certain of its accuracy, though once a chart *is* accurate, each way of assessing timing will work for that chart.

Over the course of many chart rectifications, you will find yourself using many means routinely, and develop a flexible, comprehensive approach. The following suggests many ways of thinking about the natal chart that will assist in both the flow and the technical work of rectification.

Now, to illustrate the many modes of blueprinting pictorially, again imagine that the birth chart is a house. We did this once before, but purely in relation to space, to narrow down our 'needle in the haystack' search for the rising degree to one of the imaginary house's 'rooms' before we attempted detailed work with the chart's timing.

Now we will envision this house (the 'chart/house') as representing the native and his life in total—the whole 'me and my life' composite. This is still a 'spatial house', but now it is also a 'timed house'. Its blueprints are graphic, etched into space, as are an architect's, but their *realization* is unravelled through the course of time. If we only follow them on through, we will discover how living itself reveals the manifestation and realization of the natal potential.

Now imagine that we are travelling from room to room (the equivalent of the natal chart's houses), signifying our journey through life via our rootedness in the natal chart, both on a permanent basis and through the course of time. We pass successively through the rooms, or even simultaneously (as they are all 'within us'), enhancing each—or, as the case may sometimes be, wrecking each!—in the continuing process of 'becoming more and more ourselves', or 'getting to know ourselves'. The imaginary house (the whole chart) has always been there from the beginning of life, but both its contents and its usefulness—its sum-total 'potential'—were yet to be successively explored.

Upon first entering the house, let's separate exploration of its contents from exploration of its usefulness. Of course, we want to familiarize ourselves with its contents first. The natal chart, as we know, spins about one whole rotation every twenty-four hours (actually a 360° rotation plus approximately one zodiacal degree). We can picture this as a whirling object in space which is at first indistinct, vague, apparently unformed, and as it comes closer and closer—spinning all the while—its many characteristics come into clear focus. Or you can think of travelling on a circular path throughout the imaginary house once each day, first the porch, then the living room, then the kitchen, then the den, and so on. It will take a whole day before you are fully familiar with the surroundings and are aware of what, exactly, is in each room.

Now take our house analogy and see it again as the natal chart, and say that this particular chart has a rising Saturn (Saturn in the first house). You are not going to be able to distinguish the many characteristics that imparts to the native when he is a new-born baby, but what will happen is that he will *develop into* a 'rising Saturn' type of person, both physiologically and temperamentally through the years of growing up. Perhaps he develops a reserved, cautious demeanour, exercising careful, serious discernment before committing himself to a course; he looks first, before he leaps, long and hard. He might have skin that is pasty pale, cheeks flat, his legs might be short, his eyes might have a 'goat-like' look about them— wide-set, bulbous, large. He has a hard-edged, flat-sounding voice. These are all characteristics that are plausibly 'Saturnine'.

Remember, we are still exploring the basic 'contents' of the imaginary house, 'contents' corresponding to the fixed spatial layout of the chart. 'The Chart as a Mirror' viewed this in its static form,

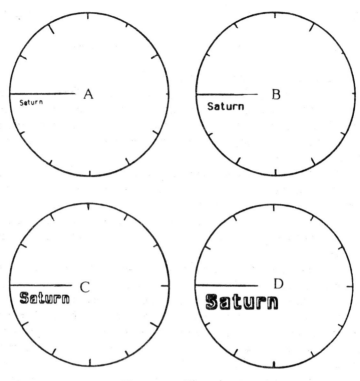

Figure 15.   Blueprint 1

but now we can also see that the development of the permanent, visible 'up front' rising Saturn characteristics developed, in part, from the native's recurring experience through time, of the front door of his imaginary house—the equivalent of the *natal ascendant*—which—in his case specifically—was strewn with rocks (Saturn indeed!). So in his experience, his contact with the world (the ascendant) has a *hard* quality: it implies barriers and obstacles, restrictions and the need for cautious discernment. Those Saturn qualities so close to the surface in him (ungracefully represented here as a pile of rocks) both sets his appearance gradually in a Saturnine mould, and also serves as both a magnet and a transmitter of Saturnine energies from the doorway of his own personal world.

This continuous, recurring, repetitive whirl through the chart/house is the most rudimentary type of chart/blueprint, because nothing has changed positionally in the chart, it just gets reinforced again and again through the characteristic ascendant/Saturn experience of the native.

Figure 15 suggests what happens in a graphic form.

Blueprint 2: Selective Highlighting

The second type of blueprinting goes beyond exploration of the contents of the imaginary house into exploration of its usefulness: how does it function, what does it do in the life; when something (a planet or a house cusp) activates it, what characteristically *happens* in the native's life?

Although the natal chart, the transits, the progressions and other directions are all 'within you' from the moment of birth, the natal positions are activated selectively at *specific times* in the life. Each experience brings to the fore different *components* of the natal chart, which correspond to the character of what is happening in the life at that time.

Thus are different parts of you 'realized' or 'actualized'. For example, perhaps you have had some notably Venusian periods in your life. Let's say that one, notably (a common example), was when you fell in love with the progressed seventh cusp trine the natal Venus, i.e. your natal Venus was to the fore. Your own special Venus qualities, the capacity for love and romance and harmonizing one's life with another's, and that Venus complete with sign and house location and its natal aspecting (which is personal to you) was being 'realized'. This is an example of blueprint 2: how the timing of life experience brings the natal potential to the fore.

Now we are not simply making our characteristic pilgrimage through the entirety of the imaginary house, but at specific times are centred, or focused upon the kitchen, or the guest bedroom, and so on. Each experience brings to the fore different components within the chart, or 'different parts of you' until the paper blueprint (the natal chart) becomes an actual *living* blueprint in a realized form. 'Self-actualization', if one will. (Traditional teaching is that you have to analyse all that happens in the life in relation to the *natal* chart. If something is promised there, the appropriate aspecting could land it for *you*.)

To review thus far, blueprint 1 is the gradual realization of the whole of the layout of the natal chart, which is purely a fixed layout of space, but which becomes more and more 'itself' through the course of time. Blueprint 2 brings to the fore (centres, focuses, or however one might express it) specific components of the whole you

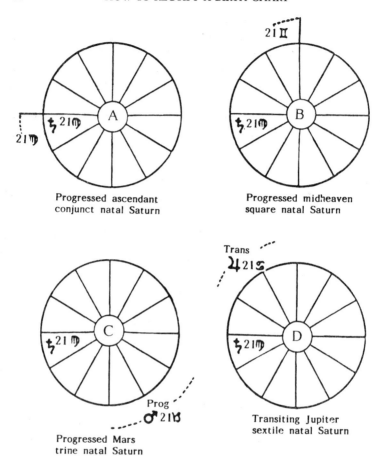

Figure 16.   Examples of Blueprint 2

as they are successively activated in your own natal chart at some specific time period(s) in the life.

Figure 16 illustrates this in graphic form for a natal Saturn.

Blueprint 3: The Structure of Events
Both blueprints 3 and 4 relate to the timing of the chart in terms of specific dates (or time periods) of specific changes in the life. They are both essential parameters of the 'whole astrological picture' of those key junctures in life we call 'events'.

First we will continue our exploration through our imaginary house. Imagine that certain things happen in the larger, house-as-a-whole which affect specific rooms or specific structural characteristics of the house. Let's say that figuratively, you have gone through blueprints 1 and 2, and you discover upon exploration, that you function most effectively in the living room of the house. Let's say that the living room is the equivalent of the astrological *house of your chart* where you find the Sun or the Moon. Maybe you had some fear the first several times you entered the 'kitchen' of the imaginary house, where your natal Saturn is hiding out, or feel invigorated whenever you come anywhere near the 'porch', the imaginary location of your natal Mars.

This type of blueprint characteristic—how you personally function in some part of the imaginary house—is individual from person to person; that is self-actualization that is specific to any native's natal chart. But in blueprint 3, the rooms of the house have a larger, more general significance that is in common to everyone, whatever the particulars of their own natal chart.

For example, everyone's house has a master bedroom. Let's say that that is the area of the chart/house which corresponds to one's *parents*. In terms of the natal chart, that is shown structurally through the meridian of the chart (tenth-fourth house axis) *irrespective of* any of the more personalized contents of the chart. You may have the Sun in the fifth house and someone else has the Sun in the twelfth, but for both of you, and everyone else in the world as well, the parents are shown through the meridian.

Now let's say that a parent dies. That is an event that happens to nearly everyone at some time during their life. If and when it does, then in *everyone's* imaginary house, the 'master bedroom' (analogue for the chart's meridian) will be put under great stress structurally *at the exact time the parent dies*. The supporting beams of the strength of the walls or the character of the environment of *that* 'room' of the imaginary house will be affected for chart A, chart B, chart C alike, and so on *ad infinitum*, notwithstanding that the living room may be the main hangout for the chart A native, the den for the chart B native, and the dining room for the chart C native.

Thus blueprint 3 is the basis of how 'the astrology of events' works. It is not rooted in psychology, philosophy, our attitudes or our creative interpretations. This type of unfolding blueprint is *structural and objective*. Everyone has a mother; if something affects her, the chart's meridian is where to look. Everyone has a physical body; if it is injured, the ascendant axis is where to look. Everyone has a health outlook;

if it is affected, the sixth house cusp is where to look.

We might say that blueprint 3 gives us the 'X-ray' of a chart for any given event, or—with our imaginary house—just the structural beams minus the surface of the walls and the interior decoration. The latter is filled in by blueprint 4 coming up, 'The Content of Events'.

Figure 17, A and B, shows examples of how blueprint 3 works.

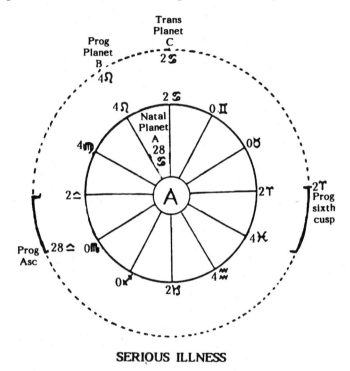

SERIOUS ILLNESS

Structural requirements:

1. **Affliction(s) involving natal and/or progressed ascendant:** Transiting planet C (2 CAN) square natal ascendant (2 LIB); progressed ascendant (28 LIB) square natal planet A (28 CAN).

2. **Affliction(s) involving natal and/or progressed sixth cusp:** Progressed planet B (4 LEO) quincunx natal sixth (4 PIS); transiting planet C (2 CAN) square progressed sixth (2 AR).

3. **Common involvement of quincunxes for illness:** Progressed planet B (4 LEO) quincunx natal sixth (4 PIS).

Figure 17A.   Examples of Blueprint 3

Figure 17, A and B shows examples of how blueprint 3 works.

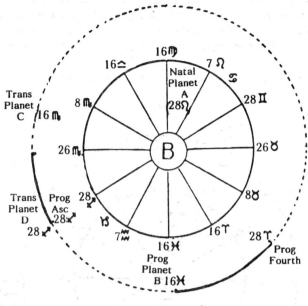

SALE OF HOME

Structural requirements:

1. Fourth cusp involvement for the home: Progressed fourth cusp (28 AR) trine natal planet A (28 LEO); transiting planet C (16 SCOR) trine natal fourth (16 PIS); progressed planet B (16 PIS) conjunct natal fourth (16 PIS).

2. Ascendant involvement for effect upon native: Transiting planet D (28 SAG) conjunct progressed ascendant (28 SAG); progressed ascendant (28 SAG) trine natal planet A (28 LEO).

3. Second/eighth cusp involvement for monetary transaction: Transiting planet D (28 SAG) conjunct natal second cusp (28 SAG); progressed fourth cusp (28 AR) trine natal second cusp, progressed ascendant and transiting planet D (all 28 SAG).

Figure 17B.   Examples of Blueprint 3

Blueprint 4: The Contents of Events

Blueprint 4 is superimposed upon blueprint 3, but it corresponds to the specific *character* of the structural changes of 3, and also our response to those circumstantial changes, together loosely termed the 'content' of events, because they describe exactly what happened and its effects.

A word of clarification is called for here, as some astrological pedagogy suggests a separation between what *happens* to the native and the native's *response*. This is a schism which astrology, in its natural unitary design, does not bear out. Note that *both* what happens and our response is shown by the aspecting at the event date. Indeed, if indicators signifying each are both in aspect to the ascendant, they are registered in exactly the same indicators, such as a *sudden* event, registering in Uranus aspecting, producing a reaction of *shock* in the native, shown by the same Uranus! The astrology itself shows *what type of event* happened (blueprint 3), *how* it happened (blueprint 4) and the effect upon the native (aspects to the ascendant and other specific cusps). All these facets of experience happen simultaneously and, in a sense, what we are doing here is simply 'breaking down how to walk', obviously a unitary action which could, nevertheless, be 'broken down'.

Blueprint 3 established guidelines for the 'outline' of an event, upon which blueprint 4 will fill in the specifics. What type of event happens registers in aspecting to specific *house cusps*, specifying what circumstance or area of the life is affected, such as the example cited of major aspecting to the meridian at the time of a parental death. Using our 'house' analogy, let's say a parent dies and you find the expected structural damage to the master bedroom (i.e. the meridian). That will be common to a parent dying for *any* native. But is the damage an earthquake, water seepage, a fire? That is analogous to asking did the parent die of a heart attack (Mars affliction), stroke (Uranus), a chronic illness (Saturn), in pain (Mars), in a coma (Neptune), at peace (Venus), and so on.

Also, was the native hysterical at the damage (Uranus)? Calm (Venus)? Grieved (Saturn)? Relieved (Jupiter)?

We also have to consider the *manner* in which the event arrived, shown by the aspecting. A square (sharp, definitive and/or a cut-off)? A conjunction (with direct impact)? A quincunx (gruelling, entailing suffering, a situation difficult to reconcile)?

Each aspect and the aspecting planet will give information specific to the parental passing *for that particular native*, describing both what happened and his experience of what happened, notwithstanding that the fact of *some* major structural aspecting upon the meridian will be consistent from chart to chart.

Now we can identify blueprints 3 and 4 as both relating to the astrology of events, but 3 on the general and objective levels, and 4 on the specific and subjective levels.

What this means in the context of actual astrological practice is that when you look at the date of a parental death, and you do see major aspecting involving the meridian you might say, yes, this *could* be the timing of the event because there is *some* recognizable appropriate blueprint. If that much is absent, then you have to rule it out and go no further, because that general and objective criterion must be met.

But then you go on to blueprint 4, examining the manner of and circumstances surrounding that *specific* parental death and the effect upon the native. If those specifics are reflected literally in the types of aspects involved and the component planets, you might well have a true confirmation that your chart is accurate. Or, by contrast, you may see that yes, there is heavy aspecting involving the meridian (blueprint 3), but the aspects and planets involved do not match up with the native's description. So you say 'Yes, I can see where a parent could have died at that time *but not how you're describing it*', and then seek clarification and/or seek out another adjustment of the chart.

Care in following the criteria for blueprints 3 and 4 also will provide cross-checks in your work, so that it is both grounded in factual reality (blueprint 3) and also gets to the 'meat' of what happened and its effects upon the human life (blueprint 4). It is astrology itself which, remarkably, naturally provides the bridges between objective and subjective experience. The same structural changes that activate objective events in the life also set off strong subjective responses. We don't have an actual, physical life 'versus' a life in our consciousness; they are inextricably intertwined.

In actual practice, the main problem in accomplishing accurate rectification has not been the concentration upon objective events or subjective responses *per se*, but the failure to view them as an integral whole. The way to facilitate that view *technically* is that when the native is recounting his life story, and you are presented with what seems like a wholly subjective level of response, like 'I was really upset through that whole period', you, the rectifying astrologer can enquire, 'But what actually *happened*, and *when*?' If, on the other hand, you are told a series of surface details like, 'Well, first I got married and then we moved and then . . .', you can enquire, 'What were the surrounding circumstances and how did you *feel* at the time?' That way, both structure and contents will be verified. If you concentrate on one pole to the neglect of the other—whichever pole

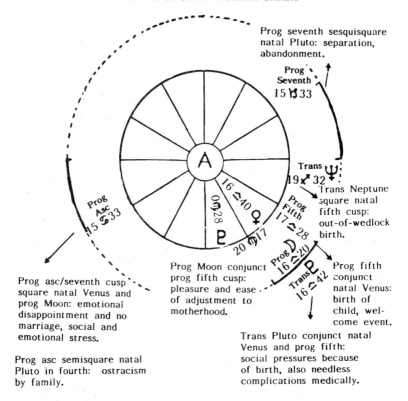

Prog seventh sesquisquare natal Pluto: separation, abandonment.

Prog Seventh 15 ♑ 33

Trans 19 ♐ 32 ♆

Trans Neptune square natal fifth cusp: out-of-wedlock birth.

Prog Asc 15 ♋ 33

16 ♎ 40

0 ♎ 28

♀

♇

20 ♍ 17

Prog Fifth 17 ♎ 28

Prog ☽ 16 ♎ 20

Trans ♇ 16 ♎ 42

Prog fifth conjunct natal Venus: birth of child, welcome event.

Prog asc/seventh cusp square natal Venus and prog Moon: emotional disappointment and no marriage, social and emotional stress.

Prog Moon conjunct prog fifth cusp: pleasure and ease of adjustment to motherhood.

Prog asc semisquare natal Pluto in fourth: ostracism by family.

Trans Pluto conjunct natal Venus and prog fifth: social pressures because of birth, also needless complications medically.

Birth of Child
Figure 18A.   Examples of Blueprint 4

it may be—you are much less likely to do accurate work. Blueprints 3 and 4 together provide most useful crosschecks to round out your work.

Figure 18, A and B, shows two examples of blueprint 4, with planetary and cuspal components identified as to the exact details they provide.

Figure 18A highlights the key astrological directions of the birth of a child. This was an out-of-wedlock birth, self-described by the native as a very happy event surrounded by exceptionally stressful circumstances.

The fifth cusp is, of course, a key indicator for the birth of a child. Either the progressed fifth cusp in exact aspect with a natal planet or a progressed planet in exact aspect with the fifth cusp is generally

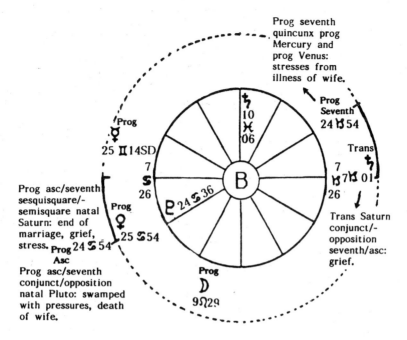

Prog seventh
quincunx prog
Mercury and
prog Venus:
stresses from
illness of wife.

Prog
Seventh
24 ♑ 54

Prog
☿
25 ♊14SD

Trans

7
♐ 7 ♑ 01
26

Prog asc/seventh
sesquisquare/-
semisquare natal
Saturn: end of
marriage, grief,
stress. **Prog** 24 ♋ 54
Asc

Prog
♀
25 ♋ 54

Trans Saturn
conjunct/-
opposition
seventh/asc:
grief.

Prog asc/seventh
conjunct/opposition
natal Pluto: swamped
with pressures, death
of wife.

Prog
☽
9 ♌ 29

Death of Wife
Figure 18B.   Examples of Blueprint 4

featured. Preferably the aspect will be harmonious (stressful aspects
affecting the fifth cusp often produce complications), and if the child
is especially loved and wanted, Venus, Jupiter and/or the Moon might
be featured prominently.

The specifics of what happened show in blueprint 4. Here we can
acknowledge the native's rendition that she wanted the child and
took readily to motherhood as accurate: note that not only has the
fifth cusp progressed to conjunction natal Venus at 16 Libra, but
the progressed Moon reinforces with an additional conjunction.
Under such aspecting, the mother would have a close bonding with
the child almost regardless of the surrounding circumstances.

The most immediate, obvious qualifier to the joy of childbirth
was the transiting Pluto, *also* at 16 Libra. The native was very nearly
'obliterated' in the eyes of her family, who not only gave her no
attention or congratulations at the time but had thrown her out of
their home several months earlier. Pluto here signifies social pressures,
ostracism, depersonalization.

Pluto's difficult influence is doubled and tripled. The progressed ascendant at 15 CAN 33 is semisquare the natal Pluto at 0 VIR 28, with Pluto in the fourth, signifying the harsh manner in which the family cut this young woman out of their lives. Also note that *transiting* Pluto, although at 16 LIB 42 very slightly past the square to the progressed ascendant, will have been skirting in and out of exact range of that square for many months surrounding this event, as it moves so slowly. In fact here, the progressed Moon at 16 LIB 20 tends to translate that square back to exactitude.

Moon/ascendant squares, such as we find here between the progressed ascendant and progressed Moon, are oft-times part of signatures of social and emotional inconvenience and discomfort. We can also note that the progressed ascendant is beginning to move into the square to the natal Venus at 16 LIB 40, so life might continue to be somewhat disappointing for a period of a year or so following the birth, with the native subject to self-consciousness about who likes her, who approves of her and so on.

Transiting Neptune at 19 SAG 21, square the natal fifth cusp at 20 VIR 17 marks the child's so-called 'illegitimacy'—a common indicator generally where parentage is uncertain, where no-one claims responsibility for the child or other hidden, neglectful or confused circumstances.

One thing interesting to note here is the marked contrast between Pluto, a compelling factor and the Moon and Venus, easeful factors both in aspect with the progressed fifth cusp, which was also reflected in the birth experience itself: the native related that the doctors kept trying to induce (i.e. force) the birth without success (Pluto). Only when they stopped trying to induce it, did the baby come in its own time, and with very little difficulty (Moon and Venus)!

Figure 18B highlights the key astrological directions for the tragic death of one native's young wife, leaving an infant in his care.

First, the structural requirements are affliction(s) involving the seventh cusp (the wife) and the ascendant (the effect upon the native), and the eighth cusp (death) as well. Quincunxes are also commonly found for deaths, as well as for illnesses and situations of great stress in the life.

There are two serious afflictions involving the progressed ascendant: conjunct natal Pluto and sesquisquare natal Saturn. Note that the progressed seventh also afflicts both these natal planets, opposition Pluto and semisquare Saturn.

This would have been a difficult year for the native in any case, Pluto and Saturn both debilitating the personal energy. Saturn in aspect to the ascendant (note it will also afflict by transit) is frequently involved in configurations of grief, and the Pluto/ascendant progression is highly descriptive of what the situation actually was, preceding and during this period in the life. The native was literally 'swamped' (Pluto) with pressures. He had to cope with a chronically-ill wife during her pregnancy due to a congenital health condition, and was already caring for the baby, as well as holding down a full-time job at the time his wife died. This slow progression well describes the gruelling effect of such circumstances.

Of course, the progressed *seventh* cusp opposes the Pluto, marking the end of the marriage by death. (Note: such an aspect would *not* signify divorce or other chosen estrangement. Pluto keeps one where one is, and applies the pressures of social conformity.)

The progressed seventh cusp at nearly 25 Capricorn applying into quincunx progressed Mercury at 25 + Gemini and progressed Venus at 25 + Leo, describes the wife (seventh cusp) becoming progressively more ill. Note also that with the natal eighth cusp at 26½ Capricorn, the progressed Venus at nearly 26 Leo is also at the quincunx angle to that cusp. The progressed Moon at 9½ Leo is quincunx the natal Saturn, both stimulating and stifling grief.

A situation such as this, where there are *a lot* of quincunxes afflicting various key points, will invariably mean that the situation (whatever it may be) caused much distress to the native and was slow to resolve.

The factor of immediate expression of grief also registers strongly here with Saturn at 7 Capricorn opposing the natal ascendant, and just a few days from station, so its effect is intensified.

(A more thorough view of the aspecting for this event, including aspects to the natal and progressed eighth cusps is included as a demonstration of the technique of partials, 'Event 2: Death of Wife', pp. 138-148).

6.
READING THE TIME OF LIFE:
THE BIRTH CHART AS A CLOCK

The Chart as a Personal Clock

The 'blueprinting' of a chart gave models by which to explore the life path in some systematic fashion, recognizing guideposts signifying the different areas of life and our experiences in their respective domains.

But now we suddenly remember that the house, as well as its many blueprints, was not a literal house of brick or wood, but one built of time and space. So imagine now, if you will, that we are going to lift the house into the air and begin twirling it upon the imaginary axis that we have suddenly realized is its true foundation—the very whirling of the Earth itself! Now we turn it face up and bring it to a halt. We had a 'chart/house'. Now we have a 'chart/clock'.

This analogy is already familiar. We have begun looking at how moving astrological indicators mark off important changes in the life much as an ordinary clock strikes noon, or five o'clock or nine o'clock. We also explored the clock parallel to demonstrate how different *scales* of time work, using the hour, minute and second hand as a working model to understand the motions of many planets moving at respectively different speeds and in different time *frames*, usually corresponding to the different 'orders' of time, such as progressed and transiting.

Conceiving astrology in 'clock-like' terms is also familiar to those astrologers who emphasize planetary *cycles*.

What all these 'clock' views of astrology have in common, of course, is their very 'clock-like' qualities!—recurrence, regularity, and the 'sameness' of their measures. The Saturn cycle, for example, is twenty-eight years, so at every seven-year phase, and especially every twenty-eight years, certain kinds of characteristic changes pervade the ongoing flow of life for *everyone*. Units of time for any time scale—such as

57′ per day for the natal Sun at summer solstice—are constant from the progressed Sun of one summer solstice chart to the progressed Sun of another. Everyone experiences new and full Moons, and the cycle of waxing and waning Moon is a constant of life for everyone.

However, rectification work homes in on the *distinctiveness* of each chart, not its characteristic sameness with others. Only you show up in the astrological 'mirror' which is your chart. Only your 'house' has its characteristic layout of crowded or empty rooms with their specific contents and functions, designs and patterns of change we are calling 'blueprints'.

Likewise, your own personal chart, or anyone else's, has its own uniquely calibrated built-in clock—the natal chart, progressions and transits that are 'given' from birth—which the generalized cycles and phases of astrology neither describe nor explain.

The orbital clocks of the transiting planets register *against* the natal chart but are not the chart/clock itself. The chart *itself* is your own personal clock, independently generating unique configurations every moment of the day specifically for you. On an ordinary clock, we find at some time each day (for example), the hour hand midway between '4' and '5', the minute hand at nearly '8' on the dial and the second hand at '3', which we call 4.39 a.m. (or p.m.) and 15 seconds. With recurrent regularity, the clock's hands will go through that same configuration twice each twenty-four-hour day. With a 'chart/clock', the same assortment of planetary 'hands' is never repeated even once, and house cusps are not regularly spaced at all, but positioned at unequal intervals of space across the circular chart.

Reading the Time of Life

Obviously, it takes very special formating to 'read the time of life' from a chart/clock, since there is virtually no repetition or recurrence. Even a planet returning to the same position by transit is invariably surrounded by a much altered context of planetary positions and cusps—something like going away and then coming home to a whole new set of parents and friends. With so much fluctuation in configurations, we need to highlight and centralize what remains stable in the overall picture and be able to assess the changing configurations against those stable reference points.

On an ordinary clock, the only unchanging, stable component is the clockface itself, with numbers '1' to '12' that never change either numerically nor in their positioning on the dial. With an astrological chart, there is *more* in the way of stable reference points (i.e. the natal cusps and planets), but even those points all swing into motion past the moment of birth.

Let's view the chart in the same graphic way that we look at a clock and the challenges will be clear. It is as though we took the clockface from '1' to '12' on the clock *plus* the hour hand between '4' and '5' *and* the minute hand near '8' *and* the second hand at '3' (4.39.15 a.m. or p.m.) and said, '*This whole configuration* is your permanent reference point for life. Whatever other times the life may pass through, this specific 4.39.15 a.m. is your permanent "time".'

Then, of course, the '12' on the dial—unlike the permanently fixed positioning on an ordinary clock—would begin slowly moving towards '1', the '1' towards '2', and so on. The hour, minute and second hands would all do likewise at their respectively different speeds. By the time the clock read 6.21.47 a.m., the '12' might have moved on to nearly '2', the '1' to '3' and so on.

Then you would need to take all the separate moving 'second hands' (the many transits) and all the separate moving minute hands (the many progressions), plus the moving numbers on the dial (the moving house cusps) and scrupulously *compare* each of their positions with your 'permanent time', 4.39.15 a.m. to arrive at the true 'time of life' under examination.

Mistakes in reading the clock would be endemic. Schoolchildren would wander about in a daze because their poor parents could not figure out their bedtime the night before, while highschoolers would cram for their college entrance exams with crash courses in 'telling time'. Dinner might be served at 9.30 in the morning; shops wouldn't open until 3 p.m. Emergency legislation would have to be drafted to keep astrologers from running (i.e. *ruining*) the country. Meanwhile, books would be rushed into print claiming 'absolute proof that astrology doesn't work'—finally!!

It may sound very silly in this exaggerated form, but it is true enough to say that *astrological time really isn't very easy to tell!* We need to devise means to simplify it, and to read it visually.

To establish a simple, effective format for astrological time-telling, we would begin first with its stable components. That could be the natal chart in its entirety, which remains constant throughout the life. However, not all its components are central for *timing*. Timing events means timing the changes in life *circumstances*, and that means the house cusps, especially the perpendicular axes that define the structure of the life, the angles.

The Tri-circled Model

What is the simplest, most explicit format to keep the chart's stable reference points intact? One which highlights the key *timing* indicators, especially the 'steering wheel' of life, the angles. Another convenient consideration in favour of keeping the chart's cusps intact for graphic representations, is that they are points, not planets, and do not create the type of visual 'clutter' that a full complement of natal, progressed and transiting planets would. The eleven separate 'minute hands' and eleven separate 'second hands' may not each even be relevant, much less central to the particular event in question.

A clock that is simple enough to readily read, yet specific enough to spell out the 'time of life' will feature *selected* positions to show the focus and direction of the life *at the specific time in question.* Certainly if we were on a boat taking a cruise around the world and reporting on the journey, we wouldn't show a map of the whole world at once, but pinpoint the location of the boat itself and detail in what direction it was headed at the time.

Figure 19 shows a basic model for a 'clock' which will enable the astrologer to 'tell astrological time' explicitly. It will show the natal house cusps marked, as usual, with a circle divided into twelve houses. The middle circle, for progressions, will leave the house cusps

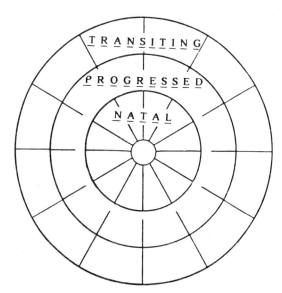

Figure 19   The Tri-circled Model

unmarked, as the progressed cusps will fall in different locations to the natal ones; also, it will only be necessary to mark in the ones that our blueprinting requires. The outer circle is for transits—that is, those *in exact aspect with* natal and/or progressed indicators.

How do we read these selected slices of life? Ideally, we will develop the facility to read them in terms of unified perceptions, much as we read words rather than letters, sentences rather than disconnected words, and—yes—'the time', rather than 'the hour hand is here, the minute hand is there, the second hand is there'.

To facilitate developing skills in reading these astrological clocks, we will illustrate by a few simple examples which use variations to make the point. Figure 20 A–E all show one basic kind of year in the native's life: progressed midheaven square natal Uranus, which could be precarious, risky, shattering, scandalizing, bankrupting, disruptive, shocking, dislocating and/or characterized by dramatic shifts in terms of the career (tenth house), standing in the community (tenth, also fourth), security (fourth, also tenth), family and home life (fourth) or basic direction in life (the meridian). A native subjected to this *could* have the life 'swerve off course' during such a period, to be later reorganized on a different basis.

It could also, in some cases, refer to a parent (the meridian). Let's say this might be the year when someone's emotionally unstable mother really went 'off her rocker'. Certainly in a child's chart, it could be a year of great dissension in the home and/or divorce.

Yet this is only one indicator, and devoid of context. Much depends on what preceded it, the relative strength of the chart as a whole and, most certainly, the surrounding aspecting, which might specify further what happened, intensify it, qualify it, or put it in some unconsidered light. It is training in organizing the aspecting in a holistic way, to which our 'clock' model is directed.

Figure 20A shows the progressed midheaven square natal Uranus plus progressed ascendant trine the natal Sun. The first aspect is disruptive of the career/home/standing; the latter aspect is stabilizing of the native *personally*. This shows the personal energy, confidence, backlog of personal achievements, staying power (or other references specific to the Sun), to offset what could be the considerable loss suggested by the midheaven/Uranus square. Perhaps during this year, there was what the world perceives as a 'bad twist of fortune' for the native (progressed midheaven square natal Uranus). But it is also a year where he can use his personal (ascendant) energy, confidence, backlog of achievements to offset its effects. Personal

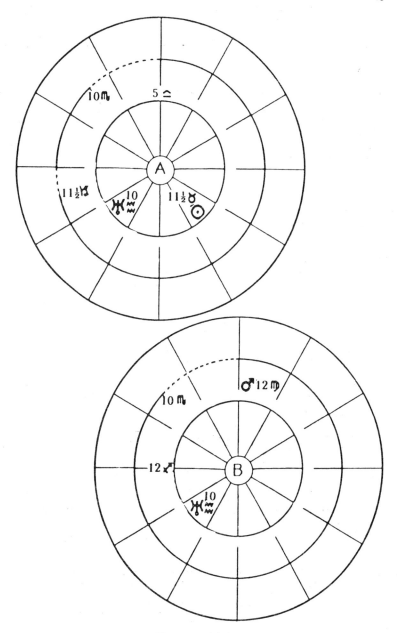

Figure 20A & B.
The Tri-circled Model to Highlight Contextual Differences

resilience and vitality might actually 'save the day' and enable the native to regroup his life constructively.

Figure 20B contrasts the above scenario dramatically. The midheaven-Uranus square is still intact, but now *compounded* by progressed Mars square natal ascendant. The native depicted in illustration A says, '*I* can handle this. I'd just get right in there, assert myself, stabilize the situation, restore my self-confidence and the confidence of others in me.'

By contrast, the native depicted in B is acutely aware that he is 'under the gun', and much more likely to take desperate, rash, or a variety of 'overkill'-type measures to cope with the turn of events. He may wind up accident-prone (Mars in combination with ascendant), or overtax himself (Mars/ascendant square) in efforts to cope with whatever jolt (Uranus square) has befallen his family (square fourth cusp). Remember, as well, that this is not like a Mars *transit*; this relatively long-range progression will be in orb for well over a year (with, let's say, Mars progressing at the rate of 37' per year in this instance).

Figure 20C shows three possible Jupiter transits against this chart at the specific time that the investment backfired, or bad publicity struck the firm, or a family member suddenly took ill, throwing the native's lifestyle and plans into havoc. For C-1, transiting Jupiter at 5 Gemini trine the natal midheaven at 5 Libra and sextile the natal fourth at 5 Aries, help of some sort or another is on the way. The bank extended a loan, or neighbours pitched in to help out, or the native's good name was upheld against what was viewed as the onslaught of 'circumstances' (i.e. not his fault, not to be held personally accountable).

For C-2, transiting Jupiter at Scorpio conjunct the progressed midheaven, note that we generally consider Jupiter a 'benefic', but here its positioning on the progressed midheaven also means it is square the same natal Uranus. Perhaps some new stroke of luck enables the native to expand his resources out even further than he had done previously, but here—square the Uranus—with a keen liability to misjudge or take too big or too costly (Jupiter) a risk (square Uranus). Or someone may come along and 'bail the native out' (not necessarily financially, though with Jupiter that could certainly be involved). He could easily wind up 'rescued but in debt' with a Jupiter so placed. Or the native might project confidence (Jupiter) in the face of hard knocks (square Uranus), which could help him solicit

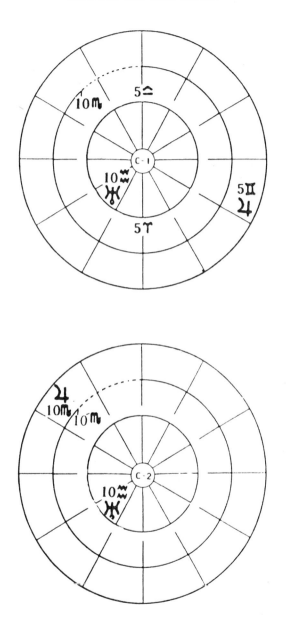

Figure 20C 1 & 2.
The Tri-circled Model to Highlight Contextual Differences

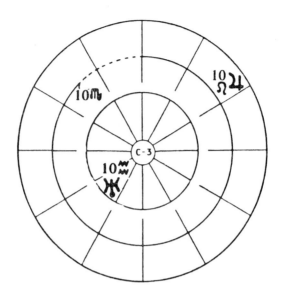

Figure 20 C3.   The Tri-circled Model to Highlight Contextual
Differences

support and/or backfire (as afflictions to Uranus can).

With C-3, the transiting Jupiter at 10 Leo—square the progressed
midheaven at 10 Scorpio and opposition the natal Uranus at 10
Aquarius—could well magnify the problem rather than signify a
solution. This native could be clearly over-extended (Jupiter), and
moreover predisposed to over-react (Jupiter square). Yet, given more
supportive aspecting with some other, unknown components of this
picture, he might yet have the buoyant energy to thrash his way into
new territory—perhaps ill-advised, perhaps overshooting the mark,
but in true, whole hog Jupiter style.

Figures D and E are designed to show a sharply contrasting context
of surrounding aspecting for the main midheaven/Uranus aspect
under consideration: maximum intensifying surrounding aspecting
for D and maximum qualifying surrounding aspecting for E.

Figure D is really a full-blown disaster! Note first that
compounding the progressed midheaven square natal Uranus is the
transiting Uranus (5 Aries) opposition natal midheaven (5 Libra) a so-

called 'double whammy'. Whatever he thought was 'stable' in his life circumstances prior to this point, it is scheduled to be severely disrupted. This fellow might best cut his losses and run. If he can,

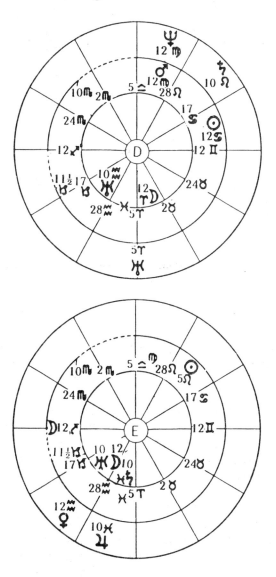

Figure 20D & E.   The Tri-circled Model to Highlight Contextual Differences

that is, and the surrounding aspecting makes that quite doubtful. For one thing, Uranus aspects, of themselves, can provoke drastic breaks but also leave 'fall-out'. Someone has to pick up the pieces that have been splattered about.

For another, there are several factors here that suggest the native's life circumstances will not be that well-expedited, but subject to quandaries and to misjudgements. Notable is the involvement of *quincunxes*, which show internal stress, forks in the road, and no clear way through; this necessitates partly-satisfactory, partly-unsatisfactory solutions, however approached. Note that both the progressed Mars at 12 Virgo and the transiting Neptune also at 12 Virgo are not only in conjunction with each other, but in affliction to both the natal ascendant (square) at 12 Sagittarius and the natal Moon (quincunx) at 12 Aries. A Mars/Neptune conjunction of itself is precarious when rapid decisions need be made, because Mars *acts*, but Neptune clouds circumstances, enticing one to 'go blind' or by the 'feel' of things, so a choice may be made only to be later regretted. To have the Mars/Neptune conjunction quincunx the fourth house Moon, when the fourth house both natally and by progression is sporting Uranus afflictions, is nearly an invitation to either quick moves in the wrong direction, or a kind of acute (Mars, the Moon in Aries) emotional (the Moon) confusion (Neptune) enmeshed in circumstances which defy ready reconciliation (the quincunx). With the same Mars/Neptune conjunction square natal ascendant, the native, in effect feels both rash (Mars square) and insecure (Neptune square), a most difficult state to endure, much less act upon.

Cutting back further on the native's power of effective action is that the progressed Sun at 12 Cancer is square the natal 12 Aries Moon —an aspect under which it is difficult to achieve what one wants even under considerably better overall aspecting. Here we find a native who might well be cut off from the support of family as well, given the Moon's location in the fourth house.

Compounding the numerous afflictions to the natal Moon is the progressed ascendant square from 11½ Capricorn. This makes supportiveness from others (the Moon) an *issue*, but a struggle which presents many obstacles. Moon squares generally, as a rule-of-thumb, make accommodations and adjustments in the life *inconvenient*. The 'climate' of a situation does not permit things falling into place.

Last is the transiting Saturn at 10 Leo, opposition the natal Uranus at 10 Aquarius and square the progressed midheaven at 10 Scorpio. The native feels responsible, or is made to assume responsibility for this unenviable life juncture. Resources may be impoverished as well.

The native represented in Figure E has a much less devastating time indeed, notwithstanding that the original aspect, progressed midheaven square natal Uranus remains intact. Notably, there are two major progressed aspects involving the midheaven that are favourable and stabilizing: progressed Sun at 5 Leo, sextile the natal midheaven at 5 Libra, and progressed midheaven at 10 Scorpio trine the natal Saturn at 10 Pisces. Taken alone, these two would spell out a period of prestige (as much as his accomplishments to date would merit, of course), stabilization of responsibilities and a firm grounding in life generally. In fact, if these two aspects are considered a 'modification' of the original aspect—which, note, could just as easily be considered a modification of *them*—it is one that could change the complexion of events entirely. Native D was in desperate crisis; native E may be experiencing genuine difficulties, but is well-buffered against things getting out of hand. So if half the firm quits, he still has the leadership and soundness of purpose to keep the company afloat. If his wife is in hospital, there are plenty of resources to keep the home running in good order. If he has to move because his rent is tripled, he finds an even more suitable dwelling elsewhere.

Transiting Jupiter is fortuitously placed at 10 Pisces, trine the progressed midheaven at 10 Scorpio and atop the natal Saturn at 10 Pisces (note, this is quite different to Saturn arriving on the Jupiter). This native can take hardship with a smile and find a way out. The progressed Moon at 12 Sagittarius conjunct the natal ascendant, and transiting Venus at 12 Aquarius, conjunct the natal Moon, and sextile the ascendant and progressed Moon at 12 Sagittarius pretty much guarantees this native a friendly, helpful boost from others.

Why, this progressed midheaven square natal Uranus almost looks 'lucky'!

Now we have a somewhat better grasp of the 'grammar' of events as astrologically defined. Never just a word, but a sentence, a paragraph, a whole episode, which the astrological configurations 'spell out' for us to 'read' in whole, succinct units. Like a book in our hand, or the clock on the wall, the time of life may also be 'read', in a visual, succinct format.

This tri-circled model will also become the main visual tool for the technique of 'partials', to be developed in Part Three. Now, having been introduced to several observational and visual skills indispensable for our rectification work, we are about to embark upon a systematic, step-by-step guide to the technical work of rectification, to begin using these many skills in the context of actual chart rectification work.

PART THREE:
METHODS—THE TECHNICAL
WORK OF CHART RECTIFICATION

7.
PRELIMINARIES

Whose Chart to Use

Begin with the chart of a relative or friend, or a client willing to share information about their life. Don't begin with the chart of a celebrity or a total stranger, for several reasons:

Birth time accuracy: With celebrities especially, the birth time released to the public may not be correct. Some celebrities mask the true data, especially if they do not want the public delving into their private life, which a correct birth time would facilitate. (See a copy of the birth certificate if you can.)

Rounded-off times: Even if you are given an allegedly correct time, it is likely to be rounded-off since the celebrity, the celebrity's mother or other source for the time does not understand how important an *exact* time of birth is. The same problem could well occur with any birth, but a rounded-off time *plus* lack of personal contact with the native is a great barrier with beginning rectification work especially.

Public image: The public image of a celebrity may not correspond with reality. This makes for poor example cases because you may be hunting for publicly-touted characteristics which are absent, or discovering characteristics which contraindicate the public view.

Need for personal contact: You will get sketchy information at best unless you either interview the native personally or have a rather complete and accurate biography. But for a living celebrity, there are always open questions.

When you are experienced with rectification work, it is exciting to work on rectifying the charts of historical figures, but it is not the place to start. When you work on a basis of personal contact, you can obtain direct feedback and thorough answers to your questions regarding life events. This will provide a much more complete picture to match up with the appropriate astrological confirmation.

Using Your Own Chart

Your own chart—if you have a reasonably close birth time—may be an ideal place to begin. You know yourself and have experienced your life at first hand, so you will have the maximum means to assess the chart's accuracy. However, it should be noted that you might not be the most objective judge—not because you do not know your own life, but that having looked at a *wrong* chart for a long time (if your chart has never been adjusted) can produce an internal mind-set that makes consideration of alternate times difficult. This can slow your work down.

There isn't any rule as to whether your own chart may or may not be the best place to start. However, I would recommend that you begin by *looking in the mirror* rather than with mathematical computations. Confirm the ascendant and prominent planets in your own appearance just as you would begin with others, and you've a much better chance at it.

How Close Should a Birth Time Be

With your initial work, choose a chart for which the birth time is already very close, even exact, so far as is known. The reason is that rectification is really the same as *verification* of the chart's accuracy. See how everything works together for a correct chart before attempting to adjust charts with a wider margin of error.

What Sources are Reliable for Birth Time Data

This commonly-posed question oft-times has discouraging answers.

You can short-circuit many a time-consuming astrological wild goose chase if you consider one basic principle prior to assuming that any birth time is exact because the source seems so 'reliable'. That is, that it is the *astrology* that will prove or disprove the birthtime, not a document or a person's memory. It is also the astrology that will give the *exact* birth time, whereas many birth times from so-called 'reliable sources' will give rounded-off times, which are not as likely to be accurate.

This does not mean that any record or report is to be discounted. To the contrary, every scrap of 'evidence' gives a guide, and perhaps a true one. But only astrology will give you the *answer.*

Remember that only an astrologer, or some inveterately careful record keeper (such as a hospital nurse—*some*, that is, hardly all) is likely to consider an exact-to-the-minute birth time important. Even at that, you don't know for sure what they're timing. One mother who had four children said *all* her children's births were timed ten minutes later than when they were born. She thought they probably didn't make any note of it until they were cleaning up the afterbirth. 'Ten minutes' is two-and-a-half years worth of many astrological timers!

The commonly-used sources for birth times each have special considerations:

The memory of relatives, including the mother. It is rare that a relative's memory of birth—*especially* the mother's, who was not looking at a clock—will be exact-to-the-minute. (I recently met a *four-day-old* infant, whose parents were *both* present at the birth, and neither knew the birth time within closer than a half an hour.) Always remember how much difference each minute makes once you begin spinning the chart's timing out on different time scales.

You might be told that the mother was sure the birth was 'before breakfast' or 'after dinner' or 'some time in the afternoon'. If the birth time is expressed in terms of marking points in the day, such as 'breakfast', find out what time breakfast was served in that family—7 a.m. or 9 a.m., for example.

Every now and then you'll be lucky, and the mother will have been hearing the church bells chime six exactly, just as the native chimed in his first cry, but this is the unusual case. More often, the time will be expressed as a range ('somewhere between 2 p.m. and 6 p.m.') or in relative terms ('just before lunch').

Also remember that some mothers have better memories than others, and the birth happened a long time ago. If the circumstances surrounding the birth were difficult, the mother may block out or distort the birth time. In a family with many children, birth times may be inadvertently confused. 'No, my mother isn't really sure. That may have been when *Johnny* was born.' An hour into a confounding rectification. Frustration galore!

Birth documents: Many birth documents round the birth time off to the nearest hour. Even a time rounded to the nearest half-hour is reason for suspicion. Occasionally a birth occurs exactly so, but usually not.

Even in countries which usually record the time on the birth certificate, it is often rounded off. Practices for hospitals within the same city may vary. Circumstances of recording the birth time can vary, even within the same institution. One hospital worker who noted the time may have been personally present at the birth but rounded off the time as it was hospital procedure. Or worse still, the time may have not been recorded immediately (when the hospital staff was busy with the mother) but later on, even the end of a shift, which makes inaccuracy more probable. Not realizing a birth time is important makes inaccuracy more likely still.

If you do see an exact-to-the-minute time, however, such as 9.47 p.m. or 6.59 a.m, chances are good that if it is not exact, it may be quite close. However, the length of labour varies, and with a birth involving complications, the clock may not have been consulted until mother and child were both clearly out of danger. There is no-one stationed in the delivery room solely for recording the birth time! Any number of factors could result in an inexact birth record.

It is generally much easier to work with exact-to-the-minute records, but do not make assumptions. The time has to be verified *astrologically*. (Note: This is true especially when the time is near the division between two rising signs.)

Extra Pointers
A.M./P.M.: Some people will offer the time on their birth certificate, which they remember, but then give a.m. instead of p.m. or vice versa! Every astrologer of long practice has run into a few of these.

A note about computer charts: A computer will readily calculate a chart for some exact birth time, but *this has nothing whatsoever to do with whether that birth time is correct*. A perfectly-calculated chart for a wrong birth time is still a wrong chart.

What Types of Events are Suitable to Use
The basic fare of rectification work is common events such as marriage, deaths in the family, serious illnesses, major career moves, major relocations and the life. This is not because there is any set list of events to work with, but rather that events such as these generally affect the native overtly and markedly, altering the circumstances of his life, which is reflected definitively in the astrology.

The surest guide is to use anything which has had a major impact on the life; the greater the change in the native's life, the more suitable for rectification purposes. It could be a breakthrough or a major disappointment, a special opportunity which changed the life course, or discovering an interest or organization that transformed the personal outlook. For a writer, it might be publication of the first book. For a housewife, the first chance to achieve something significant outside the home. For an athlete, his first big championship.

It is also *very important* to use one, preferably more events for which the native had *no control whatsoever over the timing*. This may be a chance meeting which turns out to vastly change the life, a death, an unexpected boon, an accident or illness. Such events show up with great vividness and clarity.

Why Use Major Events

When something 'major' happens in the life—because its *impact* is major—it registers in many simultaneous ways, not just one. This makes it easier to spot if you are on the right track. Also, something major will impact upon different *areas* of the life, so many house cusps might be affected simultaneously. For example, if a marriage is dissolved, major aspects will affect the natal and/or progressed seventh cusp as primary indicators, whereas the native's personal response will show in aspecting to the ascendant. Perhaps the native also had to move house (fourth cusp), or get a job (tenth cusp), or relocate (ninth cusp). The financial situation (second/eighth house axis) and social life (fifth/eleventh house axis) are also subject to change. Although we experience changes in a unitary way, astrology still shows each distinct area of change.

Notably, genuinely 'major' events will invariably register through the chart's *angles*, which is our key focus in the rectification process.

How Many Events to Use

Three major events are a minimum, even for a very close birth time, though five is always more secure. I don't like setting any 'rule' about this, because charts vary as to the ease or difficulty in rectification. Usually, the more uncertain the birth time is, the more back-up you will need. There, the important thing is not to do patchwork, but establish cohesive linkages across spans of many years.

More important than the *number* of events used, is the types of tests the chart withstands. It must describe the physical native, and only then proceed onto events. Events should show convincing partials which describe exactly what happened in the life, and a range of many years' sequencing should match up against the native's life. (See 'Partials', pp. 128-148, and 'Sequencing', pp. 148-158.)

Setting Up Worksheets

An indispensable aid to accurate work is clearly-organized worksheets.

As a preliminary step, compile a chronological list of major events in the life. List what happened and the date. Obtain as many *exact* dates as possible. If the time of day is available, use it, because the more rapidly-moving transits may move one or two whole degrees per day. The transiting Moon, of course, is unusable unless the time of day is available, as it moves 13° per day on the average.

If the time of day is unavailable, use midday positions for locations within a few hours from Greenwich. For locations very distant from Greenwich, such as Australia, use whichever midnight positions come closest to the middle of the day's planetary positions for that location. For Australia, for example, nearly a half a day *east* of Greenwich, use midnight positions for the date of the event. For a location such as the Hawaiian islands, nearly half a day *west* of Greenwich, take midnight positions for the day following the event date.

Then take an entire sheet for each event. At the top, identify the individual event, such as 'Marriage', 'First Trip Overseas', or 'Founded a Business'. Next to this notation put the event date. If you have been given several events but few exact dates, it is generally better to work with exact dates first. If you have several exactly-dated events, it is advisable to work with the most significant-seeming events first, since they will be marked in more definitive ways than lesser junctures in the life.

On the sheet for the first event, make notation of the *adjusted calculation date* in the upper right-hand corner (abbreviated 'ACD'). This is the date that the day of birth in the ephemeris 'equals' for calculation of the secondary progressions.

Underneath the ACD, note the index date closest to the date of the event, which will show the adjusted calculation date at the *year* closest to the event date. (For methods of rapid calculation of the ACD and Index Date, see 'Quick Computation of the ACD', p. 185.)

Be sure to leave space on your worksheet, preferably near the top, to transfer all the information you have gleaned about the event onto your worksheet, such as 'the most happy time of life', or 'very confusing and unsettling', and the like. In other words, condense everything relating to that particular event onto its individual worksheet. You will need to be looking back and forth between worksheets for other reasons, and you want your work to have a visual economy that will make it manageable.

There is also pragmatic value in having descriptive information on the same page as the relevant calculations. You want to be able to compare the native's rendition of life circumstances and reactions against the astrological specifics, so you can 'read' where the native was depressed, or 'read' where the change in question meant an increase of income in the life.

It is also helpful to leave space at the bottom of the worksheet (or on the side, if the sheet is held sideways). You may need to adjust the chart's angles back and forth, to experiment in finding the perfect match. (See 'Sequencing: Time on the Horizontal', pp. 148-158.) You need space to do so.

Each separate worksheet will have a standard format of three columns: from left to right, Transits (abbrev. Trans), Progressions (abbrev. Prog), and Solar Arcs (abbrev. SA).

Transits: Under the Transits column, list all transits for the event date all the way out to Pluto. (Most ephemerides do not include positions of the new planet, Chiron, which can be invaluable. A separate ephemeris for this may be obtained from CAO Times, P.O. Box 75, Old Chelsea Station, New York, New York 10113, USA).

Also include the position of the transiting North Node, which can indicate whether the event in question opened a clear pathway in the native's development (harmonious aspect to some key point in the chart) or frustrated it (an affliction). The South Node renders whatever it touches by conjunction vulnerable.

Progressions: Calculate the secondary progressions. It is relevant to enquire here, since the birth time is inexact, will this not affect the progressed positions as well?

Your first endeavours will be with near-accurate birth times, so only the rapidly-moving Moon will be significantly affected, at the rate of about ½° per one hour's discrepancy in the time. It is good to be aware of that, and whether an adjustment of the time will alter the Moon's position forward or back in the zodiac, but it should not present much of a problem for a birth time that is genuinely close (let's say within twenty minutes of accuracy, which is approximately 11′ of Moon motion). With the other planets, the difference will be rather negligible. Even with a rapid Mercury (2° per day or upwards), a whole hour's discrepancy will only result in 5′ difference in the position of the natal and/or progressed Mercury.

Calculate the progressions out as far as Saturn only. Uranus, Chiron, Neptune and Pluto progress very slowly. Sometimes a progressed outer planet *will* be significant, and these planets should be monitored lest this is the case. But this is a relatively subsidiary consideration when first learning chart rectification. There are many other definitive, more primary ways of ascertaining the accuracy of your work.

Solar Arcs: To compute the solar arc for an event date, take the difference between the progressed Sun from the Progressions column and the natal Sun from the birth chart. This will give you the SA at the event date in degrees and minutes.

The SA column on the worksheet will always include three figures: SA, the Solar Arc itself; Progressed Midheaven (abbrev. Prog MC); and Progressed Ascendant (abbrev. Prog Asc). Other, intermediary progressed house cusps are optional, depending upon the type of

WORKSHEET

Event: Date: ACD:
                                               Index Date:

Description:

Transits	Progressions	SA's
Sun	Sun	SA =
Moon estimate	Moon	Prog MC =
Mercury	Mercury	Prog Asc =
Venus	Venus	(any other
Mars	Mars	relevant
Jupiter	Jupiter	house
Saturn	Saturn	cusp)
Uranus		
Neptune		
Pluto		
Chiron		
North Node		

Chart Setting Experimentation

Natal MC	Solar Arc	Prog MC	Prog Asc
_____	_____	_____	_____
_____	_____	_____	_____
_____	_____	_____	_____
_____	_____	_____	_____
_____	_____	_____	_____

Figure 21.   The Worksheet

event, such as ninth house for a legal matter or sixth house for health.

To find the progressed midheaven, add the Solar Arc of the event directly onto the natal midheaven. (I'd advise using a separate scratch sheet for calculations as you go along, to prevent cluttering the worksheet.) This will give the progressed midheaven at the event date.

Take this newly-progressed midheaven to the Placidus Table of Houses. After you have located it in the Table, locate the newly-progressed ascendant at the same latitude as at birth. (Note: the progressed house cusps of the *birthplace* will be effective throughout the life, even if the native relocates away from the birthplace. A relocated chart may be superimposed upon the natal and progressed birth chart, but anything major has to show in the original birth chart, which remains primary.)

Figure 21 illustrates a sample worksheet. Note that extra room is allowed to experiment with different settings of the natal midheaven, and the results they produce for the given event.

8.
THE SEVEN RULES

Introductory Note
Each chart is unique, and your continuing judgements will be tailored to their appropriateness for any particular native. However, certain structural criteria are the underlying basis for *all* rectification work. The seven points detailed below will be satisfied in relation to each major event/turning point in the life when the natal chart is accurate.

Perhaps, scientifically speaking, this gives the best body of evidence available that astrology's correspondence to real life experience involves natural laws which are thorough, explicit and consistent. Speaking purely pragmatically, when you work consistently with the Seven Rules, your work will be reliable and accurate.

Rule 1: Placidus Table of Houses
Different house systems are effective for different purposes. The Placidus house system is the one which times the outer events of the life with great precision. It is not possible to substitute Koch or any other house system and obtain the same results for chart rectification.

Note: the midheaven and ascendant are the same whichever house system is employed; it is the intermediary cusps which differ.

Rule 2: Major Aspects
Major aspects are the only ones allowable for rectification work. This includes conjunctions, squares, oppositions, sextile, trines and quincunxes, although semisquares and sesquisquares can certainly be contributory. (See 'Aspect Guide' in 'A BOOK OF REFERENCES' p. 303.)

Not all astrologers consider quincunxes a major aspect, but its major aspect status is confirmed in rectification work. It is prominent in situations of great stress, illness, forced decisions, deaths in the native's circle, quandaries and other situations signifying difficult forks in the road.

(Note: the quincunx is a major aspect, but the semisextile is not. There is no similarity in the workings of these two aspects.)

There are other astrological aspects, the so-called 'minor' aspects: the quintile, nonile, septile, golden section. 'Minor' does not mean unimportant, so far as natal analysis is concerned. However, these aspects work on internal levels. It is the major aspects which bring events into outer manifestation.

Rule 3: Tightness of Orb
Natal delineation allows for a relatively wide orb for aspects, such as a six- or eight-degree orb for a trine, according to many texts. Since natal aspects describe general personality traits, they do not have to be very narrow to be effective.

With material changes in the life, however, we are moving through many relatively tiny mathematical windows at once ('multiple convergence'). For an aspect to be effective for timing purposes, it must be within a single-degree orb *maximum*, very frequently less. Commonly, at least one major progressed aspect involving a natal or progressed angle will be within only a few minutes of arc orb.

Major events also feature a preponderance of applying rather than separating aspects, though this rule is relative, as applying aspects can sometimes translate a slightly-separated aspect of a slower-moving chart component (slower-moving than the applying planet, that is) back to partile. Generally, there will also be one or more key *transits* applying within just a few minutes of arc.

Rule 4: Multiple Simultaneous Aspects
Multiple major aspects at the time of a major event is the norm, involving the natal and progressed chart. Any one aspect alone does not have a strong enough effect, or force, if one will, to make for a major life change. It seems to take many simultaneous aspects to 'push energies through' from a metaphysical plane to the physical one. Ordinary language does not provide a universally-understood expression of this phenomenon. Again, a pragmatic view will suffice: it is what works!

Rule 5: Aspects, Planets and House Cusps Appropriately Describe as Well as Time the Event
'Timing an event' must be taken to mean that the appropriate aspects

are partile (i.e. exact) or very nearly so *at the time of the event itself.*
To illustrate this, for many years the deaths of American Presidents
were linked to periodic conjunctions of Jupiter and Saturn. However,
closer examination revealed that although the conjunctions occurred
'somewhere' near the respective deaths in office, none occurred *at
the time of* any Presidental death; in one case, the conjunction was
never exact at all until *after* the President was long gone. Aspects,
to be effective, have to be in orb at the event date, not earlier nor later.

Planets, aspects and house cusps 'appropriately describing' what
happens in the life is a whole book's worth of material to be considered
planet by planet, aspect by aspect, house cusp by house cusp and
various combinations thereof. It is clearer in actual practice than it
might seem, however, because specific functions are served by each
of the respective components that are not duplicated by the others.
(Reference guides are provided in 'A BOOK OF REFERENCES',
pp. 287-312, under 'House Cusp Guide', 'Planetary Guide', Aspect
Guide', and 'Event Guide'.)

Rule 6: Involvement of the Chart's Angles
The chart's angles define the structure of the native's life: the physical
person and personal responses through the ascendant axis
(first/seventh cusps) and the course of the life-path (including but
not confined to the career) by the meridian axis (tenth/fourth cusps).

Major events and turning points will register through the angles
of the chart, natal and/or progressed. It is not uncommon to find
both angles involved, though this is not a hard-and-fast rule; it
depends upon the exact details and the effect upon the native.

Rule 7: Different Orders of Aspects Simultaneously
'Different orders of aspects' means transits *and* progressions *and*
aspecting involving natal planets and cusps. (Solar arc directions are
included under 'progressions', as they are derived from the position
of the progressed Sun.)

With a major event, components of the natal chart are always
involved. Generally, at least one major progressed aspect will involve
either a progressed planet in aspect to a natal angle or a progressed
angle in aspect to a natal planet. Commonly, this will be reinforced
by aspecting involving transits.

Representation of all orders of aspects seems to be a key component
of events coming into material manifestation—metaphorically, this
has already been likened to the climax of an orchestral piece, where

all sections of the orchestra—string, winds, brass and percussion—are heard, and in some striking synchronization. In terms of *timing*, we can see how the different orders of aspects correspond to time frames: natal components of the chart (permanent), progressions (longer time frames), transits (shorter time frames). In terms of the *meaning* of the several respective orders of aspects, we find the inevitable overlap of what you are (natal), how you are changing (progressed) and what happens to you (transiting), all of which comes into play at times of major change.

9.
SPECIAL METHODS:
PARTIALS AND SEQUENCING

How to Approach Analysis of Events

The Seven Rules can be checked point-by-point for major life events. Training with charts that are already accurate will provide the best material for practice in making such checks routine.

There are, however, logical guidelines for what to watch for first, to forestall the astrologer going too far into the rectification process before realizing that something might be wrong and/or undertaking unnecessary work. The greatest potential stumbling-block in rectification is not that any single step is very complicated, but that there are so many things to take into account. Establishing their priority of importance and the sequence in which they are approached is at least as important as skill in delineating their meaning.

The first priority is to establish the 'backbone' of the particular event in question. What is expectable for this *type* of event in terms of house cusp involvements? For a career change the tenth, for illness both the ascendant (the physical body) and the sixth cusp (the effects of stress and adjustments), for a faraway move the fourth (the home), ninth (distant relocation) and the ascendant (the affect upon the native personally).

Note all the above examples include at least one angle, referring back to Rule 6 of the Seven Rules. The meridian and ascendant axis are the constant backbone of the chart, so your initial analysis of events often begins with them.

If you find suitable angular involvement combined with suitable involvement of the appropriate intermediary cusps, things may look promising. But then go right to Rule 5, that the astrology appropriately describe as well as time the event in question. Do the planets and aspects describe what was happening? For example, if the native gets a big promotion, accompanied by a rise and other desirable benefits, you will find key trines and/or sextiles involving the midheaven, or conjunctions from benefics to same. You may not be sure whether you are looking for Jupiter, Venus or the Sun, but you can certainly see that if you don't have some convincing favourable aspecting to back the native's rendition up, the chart is in error. You can also see that if you are discovering, instead, Uranus squares or Mars quincunxes or oppositions from Neptune, Rule 5 is definitely violated!

Conversely, whatever you do discover of a 'backbone' nature will need to correspond with the native's life. For instance, if the midheaven has progressed to square natal Neptune, effective for approximately a year, that was a time for career uncertainty and/or lack of confidence and/or unfair treatment, not career *advancement*.

The key point here is to discover a plausible overall picture for the time period in question *before* attempting more detailed work. If it's plausible in the broad outline, then the chart might be correct. If it's not plausible and you move ahead nevertheless, you could be in for a great deal of wasted time and work.

Once the backbone of an event is established and it corresponds with the native's rendition of what happened, there are basically two kinds of approaches that will build a securely rectified chart.

We can fill in more astrological information relative to any one single event. In effect, we will be looking 'into' time, into the event date and filling in its details. I call this 'time on the vertical', because we not only look into the structure of a single moment of time, but we represent it with vertical lists of transits, progressions and solar arc directions.

Looking into time is achieved by a method called 'partials', which was preliminarily introduced in 'The Tri-circled Model' (pp. 101-110).

The second means of approach is looking 'across' time, which I call 'time on the horizontal', because it examines *spans* of time in the life as seen in continuous sequence. Appropriately, it is called 'sequencing', which was preliminarily introduced in 'Sample Models Incorporating Natal, Progressed and Transiting Positions' (Figure 3, pp. 29-30).

When the necessity for working with *both* space and time was introduced, it was likened to needing both the warp and woof of a fabric to keep the weave secure. Working with both partials and sequencing is similar conceptually. If you are skilled at looking both *into* time (partials) and *across* time (sequencing), you have secure methodology for validating your work. You'll see both the *span* of the life (through sequencing) and its *specifics* (through partials).

Note that sequencing is sometimes worth getting sketched in first, since it is less time-consuming than partials. However, it has the liability that the astrologer only has one or two major aspects by which to initially gauge whether the timing is right for each individual event; furthermore, some aspects may 'resemble' each other in their effects, so greater thoroughness is needed. Between the two major methods, however, very sound chart rectifications can result.

PARTIALS: TIME ON THE VERTICAL

What Partials Reveal

The method of 'partials' cuts through the apparent clutter of tens of zodiacal positions on the worksheets. We want to look at relevant extracts from those positions *selectively*, since life itself is selective. For example, you don't get married at one time or another by 'accident'; it is when the *seventh cusp* is selectively highlighted. (No, you don't get married *every* time the seventh cusp is highlighted. But if you get married, it certainly is at such a time.) Partials enable the astrologer to relate to that selective highlighting *visually*.

On the worksheets, transits, progressions and progressed house cusps (the 'SA' column) are listed vertically in separate columns. In nature, all three sets of figures are not 'vertical' at all, but rather superimposed upon one another around the circular zodiacal band. We want to retain the circular format, since we can literally see aspects by their distances apart in a circle, and also view many aspects as a unit. But we also want to separate natal, transiting and progressed components visually, both because different orders of aspects function differently in the life and to check for representation in all orders.

The tri-circled model was introduced in a section of the same name, p. 101-110, showing natal positions in the centre circle, progressions in the middle circle, and transits in the outer one. This format, of itself, is not new. Older astrologers used a similar model routinely to show various junctures in the native's life. But they retained the clutter! Perhaps that is why this method was by-and-large dropped; meanwhile, now it seems more convenient to just look at a computer print-out of planetary positions which, however, brings us back to *lists*, removing the perceptual connection of seeing aspects visually as they naturally occur within circles.

Partials is a way to extract selectively all the *exact* aspects (i.e. orb of less than one degree, as per Rule 3, Tightness of Orb) from a full complement of planetary and cuspal positions, such as natal MC 5 AQ 34, progressed Moon 5 SCOR 09, and transiting Jupiter 4 LEO 52. Thus the term 'partial', since it shows *part* of the astrology, not the whole thing at once. It isn't that 'partials' aren't thorough, however. Inclusion of *every exact aspect* in the partials for any one event is *very* thorough. The rest is not effectively operative in bringing the event into materiality, anyway, so inclusion would be the very 'clutter' we desire to eliminate.

Meanwhile, the Seven Rules ensure that we will not just use a few exact aspects to make assumptions about astrological correspondences to real life events. *Are* the appropriate house cusps affected? *Do* the planets in exact aspect to them appropriately describe what happened? *Is* the aspecting reflective of the energy form in which the happening arrived? Are *all orders* of aspects represented? Are they in *very narrow orb*?

Partials is an 'astrological shorthand' which provides immediate visual confirmation or denial of all these key questions. It also gives the option of constructing as many partials as are necessary to ensure visual clarity. Some events can be shown through two clearly-spaced, uncluttered partials; some require four. Sparse is easier to read, but the astrologer can also be selective in other ways. Showing one partial with all the aspects to *the natal and progressed midheaven*, for example, will show everything relevant to that particular backbone area of the chart. Another partial can show exclusively all the exact aspects to *the natal and progressed ascendant*. Or perhaps one partial can show both aspects to the natal ascendant and to the progressed sixth cusp which, let's say, were at the same degree number (i.e. the sixth cusp has progressed to the place of the natal seventh cusp), when the native fell ill, such as natal ascendant at 19 Pisces and progressed sixth at 19 Virgo and both under serious affliction. Or we could show all aspects involving the natal and progressed Moon, or all the transiting malefics, or all aspects to the natal seventh, its ruler, and the natal Venus. The character of the event and the structure of the aspecting will suggest the most readable formats.

Partials can also remedy the type of 'mathematical dyslexia' that many astrology students suffer, since their training is to consider calculations and delineations *separately*. For example, when one looks at a list of zodiacal positions, such as transiting Mars at 15 Virgo and natal midheaven at 15 Sagittarius, one thinks, well, we have Mars first and there's the midheaven and isn't 15 Virgo to 15 Sagittarius a square? Then one thinks 'what Mars is supposed to mean' and the same for the midheaven, then for a square.

There is nothing wrong with this. But when isolation of astrological components becomes the norm, with little graphic assistance in seeing the components all together in a unitary way, then foggy or otherwise cumbersome delineations become a matter of course. Moreover, it doesn't get beyond that. Single delineations each become an isolated challenge. Piecing together what is happening with *all* of the astrology at the time of an event may seem prohibitive.

However, when the same transiting Mars square natal midheaven is viewed in the context of a partial, you can *see* 'Mars square midheaven' as a single visual unit, and so *the mathematics itself sparks off a unitary delineation of all the components involved.*

So let's say, for example, the native has told you that at the time in question (transiting Mars square natal midheaven), 'My mother suffered an attack and was taken suddenly'. You can now *see* the meridian, which is the parental axis (*the mother*) and the abrasive square (*'taking' the mother*) from Mars (*an attack*). The partial 'says it' all at once.

Then, let's say, the native says that he was grief-stricken at the time. You construct a partial for the natal and progressed ascendant (since that shows the affect upon the native personally), and only that selectively. You look, of course, for *Saturn* (grief). You no longer have to hunt or speculate or rationalize some reasonable representation of the native's statement. You can *see* it.

Conversely, if it is *absent* in what you see, you can with all haste begin considering a different adjustment of the chart!

Working with Degree Numbers

The key to seeing planetary and cuspal configurations rapidly is training oneself to look at degree numbers. First take what you think is (or might be) the true degree of the natal midheaven, such as 2 PIS 29, and see what transits and progressions are within a degree of 2°29' *in any sign*, that is, between 1°29' and 3°29'. Each of those planets and/or cusps are likely to fall into a pattern of major aspects. Also note which *natal* planets are within one degree of 2°29' in any sign, since they will also fall into the exact-aspect pattern.

Then do the same for the natal ascendant, then the progressed midheaven and progressed ascendant. By then, you are likely to have a significant part of the 'backbone' of the particular event in question.

Of course, there are many events for which you will also want intermediary cusps, and they will be of equal importance as any other factor in relation to that particular event, such as the natal and progressed ninth cusp for going back to school, or the second cusp for striking it rich.

When you have had a bit of practice with looking for indicators at the same degree number as the ascendant, midheaven, an intermediary cusp and, lastly, the chart's planets, begin training to look for indicators at a 15° interval. With the 2 PIS 29 midheaven, this would mean looking for planets within a 15° interval in any sign, which would be 17°29′, so the range you would be looking for is between 16°29′ and 18°29′ of any sign. *Some* of these indicators might be at a semisquare or sesquisquare relationship to the midheaven, namely planets one sign plus 15° distance (the semisquare) or four signs and 15° distance (the sesquisquare). These would have a contributory impact upon the life situation, though priority should still be given to locating the major aspects. (See table for 'Fifteen Degree Intervals for Semisquares and Sesquisquares', in 'MATHEMATICAL SHORT-CUTS', p. 193.)

When you have determined that your graphic extracts, the partials, do indeed literally describe the event date, them comb through comparisons between natal, progressed and transiting planetary positions for any major aspects you might have missed, so called 'internal aspecting', not involving cusps, such as transiting Saturn square natal Moon, or progressed Mars trine natal Sun. But do not give such aspects priority in determining if the chart is accurate, because accuracy of the chart means accuracy of its *cusps*.

Another tip might be very helpful if you are stymied. If you have set up partials for several events and some aspects seem to fall into orb, but other expectable, key aspects do not, you might notice that *if only* the ascendant were a half a degree further ahead or the midheaven ¾ of a degree back, you would get an appropriate match consistently. If so, try it! Noting if aspects are consistently a little past or shy of the mark is an excellent way to bring the chart to exactitude.

I rectified my own chart for a class once. I discovered I had to keep pushing the midheaven back some 11′ of arc, representing a discrepancy of some *40 seconds of birth time*. It seems like hair-splitting, but the point is that nature itself splits these hairs just miraculously! The adjustment was consistent: always back and always by the same interval.

If very minor adjustments (half a degree or less) backwards or forwards do not make the difference, be a little aggressive and adjust the chart two or three degrees backwards or forwards to see if you can get a plausible preliminary match. If your initial work in narrowing the range of birth time through visual observation has been accurate, such experimentation oft-times pays off with a correct chart.

Finding Focal Points

Partials, aside from their inestimable help in locating the true time of birth, will also give your delineations ready focal points. For a partial involving the midheaven, for example, you can delineate specifically in relation to the life course, the career, the parents, or whatever the midheaven signifies *in the particular context of that event*. For a parental death, you can distinguish between how the parent passed (aspects to the meridian), how the native coped with death (eighth house) and the native's outer response (the ascendant).

Partials also facilitate finding the main thrust of the event first and then filling in the details. Examples: progressed Mars square natal ascendant for an accident-prone year, transits for a specific accident; progressed ascendant sextile natal Sun for fulfilling personal accomplishment and self-esteem, transits for when an event of that character happened; progressed midheaven square natal Moon for a period of disfavour, unwelcome adjustments and environmental changes, transits for the exact time of unwanted changes.

Quick, definitive recognitions between contrasting astrological components can be equally literalistic. For example, don't accept that a major disaster happened under the influence of trines to the angles. Don't accept that tons of luck came one's way under the major influence of a square or quincunx. Saturn is harsh; Venus isn't. Mars expedites; Saturn slows down. Pluto is gruelling and hangs on; Uranus provokes breaks. This is no time for philosophy, symbolism or archetypes. Ascertain what *happened* in the life, and locate which planetary influences, aspects, and house cusps describe it *literally*. Such clear, simple 'mediaeval-sounding' delineations will work superbly! (Note: once the chart is *correct*, you will find without exception, that your access to its 'deeper' levels is enhanced, not inhibited.)

Sample Events

We will use two sample events to illustrate the technique of partials, one constructed and one from real life, using the natal chart and the complete complement of progressions and transits calculated to exact minutes of arc. The reason we will begin with a constructed example is that it facilitates demonstrating the partials principle in a clear, simple way, unencumbered by additional figures which don't fit into the partials, overlapping aspects and the like. For the first example, we will consider only those figures which will be used for the partials, rather than a full complement of transits and progressions. Then we can move on to a real life event, with an in-depth work approach.

This first, constructed example will also allow for review of the tri-circled model, but in a somewhat more comprehensive format.

Event 1: A Career Success

This hypothetical event (Figure 22A–D) illustrates the kind of picture you will actually see in practice for an outstanding career success—well, let's say, *really* outstanding. Let's say the native gives this date for the achievement of some high position that carries honour and prestige, lots of money and the chance to use one's energy and talents. We will make this example superlative, since it will give many

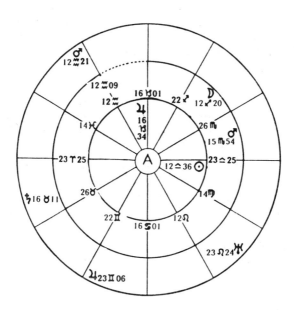

Figure 22A. Partials: A Career Success

indicators that support the same conclusion, hence provide clearly-defined focal points.

First we want to find one or more major structural indicators (Blueprint 3: The Structure of Events). Let's say this will be the progressed midheaven (career) trine the natal Sun (stable career position where one can 'shine'). So we look in the centre circle of Figure 22 (the natal planets) for the natal Sun, which we locate at 12 LIB 36. The progressed midheaven is located in the centre circle (the progressions) at 12 AQ 09, at a trine angle to the natal Sun. Note also the progressed Moon—an important supportive indicator which shows 'when the climate is right'—at 12 SAG 20, sextile the natal Sun at 12 LIB 36 on one side and sextile the progressed midheaven at 12 AQ 09 on the other.

That configuration alone—progressed midheaven, natal Sun, progressed Moon in mutually harmonious aspect—could be the key component of a signature for high profile (Moon/midheaven) career success (Sun/midheaven). Auspiciously, however, we also find the progressed Mars at 15 SCOR 54 sextile the natal midheaven at 16 CAP 01 and natal Jupiter at 16 CAP 34. *That* alone could be the key component of a major favourable career move, bringing personal energy/initiative (Mars) and resources/opportunities (Jupiter) into play in the career (midheaven) area.

For the 'icing on the cake', transiting Mars at 12 AQ 21 sits atop the progressed midheaven, trine the natal Sun and sextile the natal Moon. This lends a real 'go for it' touch to the occasion—this could well be a bright young man (or woman) on the way to the top.

Note, both the progressed midheaven at 12 AQ 09 and the progressed Mars at 15 SCOR 54 are 'long timers' in terms of time frames; they will each be in orb of their respective aspects for over a year, during which time many things furthering the career could happen. The *combination* of all these components—the two major progressions, progressed Moon, natal Jupiter, natal Sun—makes this aspecting a 'can't miss' type of juncture in the life, even if other factors detract.

We can fill in other pieces of the puzzle with the given transits. Transiting Saturn at 16 TAU 11 is trine the natal midheaven and natal Jupiter at 16 CAP 01 and 16 CAP 34 respectively. The Saturn trine midheaven shows that the new job carries serious responsibility and/or it came as a result of a step-by-step quest and/or it is work of a settled, stable character; the Saturn aspect to the Jupiter spells out both enhanced respectability and money.

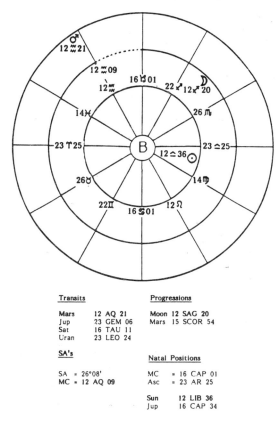

Figure 22B.   Partials: A Career Success

The opposition of the transiting Saturn at 16 TAU 11 to the progressed Mars at 15 SCOR 54 shows the native having to steel his integrity to prove himself on the job, notwithstanding that it was landed under superb aspects. (Note here that had the aspect been a square, let's say Saturn at 16 *Aquarius* square the progressed Mars, the native might be encountering overt resentment or people trying to hold him back, whereas the Saturn quincunx to the natal fourth at 16 Cancer might signify that either a personal stand was compromised to take up this job and/or that a frustrating physical move was involved and/or that he experienced stressful inner adjustments notwithstanding that he was shining so brilliantly in the outer world.)

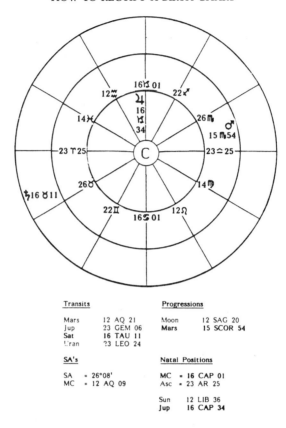

Transits		Progressions	
Mars	12 AQ 21	Moon	12 SAG 20
Jup	23 GEM 06	**Mars**	**15 SCOR 54**
Sat	16 TAU 11		
Uran	23 LEO 24		

SA's		Natal Positions	
SA	= 26°08'	MC	= 16 CAP 01
MC	= 12 AQ 09	Asc	= 23 AR 25
		Sun	12 LIB 36
		Jup	**16 CAP 34**

Figure 22C.   Partials: A Career Success

Lastly, we find Jupiter at 23 GEM 06 and Uranus at 23 LEO 24, both harmoniously aspecting the natal ascendant at 23 AR 25. The Jupiter sextile gives a boost to the personal confidence, and the Uranus trine a pace of rapid personal change which is, however, assimilated well and experienced as quite exciting.

Figure 22 B–D breaks down the whole picture into three separate partials, with accompanying read-outs of positions. The layout of partials here is straightforward: all the component at '12' degrees of a sign, all those at '16' degrees of a sign and all those at '23' degrees of a sign. This gives three sparse though potent partials (Figure 22,

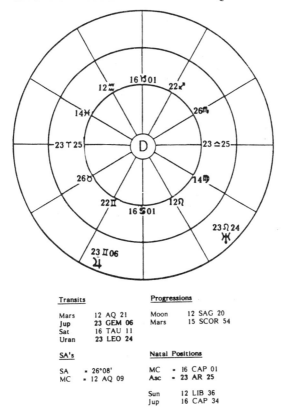

Figure 22D.   Partials: A Career Success

Transits		Progressions	
Mars	12 AQ 21	Moon	12 SAG 20
Jup	23 GEM 06	Mars	15 SCOR 54
Sat	16 TAU 11		
Uran	23 LEO 24		

SA's		Natal Positions	
SA	= 26°08'	MC	= 16 CAP 01
MC	= 12 AQ 09	Asc	= 23 AR 25
		Sun	12 LIB 36
		Jup	16 CAP 34

B, C and D). They are sparse enough that any two could be combined and not impede visual clarity—the criterion is simply clarity and readability.

Note that accompanying each partial is a duplicate readout of all the planetary and cuspal positions involved. However, in each instance, only those figures relevant to that particular partial is highlighted in bold type, to show the selective focus visually.

If you count up all the aspects that contribute to the impact of this life event, you will find eleven of them, which is not really uncommon. Remember that the astrology can only correspond to life as is, and when the natal chart is cast for the exact, accurate birth time, it *will* show that correspondence. Naturally, not every native will have 'made-to-order' successes like this! But most adults will have had enough key junctures in their lives (of whatever character) that definitive partials will allow you to zero in on the true time of birth.

Event 2: Death of Wife

This example was already touched upon to illustrate the tri-circled model (Figure 19). Now, instead of taking just a few key indicators, we will work with the full complement of all natal, progressed and transiting positions, using the worksheet format detailed on pp. 118-121.

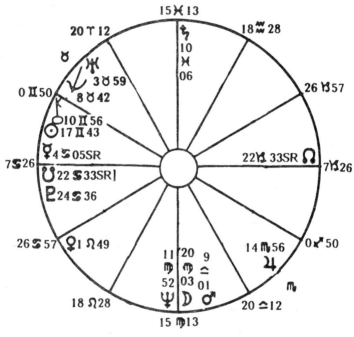

Figure 23.   Birth Chart

The birthdate for this chart is 9 June 1935, at 70W04, 40N44. To calculate the secondary progressions, we have translated the 9 June line in the ephemeris to the date it represents in the native's life, called 'the adjusted calculation date', or simply 'ACD'. (See 'Quick Computation of the ACD' in 'Mathematical Short-cuts,' p. 185.) For this particular native, his birthdate, 9 June 1935 'equals'

WORKSHEET

Event: Death of Wife   ACD: 9/6/35 = 24/11/34
Date: 9/4/59   Index Date: 3/7/53 = 24/11/58

Description: **Sudden** death after long period of ill health;
               native had to care for wife and infant, now
               left with sole care of infant.

Transits ("the middle of the night")		Progressions	
Sun	18 AR 47	Sun	10 CAN 31
Moon	3-4 TAU	Moon	9 LEO 29
Merc	0 AR 57R	Merc	25 GEM 14SD
Ven	23 TAU 18	Ven	25 LEO 54
Mars	29 GEM 23	Mars	17 LIB 09
Jup	1 SAG 16R	Jup	13 SCOR 31R
Sat	7 CAP 01	Sat	10 PIS 06R
	(near station)		
Uran	12 LEO 16R	SA's	
Nep	6 SCOR 03R		
Plu	1 VIR 57R	SA = 22°28'	
Chir	26 AQ 15	Prog MC =	8 LIB 01
No No	13 LIB 05R	Prog Asc =	24 CAN 54
		Prog 8th =	14 AQ 38

Figure 24.   Worksheet

24 November 1934 in his life, as is marked the ACD on the upper right-hand corner of the worksheet.

Every line down in the ephemeris from there on in, 10 June, 11 June and so forth, will be read as '24 November' for the purpose of computing the progressions. However, each succeeding date on down shows the next successive *year*. That is, 9 June 1935 equals 24 November *1934*; *10* June 1935 equals 24 November *1935*; *11* June 1935 equals 24 November *1936*; *12* June 1935 equals 24 November *1937*, and so on. That is called 'the index date', i.e. the index date in the ephemeris for (24 November) 1934 is 9 June, the index date for (24 November) 1935 is 10 June, and so on.

Counting down line-by-line in the ephemeris to the index date that falls closest to the event date, which will be 9 *April 1959*, we arrive at 3 July 1935 equals *24 November 1958* as the index date just before the event date, and 4 July 1935 equals *24 November 1959* as the index date following the event date. We have interpolated between these two sets of planetary positions to calculate the secondary progressions for this event.

Note that all the transits are listed all the way out to Pluto, and that the North Node is included. We have also added in two asteroids, Psyche and Sappho (representative of psychic trauma and of affectional love respectively) because the event features them so strikingly, though their inclusion is optional. (See 'Extra Information: The Asteroids', p. 173.)

Progressions are calculated only as far as Saturn. The 'SA' column includes the solar arc itself, the progressed midheaven (natal midheaven plus solar arc for the event date), the progressed ascendant (ascendant corresponding to the newly-progressed midheaven at the latitude of birth) and, for this event, also the progressed eighth cusp, since it is a death.

Underneath each partial is a readout of selected planetary/cuspal positions.

The two most 'heavily populated' partials for this event are the progressed angles of the chart, but since the quincunx afflictions are critical (illnesses and deaths are never without them), I would say specifically that it is the progressed *seventh cusp* (quincunx two progressed planets) which is the focal point of Figure 25 A, and the progressed *fourth cusp* (quincunx the natal Psyche) which is the focal point of Figure 25 C. That would be the marriage and wife (the seventh) and the home or basis of one's life (the fourth) respectively.

To begin, however, we will look at the relatively simple partial shown in Figure 25 A, which reveals that the meridian of the chart has progressed to 8 AR 01/8 LIB 01, precisely square the natal ascendant axis at 7 CAN 26/7 CAP 26. Major events not infrequently feature one house cusp progressed to the degree of another, which links the affairs of the two houses when planetary positions highlight the relationship. Here the links come through the transiting positions of Saturn and Venus. Saturn at 7 CAP 01, conjunct the natal seventh and opposing the ascendant, is a strong indicator of personal grief and loss, accentuated by its approaching station. But this Saturn, strengthened both by station and by its angular positioning, is also square the progressed meridian, albeit the square is barely within orb. Saturn in simultaneous affliction to both angles brings this life to a momentary halt.

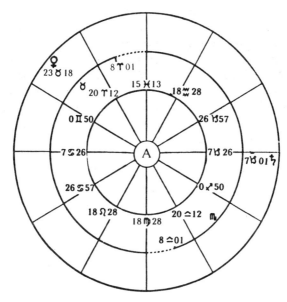

Saturn, Venus Aspects to Angles

Transiting Saturn (7 CAP 01) conjunct natal seventh (7 CAP 26),
opposition natal ascendant (7 CAN 26), square progressed meridian
(8 AR 01/8 LIB 01)
Transiting Venus (23 TAU 18) semisquare progressed midheaven (8
AR 01), sesquisquare progressed fourth (8 LIB 01), semisquare natal
ascendant (7 CAN 26), sesquisquare natal seventh (7 CAP 26)

Figure 25A.   Partials: Death of Wife

Transiting Venus is also in aspect to both angles, by semisquare
and sesquisquare divisions. It is semisquare natal ascendant and
sesquisquare natal seventh cusp; it is semisquare progressed
midheaven and sesquisquare progressed fourth. This is a component
of the disappointment and alienation of affection which is woven
throughout these partials.

The second partial (Figure 25 B) centres upon the progressed
ascendant axis, 24 CAN 54/24 CAP 54 This partial contains the
really dominant affliction of the astrology, progressed ascendant at
24 CAN 54 conjunct natal Pluto at 24 CAN 36, and progressed
seventh cusp in opposition; and also the subsidiary but important
affliction of progressed ascendant 24 CAN 54 sesquisquare natal

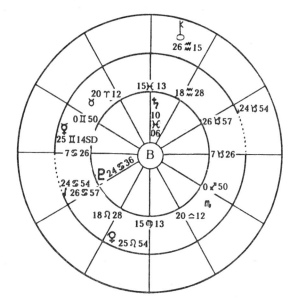

Aspects to the Progressed Ascendant Axis

Progressed ascendant (24 CAN 54) conjunct natal Pluto (24 CAN 36);
  progressed seventh (24 CAP 54) opposition natal Pluto (24 CAN 36)
Progressed ascendant (24 CAN 54) sesquisquare natal Saturn (10 PIS
  06); progressed seventh (24 CAP 54) semisquare natal Saturn (10
  PIS 06)
Progressed seventh (24 CAP 54) quincunx progressed Mercury (25 GEM
  14SD) and progressed Venus (25 LEO 54)
Transiting Chiron (26 AQ 15) opposition progressed Venus (25
  LEO 54)

Figure 25B.   Partials: Death of Wife

Saturn at 10 PIS 06, with the progressed seventh semisquare. If the
astrologer were just given this much, told it was when a marriage
ended, and asked did it end by divorce (or separation) or by death,
it is clear the marriage ended by death, because of the adhering and
binding characters of Pluto and Saturn, especially Pluto by
conjunction, which mires one into whatever life situation is at hand.
(Transiting Saturn conjunct the seventh cusp will tend to bind rather
than split as well, notwithstanding difficulties.)

Important to note here from the case history, is that the native
and his wife married when she was already near term (the infant
was barely nine months old at the time of the death), meaning that
they married when the progressed ascendant was still applying to
conjunction natal Pluto. This was a marriage fraught with

overwhelming pressures to begin with, with his wife already ill during the pregnancy.

The double quincunxes of progressed Mercury and Venus, respectively 25 GEM 14SD and 25 LEO 54 to the progressed seventh at 24 CAN 54 were previously detailed as showing the pressures of illness (quincunxes) through the period leading up to the death. Note that Mercury and Venus are not malefics, but by quincunx create considerable inconvenience, disruptions of routine, unwanted, incomplete accommodations to circumstance and the like, as the strains of caring for a sick wife, an infant, and supporting his family created for the native.

The progressed Venus here serves a double function. Note that at its position at 25 LEO 54, it is at maximum orb for quincunx the progressed seventh cusp at 24 CAP 54, but it is also just beginning to apply into quincunx the natal *eighth* cusp at 26 CAP 57. What were pressures with the wife will become the pressure of reconciling the *loss* of the wife, perhaps intensified by the opposition of transiting Chiron at 26 AQ 15 to the progressed Venus. Chiron in death situations frequently signifies ways of resynchronizing the pieces of the life into a viable new framework.

Note that with this partial, the one figure omitted is the progressed Sun at 10 CAN 31, though it is obviously trine the natal Saturn at 10 PIS 06. This helpful aspect has been reserved for a partial which will show an aggregate of helpful aspects to steel the native against what is substantially a mass of afflictions at the event date. Note also that the progressed Sun trine Saturn is a so-called 'internal aspect', not affecting the angles.

The third partial (Figure 25 C) concentrates upon the progressed meridian, of which the fourth cusp is life's very grounding. Although not all these planetary positions are in aspect with one another, this is a poignant read-out of interlinking aspects: the progressed fourth at 8 AR 01 is quincunx the natal Psyche at 8 TAU 42, which is quincunx the natal Mars at 9 LIB 01, which is sextiled by the progressed Moon at 9 LEO 29, which Moon is also quincunx the natal Saturn at 10 PIS 06.

Why is this characterized as 'poignant'? Mars, Saturn and Psyche are all potentially painful influences, the more so when in affliction. Quincunxes leave matters unresolved, mulled over, rethought, refelt, compromised. The double quincunx of Psyche and Saturn to the Mars natally gives a predisposition to suffer some acute conflicts in

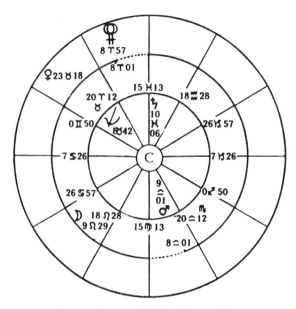

Aspects to Progressed Meridian, Progressed Moon

Progressed fourth (8 LIB 01) quincunx natal Psyche (8 TAU 42) conjunct natal Mars (9 LIB 01), opposition transiting Sappho (8 AR 57),
sesquisquare transiting Venus (23 TAU 18)
Progressed Moon (9 LEO 29) quincunx natal Saturn (10 PIS 06) sextile natal Mars (9 LIB 01)

Figure 25C.   Partials: Death of Wife

life in any case, to be activated if heavy transits and progressions come
along. Mars angular in a Cardinal sign is one who is inclined towards
action, but Saturn can hinder, quincunxes can hinder, Psyche can
make the consequences of actions painful and/or traumatic.

So first, we find that the progressed Moon at 9 LEO 29 aspects
each planet of this three-pronged configuration. The sextile to Mars
stimulates intense feelings, but the square to Psyche at 8 TAU 42
gives those feelings an inner sting, while the quincunx to Saturn
at 10 PIS 06 is both stimulating of expressions of grief and stifling
of them.

The quincunx of the progressed fourth cusp at 8 LIB 01 to the
natal Psyche at 8 TAU 42 is a significant one, notwithstanding that
Psyche is an asteroid, not a planet. Psyche afflictions at traumatic
events reinforce their traumatic impact, leaving scars which only

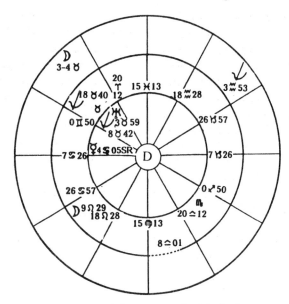

Aspects to Natal, Progressed and Transiting Psyche

Natal Psyche (8 TAU 42) quincunx progressed fourth (8 LIB 01), square
progressed Moon (9 LEO 29)
Transiting Psyche (3 AQ 53) square natal Uranus (3 TAU 59) and transiting Moon (3–4 TAU), quincunx natal Mercury (4 CAN 05SR)
Progressed Psyche (18 TAU 40) semisquare natal Mercury (4 CAN
05SR)

Figure 25D.   Partials: Death of Wife

time can heal. Here the astrology suggests that the basis of this life
has been subjected to traumatic dislocation.

The afflictions of transiting Venus to the progressed meridian have
already been mentioned. The last affliction, from transiting Sappho
at 8 AR 57 opposition both progressed fourth cusp and the natal
Mars especially, is another astrological analogue of alienation of
affection, prominent in the consciousness as it is prominently
positioned on an angle. The fourth partial (Figure 25 D) shows
the consolidated effects of Psyche, natal, progressed and transiting.
The square from the progressed Moon at 9 LEO 29 and quincunx
from the progressed fourth at 8 LIB 01 to the natal Psyche at 8 TAU
42 has already been noted. Added to this are the acute afflictions
of square transiting Psyche at 3 AQ 53 to the natal Uranus at 3 TAU
59 (and transiting Moon) and its quincunx to the natal Mercury at

4 CAN 05SR. Compounding the affliction to Mercury by transit
is the progressed Psyche at 18 TAU 40, semisquare the same natal
Mercury.

The trauma significator in astrology seems to come through Psyche,
as this partial and other practical usage demonstrates.

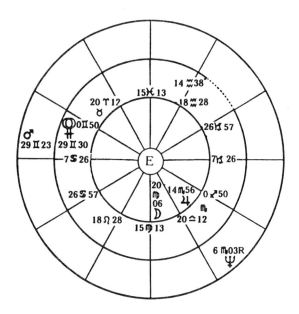

Aspects to Progressed Eighth Cusp and Natal Moon

Progressed eighth (14 AQ 38) square natal Jupiter (14 SCOR 56),
sesquisquare transiting Mars (29 GEM 23) and progressed Sappho
(29 GEM 30)
Transiting Neptune (6 SCOR 03R) semisquare natal Moon (20
VIR 06)

Figure 25E.   Partials: Death of Wife

The fifth partial (Figure 25E) shows afflictions involving the
progressed eighth cusp, which frequently is as much affected as the
natal cusp, as well as a semisquare affliction to the natal Moon (20
VIR 03) from transiting Neptune at 6 SCOR 03R.

These essentially reflect internal stresses of coping with the death
experience. It might be noted, however, that transiting Mars and
the progressed Sappho are on the same degree, 29 Gemini, a
conjunction which reinforces the effect of transiting Sappho at 8

AR 57 opposition the natal Mars at 9 LIB 01, another mark of forcible alienation of affection.

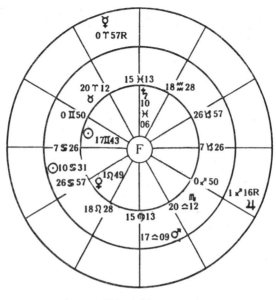

Mitigating Aspects

Progressed Mars (17 LIB 09) trine natal Sun (17 GEM 43)
Progressed Sun (10 CAN 31) trine natal Saturn (10 PIS 06)
Natal Venus (1 LEO 49) trine transiting Mercury (0 AR 57R), trine
  transiting Jupiter (1 SAG 16R)

Figure 25F.   Partials: Death of Wife

The last partial (Figure 25F) details the aspects that are helpful to the native, his reserve strength to ensure that life on a practical, functional level goes on.

Two major progressions are notable: the progressed Sun at 10 CAN 31 trine the natal Saturn at 10 PIS 06, and the progressed Mars at 17 LIB 09 trine the natal Sun at 17 GEM 43. This spells out industry, endurance, the will to work one's way through setbacks. These two trines involving the centre of vitality, the Sun, energy through Mars and persistence through Saturn are real saving graces amidst the complex skein of afflictions revealed in the other partials. But note that *the angular aspects still dominate, determining the character and overt impact of the event.*

Somewhat more subsidiary but suggestive of reason and balance in the midst of upheaval is the transiting Mercury at 0 AR 57R and transiting Jupiter 1 SAG 16R, both trine natal Venus at 1 LEO 49.

SEQUENCING: TIME ON THE HORIZONTAL

The Distinctiveness of Chart Sequences

Partials look *into* time, into the many astrological components of a single event date. Sequencing looks *across* time, from event to event, specifically in relation to the angles.

Sequencing shows the successive patterns of angular aspects across the years, which are unique from chart to chart. *No two chart sequences will be alike*, making sequencing an invaluable aid in obtaining chart accuracy.

To prove that this is true, look at *any* chart and make a list of all the planets beginning with any planet at degree '0' (such as Venus 0 Scorpio or Jupiter 0 Aquarius), then any planets at '1', then at '2' and so on through degree '29'. Then look at the midheaven degree in its particular sign. If it is at '18' of a sign, let's say 18 Taurus, see what planets are at '19', then '20' and so on, which the progressing midheaven will successively aspect. Then do it for a second chart and a third chart.

With one chart you may have three planets at '20' of a sign and then nothing until '27'. With another chart, you may have planets at '2', '4', '7' and '11'. Of course, the starting point for the sequencing, the natal midheaven, will also be at a different degree for each chart.

Even when the progressing midheaven comes upon the same degree number as a natal planet, the aspects it forms are different from chart to chart: 25 Sagittarius to 25 Aquarius is a sextile, but 25 Sagittarius to 25 Gemini is an opposition, and so on. The respective planets aspected as the midheaven progresses will also differ. A square to *Venus* for one, a square to *Mars* for another.

You won't find any two charts alike. The patterning is as distinctive as a fingerprint.

Sequencing the Midheaven

The midheaven always needs to be sequenced prior to the ascendant, which depends directly upon the progressed midheaven positions. Mathematically, sequencing the midheaven requires only a few steps, as follows.

The progressed midheaven position depends directly upon the solar arc for the event date, which is simply the difference between the progressed Sun at that date and the natal Sun, for example 19 LEO 49 progressed Sun at event date − 2 LEO 45 natal Sun = 17°04′ solar arc ('SA'). The solar arc is added directly onto the natal midheaven which is, let's say, 11 SAG 59, so the newly-progressed midheaven for the event date is 11 SAG 59 + 17°04′ = 29 SAG 03.

Once worksheets are computed for several events in chronological succession, the SA for each event may be computed using the progressed Sun's position for each respective event. Since the native is gradually getting older through this series of events, the solar arcs will be progressively greater, such as 2°17′, then 5°49′, then 11°06′, and so on. When these figures are successively added onto the natal midheaven, it will be progressing ahead in the zodiac (counter-clockwise), successively forming aspects with natal planets.

To begin with a simple example, just to demonstrate the process, we will use the hypothetical sequence introduced in an early chapter, 'Sample Models Incorporating Natal, Progressed and Transiting Positions' (Figure 3, pp. 29-30). Figure 26 begins with a reprint of the midheaven and a few of that chart's planets, simplified by rounding all figures off to the nearest degree.

MIDHEAVEN SEQUENCING CHART

EVENT	Left homeland	New home	Career problems	Own business	High profile success
DATE	1976	1977	1979	1980	1982
NATAL MC	4 SCOR	4 SCOR	4 SCOR	4 SCOR	4 SCOR
EVENT SA	28°	29°	31°	32°	34°
Prog MC/IC or PLAN-ETARY SA	Mars SA 28°	Prog IC 3 GEM	Prog MC 5 SAG	Prog MC 6 SAG	Prog MC 8 SAG
ASPECT	CONJ	CONJ	SQUARE	TRINE	SEXTILE
TO WHAT PLANET/-ANGLE	IC	JUP	SUN	MARS	MOON

Figure 26. Midheaven Sequencing Chart

The Midheaven Sequencing Chart begins with 'Event', which will identify the event in a capsule form. Here the series reads, 'Left Homeland', 'New Home', 'Career Problems', 'Own Business', and 'High Profile Success'. Underneath the event is the 'Date' line, which is provided here in its rounded-off form to the nearest year. The 'Natal MC' line is, of course, the same all the way across. The 'Event SA' is greater from column to column as the native is progressively older. The 'Prog MC' (or planetary SA) is derived from adding the Natal MC (or planet) and the Event SA.

At this point in a usual rectification, the astrologer would be looking at the natal chart to see if any aspects are formed between the newly-progressed midheaven and a natal planet. If so, what aspect it is, for the 'Aspect' line, and 'To What Planet' on the following line.

Of course, here we have constructed a 'perfect match'. The progressed midheaven aspects to planets plausibly describe the events to which they correspond. Note this is no coincidence or accident. Even this short sequence had its own characteristic pattern. First an SA of 28°, then one degree ahead to 29°, then two degrees ahead to 31°, then one degree ahead to 32°, then two degrees ahead to 34°. Not only the spacing of the sequence, but the aspects and planets involved differ, which, of course, bears directly upon delineation.

Now, one aspect taken alone may not 'prove' anything. But a *sequence* of appropriate aspects begins to build a case for an accurate chart. It is something like a jigsaw puzzle. When just a few pieces are filled in, you can't see what the whole picture looks like. Only gradually, as more pieces are added, can you see the lake, or the house, or whatever else the puzzle might depict. Moreover, the more pieces are filled in, the more apparent it is where the remaining pieces have to be placed to complete the whole picture.

With a jigsaw puzzle, of course, you will usually have a picture in front of you of what the completely assembled puzzle will look like, which is your guide to filling in the pieces. You are matching up the bits and pieces of the puzzle against the whole picture in front of you. Sequencing works on a similar principle, in that it pieces together patterns that are definite enough, and large enough that you clearly see if they 'fit' or not against the chart in question.

Even if the chart is wrong (i.e. the sequences 'don't fit'), the definitive patterning will assist you in finding the true time of birth, especially if that birth time is *close*. For example, if our sequencing chart showed exactly the same sequence as did the previous figure, with the key difference that the natal midheaven is said to be one degree later, as a result, all these aspects would fall consistently one degree earlier than for the true chart. Hence, all we have to do is shift the midheaven one degree ahead, and again the entire sequence would 'fit'.

Having an exact sequence will greatly facilitate this type of chart 'juggling', a degree ahead or two degrees back, until a definitive match is found.

Using an Exact Solar Arc

Now that the principle of sequencing is clear, it need be emphasized that it is important in actual practice to use *the exact solar arc*, not figures rounded off to the nearest degree. Rule 3: Tightness of Orb, makes clear why. Since only aspects within a degree's orb maximum are allowable, rounding off a position by, let's say 25′ is way too wide an approximation. In addition, if one has rounded off some figures up and some down, the problem is magnified, such as 13 SCOR 45 being rounded to 14 SCOR 00 whereas the applying progressed midheaven aspect has been rounded from 14 AQ 22 down to 14 AQ 00. It may *look* like a square, but its actual orb will be 37′ off (15′ ahead plus 22′ back). One is only asking for problems.

Remember, also, that not every aspect is going to be *exact*. For anything major in the life, there will be *lots* of aspects, perhaps one 10′ shy, another 21′ past and so on. Only an exactly accurate chart will register that all the many aspects in orb are truly in orb. Since the solar arc can easily be computed exactly, and the accuracy of the entire chart depends upon it, this is a prime area to work with exact figures.

Sequencing the Ascendant

The progressed ascendant is based directly upon the progressed midheaven at any given event date. After locating the newly-progressed midheaven in the Table of Houses, the new ascendant is located at the same latitude as at birth.

This means there are two extra steps needed to compute the progressed ascendant once you have the progressed midheaven. You need to take that figure to the Table of Houses, and you have to locate the newly-progressed ascendant, which generally involves interpolation, both between adjacent latitude lines and between adjacent columns.

There is another potential problem that is a little more subtle. The rate of the progressed midheaven does vary from chart to chart, but only from 57′ per year (for a birth near summer solstice) to 61′ per year (for a birth near winter solstice), which still keeps the yearly motion to *approximately* one degree per year. Gauging approximate ages when certain types of events might have happened (and then be testing with exact mathematics) can be very useful for the rectifying astrologer, and the 'close-to-one-degree' yearly increment facilitates gauging this *visually*. (See 'Working With Ages and Years', p. 153.)

With the progressed ascendant, by contrast, its rate of motion in the outer latitudes can vary from 38′ per year to 2°38′ per year. Over a forty-five-year life, for example, the *rate* of the progressed ascendant per year could have varied between 2°30′ at the year of birth to only 1°00′ by the forty-fifth year of life—meaning that unless you are some hardy soul who has effectively memorized the Table of Houses, your 'estimates' of where the progressing ascendant might be at age fifteen, age thirty-five, age fifty-five and so on are likely to be significantly in error. Visual skills won't suffice; you need to look at the book.

I would offer a few suggestions, however, to make your work less cumbersome. One is to estimate the progressing ascendant within a quarter degree until the midheaven seems secure. The second suggestion is to do some preliminary sequencing with the midheaven and perhaps the partials for an event or two, and then—when the midheaven appears that it might be accurate—calculate the progressed ascendant for the other events.

The third suggestion, which will cost less in exactitude than might be thought, is not to do triple interpolations for either progressing ascendant or progressing intermediary cusps. (See 'Simplifying Triple Interpolations', p. 181-185.)

To construct an Ascendant Sequencing Chart, use the Midheaven Sequencing Chart (since you will always need the progressed midheaven to calculate the progressed ascendant) and simply add 'Progressed Ascendant' under the 'Progressed MC/IC' line.

As you gain experience in sequencing and wish to be more thorough, check that all major progressed aspects are accounted for as follows. Put your Sequencing Chart beside the natal chart and begin tracing the moving midheaven (or the moving ascendant) with your finger, noting which aspects it makes along the way. Check this against your tabulations and see if any major aspects have been missed.

Sequencing the Progressed Planets

I am including this, because the question will naturally arise can it also be done. It can be done, though you would have to check the progressions of all the planets separately to see when they form major aspects to the natal midheaven and/or ascendant.

Many of these will naturally emerge anyway, when you work with the partials. There are really so few per planet, in any case (save the progressed Moon, but you would be watching that closely anyway). Take the progressed Venus, moving at perhaps a rate of one degree per year. In thirty years, it only has a chance of making major aspects to the natal angles twice—once to the midheaven, once to the ascendant. For slower-moving progressions, the aspects are proportionally less frequent.

For these reasons, I would rule this out as any type of 'necessary' step in the rectification process. However, when you do come on such aspects, by all means check that the happenings in the life account for them!

Nor does thorough sequencing of the progressed angles necessarily have to be performed for every chart you might rectify. However, working with charts this thoroughly is an excellent way to gradually make rectification easier to accomplish. Once you have gone the long route on paper, you will find it easier to make visual estimates as you go along, and to habitually look for sequences that will clue you in to the correct positioning of a chart.

Working With Ages and Years

When you work face-to-face with the native using your sequencing format, your task will be to verify the correspondence between the astrology and the native's life. It will mean little if you ask, 'What happened to you when your progressed midheaven squared your natal Sun?' You would rather ask, 'What happened to you when you were nearly thirteen?' or 'What happened to you in 1961?'

There are simple ways to translate sequenced aspects into their equivalent in ages and/or years. First, take the midheaven as is— your 'best bet', so to speak. Let's say that midheaven is 18 TAU 36. Let's say that when it reaches 20 TAU 32, it is exactly sextile the natal Venus at 20 CAN 32. The solar arc for that aspect is 20 TAU 32 − 18 TAU = 1°56'. In other words, this native was going on two years old at the time of the aspect, according to the setting of the chart you are reading. Of course, the native was very young at that time. You can simply ask something general like, 'Was there any

favourable turn of events for your *family* when you were about two?'
The native may not know. But they may have moved to a nicer home
then, or it may have marked the birth of a favourite sister.

Of course, for an adult, you would enquire what happened to
them under that aspect under a later age, let's say a solar arc of 21°56'
instead of 1°56'.

What you do need to do is check the rate at which the Sun is
progressing at birth, to see if it is under one degree per year or over
one degree per year. If it is over one degree, then the 21°56 solar
arc will be only about age twenty-one and a half. If it is under one
degree, the 21°56' solar arc will be a little over age twenty-two.

(For tips in rapid estimation of age equivalent of solar arcs, see
'Mathematical Short-cuts', pp. 178-180.)

Figuring Sequences Backwards
Often, you will be given a series of event dates before the natal chart
is even cast, i.e. the native will give you his birth data as close as he
knows it, along with the events you will use to rectify that chart.

Perhaps one or more of those events seemed especially striking
or outstanding like, 'the year I fell completely apart', or 'the year
I found my true calling in life'. Then, perhaps, you cast the natal
chart, and you see some progressed aspect or another that you feel
might 'spell out' what happened at that time. In that case, you might
want to see first where the chart is progressed to at the event date,
and then figure *backwards* to the natal chart, which you would then
test for the other events of the life.

I had one chart for a Capricorn Sun native, whom his mother said
was born 'before dawn'. He had a bony, rigid kind of build, a strong
jaw-line, flat face, and I certainly favoured Capricorn as an ascendant
over Sagittarius (which would also be 'before dawn'). Then I noticed
he had small, alert, bird-like eyes, very Mercurial-looking and the
natal Mercurcy was at 6 Capricorn. I couldn't go earlier than 0
Capricorn, and I couldn't go later than 9 Capricorn to keep that
Mercury very 'visible'.

Then I noticed when I cast the chart that Venus was located at
19 AQ 52 and thought perhaps he married when the progressing
ascendant reached the natal Venus. In addition, I noticed that the
natal Uranus was at 18 TAU 06, so that the progressing ascendant
(and seventh cusp) had to pass through square the Uranus before
arriving at the Venus conjunction.

I thought, wouldn't it be a stroke of luck if he divorced and remarried a little over a year apart under those two successive progressed aspects? Naturally, far from *everyone* divorces under seventh square Uranus or marries under ascendant conjunct Venus, but I thought I should check out the possibility, if the appropriate-sounding dates were offered.

Rather to my amazement (!), the native volunteered that he was divorced in November 1972 and remarried in January 1974—a little over a year's gap. Moreover, at the second of the two events, the remarriage, not only was the progressed ascendant conjunct the natal Venus, but so was transiting Jupiter, while the progressed Moon formed a lovely sextile—most fitting for marriage. So I took the sequence *backwards*, producing a natal ascendant of 7 CAP 32—most satisfactory! Not too surprisingly past that point, everything I tried with the chart worked.

Figure 27 illustrates the placement of the chart's angles at both progressed ascendant square Uranus and progressed ascendant conjunct Venus. In passing, we might note that the rate of ascendant progression here is quite rapid, with a sign of short ascension (for the northern latitudes, that is) rising—Aquarius. At 42N20, the native's latitude of birth, the ascendant is rising at the rate of 1°29′ per year. The gap between the square to Uranus from 18 AQ 06 and the conjunction to Venus at 19 AQ 52 is 1°46′, equating to one year and slightly over two months in the native's life.

Now, to figure backwards to the natal chart, the key question to pose here is, 'What was the solar arc at the time the ascendant had progressed to square natal Uranus?' The solar arc for the ascendant/Venus direction, note, would do just as well. Once we know the solar arc of *any* event date, we can simply subtract that solar arc from the progressed midheaven at the event date, and arrive at the natal midheaven.

To compute the solar arc for the event date, we need only know the natal and progressed Sun. With this chart, since the probable range of birth was initially narrowed to just nine degrees (0–9 Capricorn), at the rate of approximately four minutes per rising degree, assuming we have made the right initial determination about the rising area of the chart, then we can compute the natal Sun within thirty-six minutes (9 degrees × 4 minutes) of possible birth time. Actually, if we take the median point of that thirty-six minute span, we would be no more than eighteen minutes of birth time off for the calculation of the natal Sun. This equates to slightly less than 1′ of arc, i.e. no problem at all.

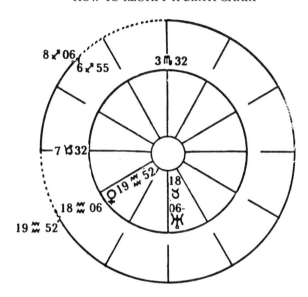

Figure 27.   Figuring Sequences Backwards

Our next step is to use the birth time given by the early degrees of Capricorn rising for the native's birth date to compute the ACD. The birth time for 4½ Capricorn rising (midway between 0 and 9 Capricorn) is 7.08 a.m. EST (Eastern Standard Time) 10 January 1940. This equates to an ACD of 10 January 1940 equals 7 July 1939.

Moving down line by line in the ephemeris to the Index Date closest to the date of the divorce, we arrive at 12 February 1940 equals 7 July 1972, and 13 February 1940 equals 7 July 1973. Interpolating between these two lines for the progressed Sun's position in mid-November 1972, we arrive at 22 AQ 29 for the position of the progressed Sun. Subtracting the position of the natal Sun at 19 CAP 06, the SA for the event date is 33°23′.

The progressed midheaven for the event date is 6 SAG 55. 6 SAG 55 − 33°23′ = 3 SCOR 32 natal midheaven, and a natal ascendant of 7 CAP 32.

Fine-Tuning the Chart Through Sequencing
There is another way that sequencing can tighten up the positioning of the chart's natal angles. Remember that with partials, we wanted the natal and progressed angles to allow for only one degree orb

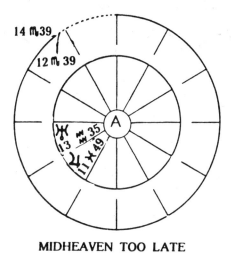

MIDHEAVEN TOO LATE

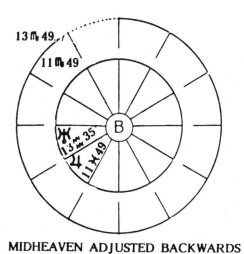

MIDHEAVEN ADJUSTED BACKWARDS

Figure 28.   Fine-Tuning the Chart Through Sequencing

maximum for all relevant major aspects. These tiny intervals can also be tightened up *across* time.

You do have that degree's maximum leeway, so you do not have to locate exactly partile aspects, such as progressed midheaven at 15 LIB 49 square natal Moon at 15 CAN 49. If the progressed midheaven is at 15 LIB 15 or 15 LIB 57, the aspect is still within range of effectiveness. This gives a tool for fine-tuning the adjustment of a chart's angles.

For example, let's say that you discover that the progressed midheaven was trine the natal Jupiter when the native had the opportunity and funding (Jupiter) to move (sextile progressed fourth cusp) to Hawaii and open the scuba diving business (trine midheaven) he always wanted (Jupiter), as shown in Figure 28, A and B. How much more 'Jupiter trine' can life get?!

In the chart as cast, let's say the natal Jupiter was at 11 PIS 49 and the progressed midheaven was 12 SCOR 39. That's an orb of 50' past partile, which does seem wide for a separating aspect as is.

Now let's say that the native's natal Uranus is at 13 AQ 35. So two years later (let's say *exactly* two years), the native's business partner suddenly absconds with the money, bankrupting the business and the native is kicked back to the family farm, destitute.

Obviously, you expected this unexpected disaster to register as progressed midheaven (and progressed fourth) square Uranus, since how much more 'Uranus square' can life get?! But instead, you find the progressed midheaven at 14 SCOR 39 (12 SCOR 39 + 2 years), more than a degree past the square to the natal Uranus at 13 AQ 35 (Figure 28A). Aspect both passed and unacceptably wide!

However, when you look back to the time of great opportunity (progressed midheaven trine natal Jupiter), you note that this aspect would still have been effective if you moved the progressing midheaven *back*. It could be moved back 50' to partile, or even more and have the aspect applying. If you moved it back 50', then the progressing midheaven at the time of the sudden breakup of the business would be 13 SCOR 49, certainly a more convincing square to the Uranus at 13 AQ 35 (Figure 28B). It could go back even further. In fact, once you have filled in more of the sequencing, other adjustments might become obvious, to bring the chart into its true balance.

Several such successive angular aspects in a row will often do the job, where separate analyses might leave one baffled. This will put a real tool for adjustment at your disposal.

10.
OTHER METHODS
AND CONSIDERATIONS

Transits Over Angles
Transits of Saturn and the so-called 'outer planets' over the natal chart have already been covered extensively in other works, so this useful aid in rectification will be given in capsule form. It should also be noted that transits over *progressed* angles will be effective as well. What you will frequently find (logically enough) is that when the transit is conjunct or in other aspect to a natal angle, this is a new component in a life situation, whereas when the transit affects a progressed angle, it is a continuation of an ongoing situation or, sometimes, a matter of circumstances catching up with one.

The newly-discovered planet, Chiron (whose orbit falls between Saturn and Uranus) is also included here, which is often a key component in life changes which feature alternative solutions, unusual growth or transformation, or altered life contexts.

Saturn and the Ascendant Axis
Saturn in conjunction with the first or seventh cusp suggests discipline, constraint, responsibility, depression, confrontation of hard reality, stabilization of material circumstances, or simply the necessity for hard work on oneself. With Saturn transits, you do find out where you stand.

In trine or sextile to these cusps, stability, security, responsibility well-assumed, a realistic grounding in life, or the undertaking of relationships and/or projects which will be of a long-range or enduring character.

Square to these cusps show constriction, depression, pressures to knuckle under, uncomfortable or painful straits, pressures to bind oneself to people or circumstances.

Saturn and the meridian

In childhood, this transit can be a component of hardship for the family, a family loss, depressing circumstances or (in a child's perception), a parent for whom the force of circumstances have alienated them from the child. For an adult, Saturn over the midheaven brings practical responsibility and the necessity for hard work in the career. If read as opposing the fourth cusp, however, it could even be involved in the loss of a home (in one such instance, the family home was sold at the time, denying the native the opportunity to inherit). Over the fourth cusp, Saturn could bring depressing circumstances into the home; however, there could also be contexts where home-building just becomes more *important* and extra effort was devoted to such.

Saturn square the meridian could coincide with loss of prestige or austerity measures in the home, or a break-off in the career but not a sudden one, as Uranus would bring. This could have been a long time in coming, or fraught with blame, guilt, responsibilities and/or resentment.

When transiting Saturn is found in affliction with the cusp governing either respective parent at the time at that parent's death (generally tenth for the mother and fourth for the father), the parent was suffering at the time of death and, as likely as not, the death was a long while in coming.

Uranus and the Ascendant Axis

Uranus conjunct or opposing the ascendant will tend to provoke a breaking of patterns and forcibly jolting one out of ruts. The action, note, is never subtle! The changes can be sudden, shocking, shattering, exciting, electric, painful and, most often, unexpected.

Uranus conjunct, square or opposition seventh cusp *can* be the hallmark of a period that brings divorce with married people, though do not assume that is the case. If it is, however, assume that the shifts in attitudes were very rapid and came as a real jolt to the person involved.

Note: Uranus will shatter what is unstable, while leaving what is built on a solid foundation alone.

Uranus trine or sextile the ascendant is exciting (for good for ill), expediting and sometimes accompanies entering into situations where one might be going willing but is still relatively unprepared.

Uranus quincunx either the ascendant or the seventh cusp produces quandaries and split decisions for the native. Parts of his personal perspective might be shattering, but parts need to be salvaged.

(A quincunx from *Saturn*, by contrast, is outright frustration and dissatisfaction.)

Uranus and the Meridian

Uranus over the midheaven can be wonderfully exciting or devastating, but again, rarely the expected. As with all conjunctions, the surrounding aspecting is the key. In extreme manifestations, scandal might hit, or one is suddenly publicly viewed as an iconoclast, or one is out of one job only to be landed in some wild new, previously unconsidered venture.

Uranus over the midheaven is also opposition the fourth, so that can mark forcible relocation or suddenly recognizing that one's life is built on a shaky basis (fourth house) or, as well, jolting one's life onto a *new* basis. One thing is sure: with Uranus over the midheaven, changes are 'high profile'. There's no place to hide.

Uranus on the fourth cusp can boot one out of a home (as in a foreclosure for which one is unprepared, or a natural disaster striking the home), or simply provoke needed changes in the life outlook, though again, unplanned for and not necessarily welcome. One could certainly suddenly lose a job (opposition tenth) under such an aspect as well, though the more usual signature for 'You're fired!' (or 'I quit!') involves Mars.

Uranus square the meridian is certainly not apt to bring any positive boon, and could be part of a signature for many an unsettled life circumstance.

Neptune and the Ascendant Axis

Astrologically, Neptune conjunct either the ascendant or the seventh can signal confusion, uncertainty or insecurity, though we also find it with inspiration and/or romance. The native does not have a clear idea what he is getting into during such periods, and the impressions and feelings may lead rather than the reason, or what we loosely term 'reality'.

When divorce occurs under a Neptune square to the seventh, as contrasted with a Uranus square, the break itself may be clean (the square) with no way of going back, but the native is left in a state of confusion or perplexity, with many loose ends emotionally. With a quincunx from Neptune rather than a square, such confusion is compounded, since the circumstances themselves might preclude a total break of contract (such as shared custody of children maintaining the tie). A Neptune quincunx to the *ascendant* makes for a period when the personal sights are hard to set with any clarity and getting out of one quandary only seems to lead to another.

When a native feels confused or in the dark about the circumstances of *any* life situation, you might find a Neptune affliction to the ascendant. Relationships entered into with Neptune involved with the seventh cusp may later turn out to be different to what the rose-coloured glasses had thought. However, you also have to look at the surrounding aspects.

Neptune trines and sextiles to the ascendant may be, but also may *not* be a blessing, because one can let things slide by, either lackadaisically or idealistically.

Neptune and the Meridian

Neptune transiting over the midheaven can leave the course of the life momentarily adrift, uncertain or confused. One is 'feeling' for one's next steps in life rather than aggressively moving forwards. Curiously, I found this indicator with one chart marking the death of the mother. I told the native it could indicate that the mother died in a coma or heavily sedated (Neptune conjunct tenth house, the mother), that the father was left in a state of confusion (Neptune opposition fourth cusp, the father) or that she herself was left unsure how to proceed with her own life (Neptune on her midheaven). She answered, 'All three!'

It is difficult for one to assess one's own abilities objectively (or for others to do so) when Neptune is transiting the midheaven, and many a strange, experimental thrust into a new life direction has been attempted under such a transit. Neptune over the fourth cusp may be equally unsettling though not as visible to the outside world. Certainly, if one purchases a house (fourth cusp) under such an aspect, or simply moves under such an aspect, one can expect that one was misled about its value or the environment, or hidden problems may later become manifest. Neptune square the meridian can be a component of a break in the direction of the life, but it might be one fraught with uncertainties.

Neptune quincunxes can mark a combination of confusion and dilemma that is difficult to cut through indeed. It is not a good time for practical decisions, though quincunxes may leave little choice. Sometimes this aspect can also be a hallmark of being badly deceived but having no ready way out. Transiting Neptune, ironically, was quincunx Johann Sebastian Bach's midheaven when he received a major appointment, one to last the remainder of his life. He had great aspects involving the midheaven and the lights, to land the appointment. But *his qualifications were considered in doubt.* He got the job by default of others. Bach! So much for the Neptune quincunx!

Pluto and the Ascendant Axis

Pluto signifies pressure, often social pressure: pressures to conform, often pressures to conform to a social mould. Its action is repressive and drives one into oneself. One doesn't break away and act freely under a major transit of Pluto unless at enormous effort, and sometimes only after the inner recesses of the personality have been, in effect, dredged and cleansed (usually the *end* of this long, ofttimes gruelling, transit). Pluto is intensive and thorough and has an utterly humourless impact upon the personality. Personal power (its expression or repression) is likely to become an issue, as instinctual drives come to the fore.

Pluto conjunct the seventh cusp brings the very ability to relate down to its most elemental level, where the native *has* to cope with it. Nothing is casual or relaxed, and if the native has not achieved an elemental honesty with himself, relations with others can get complicated and over-emotional. However, during such a period the native is inclined to stay where he is, with the depths of his emotions and/or motivations put to the test.

The square to first and seventh cusps marks times of personal emotional discomfiture and difficulty in taking actions without considering a whole range of ramifications. Trines and sextiles from Pluto to ascendant can free one's energy on deeper motivational levels, though this would probably be contributory to some event, not the main indicator. It may just show that the native is 'playing for keeps'.

Pluto and the Meridian

Pluto across the midheaven marks social pressures as they affect the career, or overwhelming responsibilities, power plays or complicated situations encumbering one's pathway ahead. One learns how to play 'hard ball' under such directions. It becomes hard to just live one's own individual life. The cost of 'making it' in the world, extreme risks and life-and-death matters may come to the fore of one's consciousness.

Pluto across the fourth cusp can have an obliterating, or at least severely challenging influence in regard to one's grounding in life. *Any* aspect of Pluto to the fourth cusp could be found as part of a life-threatening configuration though, I would emphasize, only as a component of such.

Sextiles and trines of Pluto to the meridian are certainly more comfortable than conjunctions or squares, but could be involved in matters of career and life status where the stakes are big.

A Pluto quincunx can be an unusually forcing pressure in the life, because of the combined character of pressuring Pluto and the stymieing quincunx.

Chiron

Chiron, discovered in 1977, may still be an unknown quantity for some astrologers. Chiron seems to have the effect of spontaneously altering reality, or at least our access points to it, so that we may be in suddenly different, unthought-of perspectives or contexts. In a sense, it is the only outer-planet influence which does its work without 'creating a huge mess'. Uranus shatters, sometimes into painful pieces; Neptune dissolves, clouds barriers, and can be instrumental in confusion, misunderstandings and complications; Pluto does a dredging job, and subjects people to enormous, sometimes overwhelming pressures.

Chiron, by contrast, alters perspective and context. Suddenly things are possible that were not possible before. A lesson is being learned in a previously unavailable context or environment. Inner resourcefulness rises to the surface, and major changes may be possible at an unusually rapid rate. Chiron also has a great deal to do with parenting and unusual births (like surrogate parenting, for example), and in the astrology of death, it specifically shows what components of the native's perspective are spontaneously altered by the absence of the deceased. I call it a 'resynchronizer'. (More information on Chiron may be obtained in *'Essence and Application—A View from Chiron'*, by Zane Stein, CAO Times, New York and *The Continuing Discovery of Chiron* by Erminie Lantero, Samuel Weiser Inc., New York.)

Chiron and the Ascendant Axis

This can bring unusual and unexpected changes into the life, not by shock, like with Uranus, but by some unseen process of metamorphosis which seems to make personal changes possible. Doors may open that were previously shut, and without any forcing effort—it is just 'there'. The concepts of personal identity are altered, though what actually happens might depend upon the person's inherent character or latent potentialities. Life may suddenly have a more 'essential' quality. One native with Chiron over the ascendant at the time of the first major surgery of her life said it was the first time she felt keenly aware of her own mortality, and that it permanently altered how she related to life.

Chiron squares give an experimental twist to the native's approach to life and relationship with others, and the motivation to change can be keen. Chiron changes are often out-of-the-ordinary—education in a new field, or experimental therapy, motivation of some newly-discovered talent, fitting into a new environment.

One native had three very major life changes over a period of many years, each involving relocation, change of occupation, life perspective, income base, and so on—'everything all at once'. The one common factor astrologically was the presence of transiting Chiron on a natal or progressed angle for each of the three changes.

Chiron and the Meridian
Exceptional or unusual career opportunities may come along with Chiron contacts to the midheaven, or transformed attitudes towards one's parents or towards one's own development. One's very concept of what constitutes a career, what is one's status in life or one's *purpose* in life may be altered. Chiron across the IC can subtly but pervasively redirect the life on internal levels and set a new inner compass.

Planetary Stations
When a planet is about to change direction, whether from direct to retrograde or retrograde to direct, it moves very slowly for several days applying and separating from the directional change. During such periods, its effects are intensified. It is frequently like getting a 'double dose' of the planet, and can be an aid for rectification work.

With one chart with birth time unknown, the native was tall and statuesque, though very sturdily-built with a proud carriage. I thought Leo rising likely. She related that at the time of her mother's death, she was grief-stricken but could not express her feelings; but that six months later, suddenly her feelings erupted in a public setting. At the date of the death Saturn (a repressant) was at station at 6 Aquarius; six months later Mars (an eruptive influence) was at station at 6 Leo! Using 6 Leo as the ascendant, the timing of all given events of the life worked out perfectly! That is probably the exceptional case, in terms of ease of rectification, but planetary stations should always be given special attention.

Progressed Moon
If you have calculated planetary positions for several events, look at just the progressed Moon for each and are not finding convincing aspecting, chances are good the chart is in need of adjustment. The

progressed Moon shows both the focus of personal emotional interest and a point at which the environment permits open interaction with the native. As such, it is most always in exact aspect with *something* at the time of an event in which the native has a personal stake. Not infrequently, the aspect is with a natal or progressed angle, or a natal planet. The progressed Moon is a bit like a magnetic needle; it shows to where the native can readily gravitate at the time in question. The Moon is almost invariably part of a signature of *change*.

Progressing relatively rapidly (one degree or slightly more per month), the progressing Moon is an excellent tool for fine-tuning the natal chart to exactitude.

Solar Arcs to Angles
The solar arcs that will register the most strongly are undoubtedly those that come to conjunction with an angle. Squares are operative as well. The effects of a solar arc planet and a progressed planet are similar. The progressed planet shows how one's orientation in relation to that planetary influence (be it Mars, Mercury, Jupiter) is gradually changing, attracting and reacting to new experiences. The solar arc planet (i.e. the planetary position natally plus the solar arc of the event date) shows that planetary drive in the native in relation to his ongoing sense of personal identity (the Sun). The interpretative results may be similar, though (with the exception of SA *conjunctions*) I'm inclined to give progressed planets greater weight.

Always important to check out in rectification work is whether there is one or more of the so-called 'malefics' near an angle at birth, especially the meridian, as the conjunction to the meridian by solar arc often marks a formative event in the young life.

Progressions and Transits: Difference in their Effects
Technically, the difference between transits and progressions is that transits show what happens to you, and progressions show how one gradually changes and develops. However, since progressions continually re-centre the native in new orientations and perspective, they effectively function to attract certain types of experiences and to react to what happens, making the progressions and transits mutually activating.

The other key difference is that most often, the progressions are in orb for a substantially longer time than are the transits. Even the relatively slower-moving outer planets may stay within a range of one degree for several weeks when at station, but otherwise considerably less; whereas even the most rapid progression, the Moon, progresses only about one degree in an entire month.

The progressions, with their relatively long time frames, give periods of *predisposition* for certain kinds of things to happen. However, without the activating effect of appropriate transits, the progressions are not manifested as overt 'events', i.e. definitive changes in the life circumstances.

Things would not 'happen' without the transits. But the transits would not be effective without the appropriate orientation, states, frameworks that the progressions describe. In practical experience, you will discover both definitively represented in any kind of major change in the life.

However, something that must be kept straight in delineation is that a transit aspecting a natal planet and/or progression is still a transit impacting *upon* that slower-moving position, and it cannot just be interpreted as an aspect involving two different planets and showing a combination of their two characters. For example, transiting Uranus conjunct natal Jupiter is very different from transiting Jupiter conjunct natal Uranus. The natal planet shows *what is being affected* in the life; the transit shows *how*.

Of course, transits can definitively activate progressed positions as well as natal ones. Not uncommonly, if the main transits to angles are to progressed rather than natal angles, it shows a situation in progress, already under way, now taking a different turn.

The Relative Weight of Transits in Event Analysis

The relative importance of specific transits can depend upon the character of the event and the transit's aspecting. For example, in major gruelling, traumatic, or action-packed changes in the life, transiting Venus and Mercury may be 'lightweights', showing comparatively minor inconveniences or aids. However, for marriage, the position of transiting Venus becomes very important, and for the signing of an important document, transiting Mercury is central. For accidents, surgery, or events that are characterized by strong personal initiative, transiting Mars is vital. In money matters, one cannot overlook transiting Jupiter, with loss and hardship, transiting Saturn, and so on.

In other words, the character of the event itself will be confirmed and specified by the character of the transits in exact aspect.

11.
CHECKING YOUR WORK: LIABILITIES AND AIDS

There are many approaches that may be used effectively to double-check a chart rectification. Many of these are listed below. It is unlikely that you will have to use all of these for any one chart, but it will give you much to fall back on if you are stymied with some apparent error in your work.

Locating the Rising Sign
Be sure you have reasonably narrowed down the range of birth time at the start, by zeroing in on the most likely rising sign and prominent planetary influences that are reflected in the native for your chosen positioning of the chart. If you have not done this, you may find yourself in a sea of unsatisfying figures, and simply 'settle' for a solution based upon a *possibility*. Remember, there is only one correct chart, and that one works consistently.

Completeness of Information
Often, a rectification will not make sense because the astrologer has simply not had enough information to go on. The following is one example of how this might happen.

Suppose the native says he received a promotion in his job. The astrologer might *assume* that this would be shown by a major aspect involving the progressed midheaven and the natal Jupiter or the Sun, or a similar aspect. Perhaps this is true, but it may not be. Maybe the promotion the native was describing wasn't really a major move upwards, or it might involve mitigating circumstances. Perhaps the native was technically in a higher position, only to encounter problems with his co-workers. Perhaps he had moved to take up the new position and there are problems either in relocation or in the new location itself. This would involve the fourth cusp (change of home), whereas the career change itself would register through the tenth cusp, so the meridian itself might receive 'mixed' aspecting.

Maybe the promotion was actually one of, let's say, three successive promotions, and it was the second or third that was actually the 'big break'. All such information will bear upon the type of expectable aspecting you would find, and assist in rectifying the chart.

Importance to the Native

In other words, 'just the bare facts' can be misleading. Using the same example as above, questions like 'Did you consider this a very *important* career change?' might spare you work.

Changes in the life are also assessed by their effects in specific areas of the life. For instance, even a career change (tenth house) can have a strong concomitant effect upon the ascendant. I have seen situations where obtaining tenure on a teaching job, for example, or having one's first one-man art show was marked by progressed Sun conjunct *ascendant*, even though technically, this was a 'career event'. In the native's experience, these were substantial *personal* achievements bearing upon the personal identity and enhancing the self-esteem, so this type of indicator made sense. I saw the same indicator—progressed Sun conjunct natal ascendant—when a housewife first achieved something substantial outside the home. The natal Sun was in the twelfth, and this native had felt much 'behind the scenes' all her life. What she actually *did* during her 'coming out' period might not have clued the astrologer in to that major indicator, but for *her* it was a progressed Sun conjunct ascendant period—she had 'arrived'.

Double-Checking the Seven Rules

If there seems to be something conspicuously wrong with the rectification in some areas, review the astrology that *did* seem correct. You may discover that you had used only one major indicator to confirm an event, such as progressed ascendant trine Mars, for example, but that that aspect had little support from other confirming, descriptive aspects, not satisfying Rule 4, Multiple Simultaneous Aspects. Perhaps there were few exact transits to support the event or weakly placed, not satisfying Rule 7, Several Different Orders of Aspects Simultaneously

Once double-checking the seven rules becomes routine, you will discover that with an accurate chart, they will be met consistently. Once you find those solutions that 'fit like a glove', your work will be cut way *down*.

Checking Patterns

There may be things that characteristically happened in the life of any particular native. With one it might be that the father left home several times during the native's childhood. If you have the dates— which may be difficult to obtain—see the kind of planets and aspects involved at the various departures. Was there one time that it was finally permanent? Maybe *that's* when you find a decisive major aspect involving the meridian and a natal or progressed planet.

The caution here is that if you are given many dates of recurring types of events in the native's life—be it successive successes, successive patterns of risk and failure, and so on—you may need to enquire which was most important, which was a turning point or if, for some reason, one event date was marked by other strong references that will enable you to specify the astrological timing.

Also to be considered in life patterns analysis is that if a pattern is repetitive, i.e. characteristic, then it is likely there is something in the *natal* chart to confirm this as well. A native with the Sun brilliantly aspected in the tenth will tend to have successive career successes; a native with a badly-afflicted Saturn in the second will tend to patterns of loss, austerity and/or anxiety in the material affairs of life.

One native who was married and divorced three times had Neptune conjunct the South Node in the seventh house natally— rather a 'marriage addict'! Each time the transiting Neptune and/or Uranus was in major affliction to the natal or progressed seventh cusp along with other, major indicators. But the divorces were specifically different, and the way this was reflected was that the 'Neptune affliction divorce' was one of many years and with children, which left much residue in its wake with continuing ties, whereas the other two divorces were 'Uranus affliction divorces' where the break was clean and the women were never seen again.

Another native who had the Moon in the ninth natally moved back and forth between Sweden and England all through childhood and youth; and invariably at the times of relocation, the progressed Moon was in exact aspect with the natal or progressed ninth, fourth or first cusps.

Keeping House References Clear

A great aid in checking your work is to ensure that house cusps relate specifically to appropriate circumstances. Death of a parent, for example, involves the meridian, the eighth cusp and the ascendant, but each signifies a different facet of the experience. The meridian shows what happened to the deceased; the ascendant shows its effect upon the native; the eighth cusp show how the experience of death *per se*, its aftermath and recovery period was handled by the native.

With the birth of a child, if the native experienced complications—such as a Caesarian—you might find a Uranus affliction to the natal or progressed fifth cusp. Yet at the same time, the ascendant might be clustered with harmonious aspects from Jupiter, Venus and the progressed Moon, showing the native's happiness and ease of adjustment to the new routine. Same birth, very different types of indicators to the fifth and first cusps, yet both reflect the circumstances as they were.

Filling in the Missing Pieces

If the chart seems correct, sequence the progressed midheaven and ascendant. If some year is marked off by prominent aspecting and it doesn't show up in your chronological listing of events, enquire what happened that year.

Don't neglect planets directed to conjunction one of the angles by solar arc. Note the approximate age in the native's life at which each occurs. Watch malefics close to natal angles for childhood traumas, early break-up of the home and the like.

Years when there are major progressed aspects involving both ascendant and midheaven, or several aspects to one angle or the other, it should be verified what happened in the life. If the answer is a blank, the timing of the chart might be seriously questioned.

Other years to watch closely are those when one house cusp has progressed to the degree number of another, if one or both house axes in question is an angle. Transits or progressions affecting one cusp will tend to also activate the other. Such convergences not infrequently mark major junctures in the life.

'Lost' Events

Most difficult to fill in may be childhood events—events which affected the family as a whole may not be remembered readily, but are registered in the chart nevertheless. Sometimes you will hear that the native doesn't remember something personally, but that the family had talked about it (such as 'they said it was a disgrace but I never knew the details') and valuable information can be gleaned from that about the character of that period in the life.

Successive Major Aspects in a Row

Perhaps you have come on a chart where many successive aspects 'resemble' each other. This can happen with a chart that has a closely-spaced stellium, such as Sun at 11 Aquarius, Venus at 12 Aquarius, Mercury at 12½ Aquarius and Jupiter at 14 Aquarius. It may be difficult to distinguish which major aspect of the midheaven referred to which event—how did the progressed midheaven differ from trine Sun to trine Venus and so on.

Astrology can only describe the life as it has been, so take the series at face value. Find out if there was a *series* of events spanning several years, an overall good time when everything went smoothly. Then see what aspects border that series of progressed aspects. Perhaps it is bordered by a progressed midheaven square Saturn a year before the series began, quincunx Uranus two years after the series of aspects, or opposition Mars somewhere in the midst of them. Any such factors will facilitate deciphering the true timing of the chart.

Somewhat easier to work with are a series of very different types of aspects in succession, such as progressed midheaven sextile Mars, then quincunx Uranus, then trine Venus, then opposition Jupiter, then square Uranus. This gives a definitive profile of conspicuously different types of fortune, which can be most helpful.

Also bear in mind, should a sequence seem frustrating or the overlaps of aspects difficult to sort out, that sequencing, although very important, is not the only tool at your disposal. Working with some partials, transits across the angles, or simply some other period of time in the life, may provide just the relief and perspective needed to allow the problematical sequence to fall into place.

Appropriately Descriptive Planets and Aspects

It is fashionable to disregard the effects of so-called 'malefics'. Things of a harsh, so-called 'negative' or stressful character do happen under the influence of Mars, Saturn and Uranus, not under Venus, Mercury and the Moon. They happen under squares and quincunxes, not sextiles or trines. Philosophies of personal growth and evolution do not alter this.

Also remember that you may be listening to 'edited' accounts of events that happened long ago. The mind can selectively remember or forget, so try to find out what *happened*. Just because the native relates everything calmly *now*, don't assume that some disaster happened under the benevolent disposition of Jupiter, for example, because disasters do not happen under such aspecting. *Ask*, 'Did it come as a shock at the time?', or 'How long had he been ill?', since slow-moving Saturn indicators will prolong an ordeal, whereas with Uranus, things can come as a bolt out of the blue.

Also, time alters one's response. Things that were exhilarating years back may be related in a blasé manner now. Often the key is to enquire what the reaction was *then*.

If the planets and aspects involved in a major event seem appropriate, also look at the surrounding aspecting, to see if significant reinforcers or modifiers are present.

If you see one aspect that seems to fit an event perfectly, but the surrounding events are questionable, it may be worth going back to the drawing board. For instance, if someone describes three reunions that were very happy and you see a Jupiter trine characterizing one of them, do not overlook the Mars squares and Saturn quincunxes for the other two.

Events that Happen in Stages

This is one of the most interesting and challenging parts of rectification work. Many things in life fall into place in stages. We may meet someone and fall in love, which dating is important, but marry that person at some later date, which is also important. We may begin a major project on one date, and see the fruits of it at a later time. Someone may have a serious surgery at one time, and die at a later time; someone else may visit a faraway place, and like it so well, that at a later date they move there. All these are events that have happened in *stages*.

It would be convenient if there were one single aspect or aspects blanketing a multi-stage happening, but most often that will not be found, nor is it necessary to have that to be descriptive of events. What you will find, of course, is that the house affected will be repeatedly aspected in successive stages, which might be viewed as a continuity reinforcing that circumstance in the life: bolstering it, battering it, stabilizing it, and so on through life's many possible actions upon us.

As always with astrology, do pay attention to *beginnings*. Whatever was first in the series will often set a special tone that colours what is to come.

Extra Information: The Asteroids

Though there is plenty to keep track of with the usual planets, some of the newly-available asteroid ephemerides prove invaluable in rectification work. Asteroids tend to be very *specialized* in their function, but no less potent thereby. You will get very satisfactory results without them, but for truly 'deluxe' work, the asteroids can be extraordinarily accurate in the extra information they provide.

The two asteroids I would personally never be without are Psyche and Sappho. Psyche is specific to vulnerability to trauma, and is invariably involved with the angles and/or affliction with planets at any time experienced by the native as traumatic.

Sappho represents affectional love. This is not just people one likes or wants or gets along with, which oft-times registers through Venus, but marks special bonds of affection in the life. They may or may not be sexualized—it will be found as often between parents and children in synastry, or between friends as it will be found between lovers or spouses. Events which reinforce, or shatter, or otherwise deeply touch or disrupt the affections will show through Sappho aspects.

Other asteroids that can be useful in rectification work are Eros, Icarus, Toro and Hidalgo. These and other asteroids, accompanied by delineation guides, are available through CAO Times, P.O. Box 75, Old Chelsea Station, New York, New York 10113, USA.

Special Aspects: 75°, 105°, 165°
States of unrest accompany these aspects. The 165° aspect appears to be more aggressive and overt than the other two. In natal delineation, this aspect signifies eternal persistence (as clarified by W. Kenneth Brown and Al H. Morrison), and works past any measure of discouragement or obstacles. In event astrology, it seems to show what effects will be left long after an event has happened.

The 75° and 105° aspects seem to appear with especial frequency with junctures in the life characterized by chronic or insidious states of affairs, unclear ramifications, anxiety, ambivalent motivations, lingering effects.

Perhaps as a correlation, both these aspects fall into 'can't make up one's mind' spots: the 75° aspect midway between the 60° sextile and the 90° square; the 105° aspect midway between the 90° square and the 120° trine.

I would give none of these aspects the same weight as major aspects in event astrology; however, it is useful to note that where they occur in abundance, the clouds in the native's life are unlikely to clear rapidly. (Note: 'Event 2: Death of Wife' in 'Sample Events', pp. 138-148, reveals these aspects in great abundance, despite the fact that it was not necessary to use them to define just what happened in the life at that time.)

Hindsight as a Help

It is often said that hindsight is very wise, but not of much help since the time for its usefulness has passed. With rectification work, this observation may be dramatically reversed. The following will clarify.

Before something happens, references *expand out in a scatter.* What does the Jupiter aspect coming up refer to? Is it money, friendship, business enterprise, a religious venture? Before an event, we might have quite a job prognosticating what a planetary influence might refer to in a particular life.

However, *after* an event has already happened, the references have *narrowed in to a focal point.* We can see if the Jupiter referred to money, new opportunities, and so on.

A Mars affliction coming up will not necessarily indicate that a person will suffer cuts; however, a person who has *already been* cut will necessarily have been so under a Mars affliction. So if the native relates that they were cut or burned, you need to locate *Mars* in an appropriately descriptive location, rather than Uranus or Saturn or Neptune. If you do not find Mars, stop right there and examine the mathematical adjustment of the chart.

Many astrologers rationalize that virtually any indicator can produce any kind of life situation. This isn't true, as applying hindsight to any accurate chart will verify.

12.
MATHEMATICAL SHORT-CUTS

The Need to Streamline the Mathematics of Rectification

Adjusting a chart to exactitude requires skilled work, both perceptually—observation of the rising degree and prominent planets—and mathematically. But it is the mathematics, notably, that has kept many an otherwise astute astrologer away from the challenging task of rectifying charts.

Two key ways of precluding tedious, unnecessary work have been previously detailed. One was to work with the *space* of the chart prior to its timing, so as to narrow down many a twenty-four-hour search to a workable range prior to manipulation of figures. The second key way of forestalling extra work was the emphasis placed upon locating the 'backbone' of an event in a chart's angles before filling in its many other mathematical components.

But mathematics is inevitably with us in any case. Prior to testing the chart at different settings (I call it 'juggling'), we have to compile lists of transits, progressions and solar arcs. Some prefer to use a computer. It might be said to be a mixed blessing, however, because a computer not only does not organize your work along a chart's own 'organic' lines, but it further schisms the astrologer from the inherent calculations/delineation unity. I've personally eschewed computers for the most part, finding that manipulating figures within my own mind sinks me into a natural succession of mathematical steps which is tailored to the problem at hand, rather than rigid and mechanical; and that understanding the mathematical flow perceptually as I go along, enables me to draw successive *interpretive* linkages as well, which correspond to the successive levels of mathematical clarification. Astrology *is* 'the mathematics of life', not living human being here, chart there, and a bunch of computer print-outs sitting off to the side of one's worktable.

Even if one claims such extreme frustration with mathematics that computers are a necessity (which is quite odd, since it is the mathematically *inclined* who so often seem to gravitate towards them), computers simply *cannot* handle much of the 'meat' of rectification work: relative judgements of meanings, gauging proportional balances, in which direction to adjust and how far, plus many other areas we generally term 'discernment'. Does the complete astrological picture at hand correspond to what the native is saying about his life? Where are the missing pieces? Where are the contradictions? Are you looking at *Mars* when what the native seems to be talking about is *Uranus*? Even subtle feelings about motivational factors, and how they are threaded through the (accurately-cast) chart, enter in. Only a trained astrologer can cope with all this. It is not a job for machines.

However and notwithstanding, all of the above still bears upon *mathematics*! Only an accurately-cast chart will answer the questions, resolve the discrepancies, will paint the native in the true living colours of his form, his actions, his experience.

Ideally, the mathematical work of chart rectification should be rendered as simple and straightforward as possible, to be a positive aid throughout a chart rectification, not an impediment, or a distraction from the delineation process. Mathematics is *part* of that process.

The guides and tables in this section are designed to help the astrologer 'think mathematically', to render mathematics, so far as possible, a natural and integral part of one's interpretive work.

The Role of Estimation in Rectification Work

An initial caution is offered that estimations, or rounded-off figures, are not recommended for the usual course of astrological work. Especially since we have seen that just a single degree's difference on the midheaven can signify *a whole year* in the native's life, we do not want to wind up with anything as crude and inexact as 'a chart to the nearest degree', for example, notwithstanding that simplifications have been offered for teaching purposes.

However, certain types of estimations are invaluable time-savers within the overall context of a rectification. It takes knowing *where* exact-to-the-minute-of-arc exactitude is critical, and where—prior to reaching that kind of exactitude—estimations will be time-saving and serve a needed functional purpose. Estimations which are too wide, or simply applied without understanding *how much difference that particular estimation will make*, can fuzzy our vision of the chart, making our work more difficult. On the other hand, other types of estimations can clue us in to the true positioning of the chart with a minimum of work, sparing us additional, time-consuming experimentation.

Can Solar Arcs be Estimated—How and When to Do It

One area where we want to minimize estimation is with the solar arc, which determines the progressed angles for any given event date. It is exactitude of the angles to which rectification work is directed, since they define the exact time of birth; so of course, we cannot subject our *central reference point* to estimation.

However, we do not need to have even the progressed Sun (which determines the progressed midheaven) exact to the *second* of arc, just the *minute* of arc. This would not be so, note, for the erection of a solar return chart, where having the position of the (natal) Sun to the exact second of arc is mandatory. There, it is the Sun's position that is the central reference point, and it takes about twenty-four minutes to move through each minute of arc, too wide a range (about six degrees on the midheaven) to round off. But for chart rectification purposes, 1' difference on the midheaven represents only approximately *four seconds of birth time*, and even the most conscientious worker would not quibble whether the native was born at 1.42.33 a.m. or 1.42.37!

The solar arc may be the first thing you would want to work with, with some rectifications. If, for instance, you see several planets fairly close to the midheaven, you might want to use solar arcs to make preliminary assessments about what might have happened at certain ages in the native's life. If the response from the native is positive and seems to confirm your chart's initial positioning, or points the way to adjustment, you will be way ahead right at the start. You'll want to be able to ask (based upon the solar arcs), 'What happened at age ten?', or even, 'What happened at age thirty-nine?' This could give you a feel for the larger sweep of the chart's timing *before* you attempt more thorough calculations of a full complement of transits and progressions for specific, dated events.

How can we quickly estimate solar arcs without sacrificing accuracy? First, the time-saver we want to apply is the elimination of the usual steps of calculating the progressed Sun for each event (step 1) and subtracting from it the natal Sun (step 2), two separate, repetitive calculations. If we can work with a basic, consistent rate of progression and simply *multiply* that by the native's age in years, we can accomplish this.

At the time of any native's birth, the Sun was moving at a rate of between 57′ and 61′ per day, depending upon the time of year the native was born—closer to 57′ if closer to the summer solstice, closer to 61′ if closer to the winter solstice. A quick method of estimation is as follows.

Note how rapidly the Sun is moving on the date of birth. The rate, of course, will very gradually vary each successive day, but from any one day to the next, that variation will be negligible. For an entire *month* of solar motions—which represents *thirty years* in the native's life with secondary progressions—the variance is only 1½′ per day by the end of that thirty-day time period at maximum variation (i.e. the birth Sun close to a 0 Cardinal point), which happened gradually in tiny integers.

If you take 58′ as the daily motion of the Sun at birth, for example, and use that 58′ as a constant rate for the first thirty years of life, your result will be less than one-half degree off at the thirty-year mark, often quite a bit less.

The second work-saver is that you don't have to multiply out the figures as in, 58′ × 17 (for age seventeen in the life), 58′ × 25 (for age twenty-five in the life), and so on. Rather, *begin with whole degrees*. In other words, if the native was exactly fifteen at the date of some event, begin with fifteen whole degrees.

Then consider that for a rate of progression of 58′ per year, 58′ can also be seen as 1° − 2′. 15 years × 2′ per year = 30′. 15° − 30′ = 14°30′ solar arc for exactly age fifteen.

Now consider the same age of fifteen for the native, but this time with a Capricorn birth Sun, progressing at the rate of 61′ per year. Take the fifteen whole degrees again, but this time you will be *adding* an increment onto 1° per year, namely 1′ per year (61′ = 1° + 1′). 15 years × 1′ per year = 15′. 15° + 15′ = 15°15′ solar arc for exactly age fifteen.

Also practise thinking this through *backwards*, as you will often spot the solar arc—the exact distance between the natal midheaven and a major aspect to a planet, for example—first, and have to figure back to what age in the native's life that arc is equivalent. Using the two examples cited above, and working this out backwards, this is how to think it through.

If you saw a distance of exactly 15° between natal midheaven and

SOLAR ARC ESTIMATION TABLE

Yrs	57'/Yr	58'/Yr	59'/Yr	60'/Yr	61'/Yr
1	57' (1° - 3')	58' (1° - 2')	59' (1° - 1')	1°	1°1' (1° + 1')
2	1°54' (2° - 6')	1°56' (2° - 4')	1°58' (2° - 2')	2°	2°2' (2° + 2')
3	2°51' (3° - 9')	2°54' (3° - 6')	2°57' (3° - 3')	3°	3°3' (3° + 3')
4	3°48' (4° - 12')	3°52' (4° - 8')	3°56' (4° - 4')	4°	4°4' (4° + 4')
5	4°45' (5° - 15')	4°50' (5° - 10')	4°55' (5° - 5')	5°	5°5' (5° + 5')
6	5°42' (6° - 18')	5°48' (6° - 12')	5°54' (6° - 6')	6°	6°6' (6° + 6')
7	6°39' (7° - 21')	6°46' (7° - 14')	6°53' (7° - 7')	7°	7°7' (7° + 7')
8	7°36' (8° - 24')	7°44' (8° - 16')	7°52' (8° - 8')	8°	8°8' (8° + 8')
9	8°33' (9° - 27')	8°42' (9° - 18')	8°51' (9° - 9')	9°	9°9' (9° + 9')
10	9°30' (10° - 30')	9°40' (10° - 20')	9°50' (10° - 10')	10°	10°10' (10° + 10')

Figure 29. Solar Arc Estimation Table

natal Pluto, for example, and then noted that the birth Sun was moving at a rate of 58′ per year, would that mean that the native was just under fifteen or just over fifteen when the solar arc became partile? It would be just *over* fifteen. Moving *less* than one degree per year, the arc would not have moved fifteen whole degrees in fifteen years, but would have arrived at fifteen whole degrees at a somewhat later time. If, on the other hand, you were working with the Capricorn birth Sun chart, with the Sun progressing at 61′ per year, at an arc of exactly fifteen degrees, the native would be slightly *under* age fifteen, because the Sun had progressed a little over a degree per year, hence would have passed the 15° mark before the fifteenth birthday.

Figure 29, 'Solar Arc Estimation Table', computes the yearly increments for ten years for progression rates of 57′, 58′, 59′, 60′, and 61′ per year. However, if you can gradually train yourself to think through the process yourself, it will streamline your work. This same type of process of estimation repeats in many areas of rectification work, and the more you can rely upon your own internal thought processes rather than many separate tables, the better your overall skills and success rate for your work.

Can Interpolations be Estimated
Probably the mathematical bane of astrological existence—even

without the challenges of rectification—is interpolations. If only one could read off where progressed Venus was for the native on 24 March 1959 without having to interpolate between the two daily figures. If only the native was born at exactly 42N latitude instead of 42N37, necessitating interpolation. If only the natal midheaven worked out to exactly 15 CAP 50 instead of 15 CAP 59, so we wouldn't have to interpolate between columns in the Table of Houses.

It is not uncommon for beginner's classes to spend three or four sessions just on calculation of the natal chart, with a bulk of effort devoted to interpolations. Rectification work, which pinpoints exact planetary and cuspal positions for times in the life span which are irregularly-spaced at best, as well as working with uncertain times which necessitates adjustment, could become a regular marathon of interpolations! Anything that can be done to minimize the work without sacrificing criteria of accuracy, will be of benefit to the rectifying astrologer.

There is one key criterion for determining where estimates can be made with interpolations and how close they need be. That is solely the one degree orb stricture (Rule 3, Tightness of Orb). If the final results of estimating an interpolation work out to 20′ off in the natal angles, for example, which is one-third of a whole degree, that's treading the borderline of allowable margin, even for preliminary work on the chart. Obviously 50′ would be far too much. But 5′, especially if it cuts down the number of mathematical steps for the astrologer is, relatively speaking, negligible.

Once one is reasonably sure of the actual minute of birth, *of course* tighten this up to exactitude. And your estimates do need to be close to *locate* that exact minute of birth. But if you tightened everything up to an exact minute of arc's exactitude all the way through a rectification, only to discover that the birth time is apparently wrong, then a lot of unnecessary work simply has to be redone. Skilled use of estimations can save time and effort, as well as definitely boosting the rectifying astrologer's morale!

Simplifying Triple Interpolations
Interpolations fall into two general categories: those involving figures in the Table of Houses and those involving figures from the ephemeris. We'll consider the Table of Houses interpolations first, starting with the standard, cumbersome triple interpolation, which we want to simplify without sacrificing accuracy.

This is usually considered a nuisance at best, even for the natal chart. The native was born at some latitude in between two latitudes, such as 50N21, in between 50N and 51N. His midheaven falls at some equally 'inconsiderate' location, let's say 20 LEO 14, falling in between 19 LEO 35 and 20 LEO 36 in the Table of Houses.

First we interpolate in the 19 LEO 35 column, in between 50N and 51N in the Table of Houses. Then we do a second interpolation between 50N and 51N in the 20 LEO 36 column. Last, we take those two latitude interpolations and interpolate between the 19 LEO 35 and the 20 LEO 36 column, to arrive at a 51N21 latitude ascendant for a 20 LEO 14 midheaven.

Rectification work would have the astrologer repeat this triple interpolation for every event given, after the solar arc for the event has been used to compute the newly-progressed midheaven. Moreover, if one has done that work and then discovers that the chart is in need of further adjustment, it's time for triple interpolation all over again! Several rounds of this, and the Table of Houses could begin to look like the Table of Horrors!

The first tip I would offer is to never do even the so-called 'mechanical' work of rectification mechanically. Keep one eye on the chart. Perhaps the native has told you about some exceptionally happy occurrence in the life. The way the timing looks, you think the progressed ascendant at that time might work out to trine natal Jupiter. You look it up in the Table of Houses under the progressed midheaven for the event date, and you see that it will fall a degree or so shy. *Stop*. Look at how moving the progressed midheaven (hence also the natal midheaven) ahead a degree will affect the figures you've already worked with. If you're still not sure that that will be right, then estimate the progressed ascendant by sight within half a degree, to give you a continuing reference point without having gone through all the steps of the triple interpolation.

The fact is, that if you do not reach the point somewhere along the line where you can say, 'Yes, I think this might clinch it—so many things work together and make sense', you might be in trouble with your rectification anyway. And on the humourous side, if there is anything more deflating than a rectification in trouble, it is the twenty-five triple interpolations you have done only to reach that troublesome point! Should some clever soul come along and point your chart in the right direction, all twenty-five of them *will have to be redone*.

But let's say that the situation looks plausible. Your preliminary sequencing shows nice results, and you've worked out descriptive partials for some single major event. You are ready to undertake the interpolations for the progressed ascendant (and intermediary house cusps as required) for the other events on your list.

We will use the example already cited for the 20 LEO 14 midheaven at 51N21 latitude. Two time-savers will be applied to the interpolation: working with fractions and cutting down the steps of the interpolation, the former first.

First, both one degree of zodiacal motion, the unit measure of the moving midheaven, and one degree of latitude, the unit measure of that co-ordinate of the native's location on Earth are subdivided into 60'. The difference of midheaven position from column to column is always approximately 60' (57'–63'), and of course, the difference from one latitude line to another in the Table of Houses, here between 51N00 and 52N00 is always exactly 60'.

Instead of doing an exact-to-the-minute-of-arc interpolation, let's try one using the closest fraction of a degree, and see how much difference it makes. Figure 30 demonstrates, by showing exact differences and the estimates of these differences in fractional form.

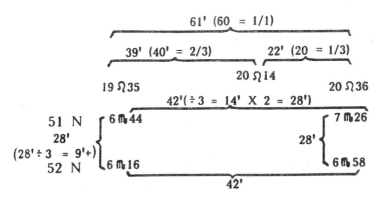

TRIPLE INTERPOLATIONS

Figure 30.   A Fractional Approach to Triple Interpolations

The distance between 19 LEO 35 on the midheaven and 20 LEO 36 on the midheaven is 61'. The figure for which we are interpolating the ascendant, 20 LEO 14, is 39' ahead of the earlier figure and 22' shy of the later one. Rounding 61' off to *60'* even, 39' to *40'* and 22' to *20'*, we arrive at the simple fraction of two-thirds (40' is two-thirds of the way to 60'). This has already simplified the later interpolation step between columns. We can interpolate two-thirds of the distance between the first column and the second. Had we not done this rounding-off, we would be interpolating $^{39}/_{61}$, which is effectively so close to two-thirds that its difference will be negligible.

The next step of the interpolation is to locate the position of the ascendant at 51N21 for the column headed by 19 LEO 35. Rounding the '21' part of '51N21' to one-third (i.e. one-third of 60' equals 20', which is very nearly 21'), we will be interpolating one-third of the way from 6 SCOR 44 at 51N00 to 6 SCOR 16 at 52N00. Rounding-off that distance, 28', to the nearest multiple of three (since we are calculating one-*third*), which is 27', our answer is 9'. Since the ascendant is moving *back* in the zodiac from 51N00 to 52N00 (which will sometimes be the case, sometimes not), we are going to *subtract* that 9' from the higher figure, 6 SCOR 44, equals 6 SCOR 35.

The step we are going to skip is the interpolation between latitude lines in the second column. We can see that the distance between the two ascendant figures at 51N00 and 52N00 is 28' within both columns respectively.

We can also see that the distance between one ascendant and the next succeeding one is 42' between columns on both latitude lines, 51N00 and 52N00. If we were to take two-thirds of 42' to interpolate on the 51N00 line, or two-thirds of 42' to interpolate on the 52N00 line, or two-thirds of 42' to interpolate at any one of the sixty subdivisions in between, the interpolation expressed in minutes of arc would be the same.

So we are simply going to take one-third of the distance on the latitude line closest to the latitude in question (51N21), which is 51N00. 42' ÷ 3 = 14' × 2 = 28'. 6 SCOR 35, which is the ascendant for 51N21 with a 19 LEO 35 midheaven, + 28' = 7 SCOR 03.

Note here that the sameness of measure between the latitude lines at the two successive midheaven positions (28' between 51N and 52N for each) and the sameness of measure from column to column (42' for 51N in the first column to 51N in the second column, also 42' for 52N) will not occur in every instance. Scorpio is a sign of long ascension in the northern latitudes, which is responsible for this. However, even with signs of short ascension, such as Aries, if you follow this method, the discrepancy for the final figure for the ascendant will still be acceptably small (within 3' for this latitude).

Interpolations in Succession
Sequencing the ascendant can present a problem if one is continually doing triple interpolations. One short-cut will still produce quite an accurate result: Interpolate the ascendant for any one event. Let's say the birth latitude for this particular chart is 39N39. To find out what the ascendant will be two years later, for example, instead of interpolating for 39N39, and then again between two columns in the Table of Houses, simply look at the 40N latitude line (the closest line) and see how far the ascendant is progressing in one year and multiply by two. The difference from one column to the next from 39N39 and from 40N will be negligible, as will the difference between some figure interpolated in between columns and the next figure interpolated between columns.

Use a few years' span and then monitor if the *rate* of progression is changing significantly, and modify your estimation accordingly if it spans over many years.

Quick Computation of the ACD
The Adjusted Calculation Date (ACD) is the date (i.e. the day and month, not the year) to which the birth date (and all succeeding days in the ephemeris) is 'equivalent' for the purpose of computing secondary progressions. Now instead of a sixty-base for our calculations, as with zodiacal longitude and geographical longitude and latitude, we are working on a twenty-four base for the twenty-four hours of the day.

From one day to the next (such as from 11 May 1969 to 12 May 1969), the twenty-four hours of the day represent an entire year in the native's life. Thus two hours are equivalent to a month of life (24 ÷ 12); every four minutes of ephemeris time is equivalent to only a day (2 hours = 120 minutes ÷ 30 days in the month = 4 minutes per day).

It is easiest to use the standard time equivalent for the birth time rather than the local mean time when computing the ACD, because any 'Standard Time' designation is some exact number of hours from the 0 point for all the time zones, Greenwich.

Begin by adding the number of hours from Greenwich if the birthplace is west of Greenwich, subtracting the number of hours from Greenwich if it is east. So a birth time 20 January 1954 at 2.05 p.m. in Berlin, Germany translates to 1.05 p.m., since Berlin is in Central European Time Zone, one hour east of Greenwich. Of course, you will also want to translate this to the twenty-four-hour clock, so 1.05 p.m. becomes 13.05. For a birth in San Francisco, California in the United States, in Pacific Standard Time, eight hours west of Greenwich, the same 2.05 p.m. birthtime would translate to 10.05 p.m., or 22.05 translated into the twenty-four-hour clock.

The planetary positions for the Berlin chart are computed for thirteen hours, five minutes into the twenty-four-hour day which begins at midnight the day of birth and terminates at midnight the following day. The planetary positions for the San Francisco chart are computed for twenty-two hours, five minutes into the twenty-four-hour day which also begins at midnight the day of birth and terminates at midnight the following day.

To calculate the ACD, we are posing the question, 'If the planetary positions for 20 January 1954 are found at 13.05 on that date for the birth in Berlin, to what date is 20 January 1954 at midnight equivalent?' That equivalent date is the ACD.

Just as we worked with fractions to simplify the work of interpolation, fractions are a great help in computing the ACD. Conveniently, there will be no need to estimate the result, however, since the measure involved, twenty-four hours ephemeris time per year in the life is perfectly consistent, unlike the varying figures of successive columns and different latitude lines in the Table of Houses.

Every two hours is equivalent to a month in the life, so first we want to see how many sets of two-hour units into the day were our computation of planetary positions for the birth date. With the Berlin birth, twelve hours into the day is equivalent to six months, which still leaves one hour and five minutes (13.05 − 12.00 = 1.05).

The one hour part of the remainder is equivalent to half a month, which is fifteen days; the other five minutes equals only one day. The total interpolation is now six months (twelve hours) plus fifteen days (one hour) plus one day (five minutes) equals six months, sixteen days. When we figure *back* six months, sixteen days from 20 January 1954 back to midnight in the ephemeris on that date, we have established the ACD as 4 July 1953.

Figures 31 and 32 give visual tools to calculate the ACD for the above example, by showing how days and hours may be divided into segments which represent months and days. Once these fractional equivalents are assimilated and routinely used, it will never be

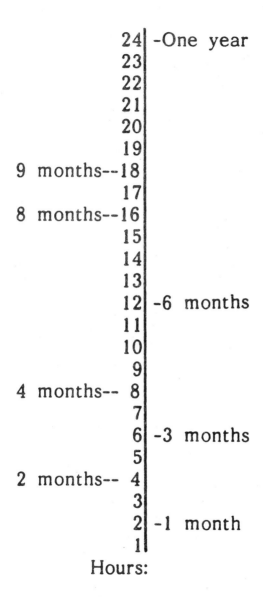

Figure 31. Twenty-four Hour Fractional Divisions

necessary to use a pen and paper to calculate an ACD.

Interpolation of Secondary Progressions

Figures 31 and 32, showing the twenty-four-hour day divided into fractions which are equivalent to months and days for computation of the ACD, may also be used for computation of the secondary progressions since the process is the same. For the ACD, we posed the question, 'If the planetary positions for the native's date of birth, 20 January 1954, are found at 13.05 on that same date in the ephemeris, to what date is 20 January 1954 equivalent?' For secondary progressions, we are, in effect, posing the question in reverse: 'If 20 January 1954 at midnight is equivalent to 4 July 1953 (the ACD), then what date and time in the ephemeris is equivalent to such-and-such event date?' We have simply shifted our reference point from the native's date of birth to the ACD, calculating the progressions in relation to *it*.

Using the Berlin birth, and working only with the first year of life, let us take a sample event date for computation of the secondary progressions. The first date will be 5 May 1954. The distance in months and days from the ACD, 4 July 1953 is ten months (from July

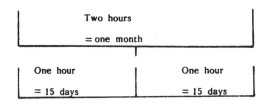

TWO-HOUR FRACTIONAL DIVISIONS

Two hours
= one month

| One hour | One hour |
| = 15 days | = 15 days |

Minutes:	4	8	12	16	20	24	28	32	36	40	44	48	52	56	60
= Days:	1	2	3	4	5	6	7	8	9	10	11	12	13	14	15

Figure 32.   Two-Hour Fractional Divisions

to the following May) plus one day (from the fourth of the month to the fifth of the month).

We can approach this one of two ways. Ten months equals twenty-two hours of the twenty-four-hour day; one day equals four minutes. If you happen to have *The American Book of Tables* (Astro Computing, Services, San Diego, CA, USA), the Interpolation Tables in the back are easy to use, and you can simply take the daily rate of each planetary motion, look up how far each has travelled in twenty-two hours, four minutes, and you will have your calculations for the secondary progressions for the event date.

If you want to take a shortcut, however, and forestall going back and forth between the ephemeris and the Table, simply consider the twenty-two hours as *eleven-twelfths* of the day, divide the daily planetary motion by twelve and subtract that *one-twelfth* from the next succeeding line in the ephemeris. The four minutes is negligible. Since there are 360 four-minute segments in the twenty-four-hour day, unless the daily planetary motion is anywhere near three degrees $(360' = 3°)$, the planet will not have moved so much as a single minute of arc. The Moon may move as much as 5' during that four-minute segment, and a rapid Mercury close to a single minute of arc, but for the other planets, it will not count at all.

However, should the twenty-two hours, four minutes have been twenty-two hours, *forty* minutes, it would need to be calculated. However, it could also be calculated with use of fractions rather than by consulting a table. As we can see with Figure 32, 'Two-Hour Fractional Divisions', that forty minutes is one-third of a two-hour segment, which is, in turn, one-twelfth of the entire twenty-four-hour day. So, for example, if Mars is moving 36' per day for the ephemeris date in question, one-twelfth of that is 3', and one-third of that is simply 1'.

Some may be more adept at computing fractions than others; some may still prefer to use tables. However, with practice, you might discover that learning to think your work through in terms of fractions will save you much time.

A good way to get used to this might be to simply count out the months between the ACD and the event date manually in two-hour segments per month using Figure 31. Once the equivalency is visual and tangible, rather than merely mental, it will eventually become natural to think in terms of such equivalencies.

Successive Index Dates

The partner of the Adjusted Calculation Date is the Index Date.

With the Berlin birth, 20 January 1954 equals 4 July 1953 gave us the ACD. The date itself, 20 January was 'equal to' 4 July in the native's life, 4 July specifically in *1953*. Once we move on to 4 July *1954*, we also have to move ahead a line in the ephemeris, from *20* January to *21* January. 21 January 1954 equals 4 July *1954*; 22 January 1954 equals 4 July *1955*; 23 January 1954 equals 4 July *1956*, and so on. Each of these successive dates in the ephemeris is an Index Date, and what it 'indexes' is what *year* it represents in the native's life.

When you are given an event date, the first thing to do is to locate the Index Date just preceding the event date and the one just following it. With the Berlin chart, for example, 11 October 1956 would be located between 23 January (equals 4 July 1956) and 24 January (equals 4 July 1957) in the ephemeris.

However, there is no need to recount the Index Date from scratch for every event date. Where you can save work is to count out the first Index Date used exactly, make a note of it, and count the next *in relation to it*. If, for example, you already know that 27 January 1954 equals 4 July 1960, then for an event in November 1963, you simply have to count ahead three more days to 30 January.

I would only caution that you count out your original Index Date *at least twice*, or you are going to risk throwing off the entire series. But with practice, it will become routine. This short-cut method is especially useful when the secondary progressions have crossed you over from one month into the next, or even two months ahead, or across the turn of a page.

Another help is that sometimes it is simpler to count by tens, i.e. if *1* February 1954 equals 4 July *1965*, then *11* February 1954 equals 4 July *1975*, and *21* February 1954 equals 4 July *1985*.

Noting the Index Date on the upper right-hand of the worksheet for the event date will ensure that you will always have a ready reference point.

Working with Fractions

The usefulness of working with fractions has already been highlighted in the sections on triple interpolations, the ACD, and the secondary progressions. Anything in your work that can be reduced to simple, manageable fractions will be a work-saver and a time-saver, and you will actually be able to figure many things out faster by sight than the time it would take to feed the information into a computer or calculator.

Figures 31 and 32, 'Twenty-Four Hour Fractional Divisions', and

'Two-Hour Fractional Divisions' respectively gives all the tools necessary for finding the ACD and the secondary progressions for an event date with a narrow margin of accuracy without resorting to tables. However, much of astrological work is done on a base of *sixty* not twenty-four or twelve. Degrees of zodiacal longitude are subdivided into sixty minutes of arc apiece, as are degrees of geographical longitude and latitude. The thirty degrees of each sign are a variant, as thirty is half of sixty.

Odd but true, though astrological calculations have been traditionally taught through use of logarithms, and more modernly assigned to the complex capacities of computers, the real key to quick, 'human' calculations—and, with practice, very accurate as well—is one's command of basic multiplication tables. There isn't any computation which cannot be rounded off to the nearest fraction. For example, 42N36 is 42 and $\frac{3}{5}$; 1°44′ is 1 and ¾; 13°09′ is 13 and ⅙.

Nor is there any division of the day that cannot be rounded off

FRACTIONAL DIVISIONS OF SIXTY

1/2's	30′								60′
	1/2								

1/3's	20′		40′						60′
	1/3		2/3						

1/4's	15′		30′		45′				60′
	1/4		1/2		3/4				

1/5's	12′	24′		36′	48′				60′
	1/5	2/5		3/5	4/5				

1/6's	10′	20′	30′	40′	50′				60′
	1/6	1/3	1/2	2/3	5/6				

1/10's	6′	12′	18′	24′	30′	36′	42′	48′	54′	60′
	1/10		3/10		1/2		7/10		9/10	
		1/5		2/5		3/5		4/5		

Figure 33. Fractional Divisions of Sixty

to the closest fraction and still not sacrifice needed accuracy (figures very close to cusps of course *always* have be done with great exactitude from scratch). 3 p.m. is ⅝ of the way through the day (15.00 = 5 × 3 hours [⅛ of the day] = ⅝; 1 p.m. is ½ of the day (twelve hours) plus ¹⁄₂₄.

Although space prevents printing all the necessary tables that give fractional divisions of all numbers from one to sixty, the basic 'sixty' division is shown in Figure 33, 'Fractional Divisions of Sixty'. If one can figure out the fractional breakdown for the whole degrees involved in a calculation, then all that will be left is some odd number of minutes (something between 1′ and 60′), which is not cumbersome to work with.

Again, the reason for using fractional estimations need be noted. It is because you may well have to experiment with different settings of the chart until you reach exactitude, and doing exact, tedious calculations all along the line will result in a great deal of work which may have to be redone with other tentative settings of the chart. Again, once you think you are *sure* of the chart, then tighten up all those figures to exactitude and carefully check the results.

Estimating Moon Motion

There is a very easy way to estimate the Moon's motion. At 12° per day exactly, a 'slow Moon', the Moon's motion will be exactly one degree per two hours. For 13° per day, the Moon's motion will be exactly 5′ *more per two hours* than for 12°, since the extra degree (from 12° to 13°), subdivided into 60′ and divided by twelve two-hour segments per day equals 5′. For 14° daily Moon motion, the rate per two hours would be 1°10, for 15°, it would be 1°15′.

Often, of course, the Moon's motion will not be close to some figure of whole degrees per day. In that case, one simply takes the excess minutes of arcs above the figure in whole degrees (such as 13°15′) and subdivides by 12′, to get a very close figure for a two-hour segment. For 13°15′, the excess fifteen minutes of arc is closer to 12′ than it is to 24′, so it would simply increase the two-hour motion from 1°05′ (for the 13°) to 1°06′ (for 13°15′).

Working with Fifteen-Degree Intervals

Using Figure 34, 'Fifteen-Degree Interval Table', take the planetary position by degree number and sign, such as 5 Libra. Add one sign plus a fifteen-degree interval for a semisquare (5 Libra + one sign = 5 Scorpio + 15° = 20 Scorpio). Alternatively, for degree numbers

FIFTEEN-DEGREE INTERVAL TABLE FOR
SEMISQUARES AND SESQUISQUARES

1	16	8	23
2	17	9	24
3	18	10	25
4	19	11	26
5	20	12	17
6	21	13	28
7	22	14	29
		15	0

Figure 34. Fifteen-Degree Interval Table

'sixteen' or over, go ahead and take a sextile (60°) and subtract 15° (−15°=45°), for example, 22 Capricorn plus sextile = 22 Pisces − 15° = 7 Pisces.

For a sesquisquare, move ahead a trine and add 15°, such as 11 Sagittarius + four signs = 11 Aries + 15° = 26 Aries. If a planet's degree number is sixteen or over, go ahead to a quincunx and subtract 15°, for example, 28 Gemini + five signs = 28 Scorpio − 15° = 13 Scorpio.

Thinking Horizontally rather than Vertically
The key to doing *any* kind of mathematics more rapidly is the ability to do accurate computations mentally instead of having to always resort to pencil and paper. Addition or subtraction involving just two figures is the most common type of calculation, and also the easiest to learn to think through, which will save time with many types of calculations.

When we first learned the simplest types of addition, such as 5 + 2 = 7, we began with it in just that form: *horizontal*; the same for subtraction. But as soon as we moved on to two-digit numbers such as 63 − 42 = 21, the numbers were stacked on top of each other *vertically*. Subtraction followed suit, as we learned to 'carry' numbers from one column for addition or 'borrow' numbers from another for subtraction.

Since many columns of addition involve many figures, and subtractions may involve several digits, it is undoubtedly easiest to use a vertical format. However, with astrology, nearly all steps of the calculations for addition, subtraction and interpolation both involve only two figures at a time and are on a sixty-base (sometimes a twenty-four-base), i.e. no more than two digits. For example, what is the difference between progressed Mercury at 11 AQ 58 on one line in the ephemeris and 13 AQ 09 on the next? How many minutes of arc between 15 TAU 34 on one line in the Table of Houses and 15 TAU 51 on the next? If the midheaven is 27 GEM 44 how far is it from 27 GEM 15 in one column in the Table of Houses and 28 GEM 10 on the other?

All of these calculations can be performed vertically:

A.	13 AQ 09	B.	15 TAU 51	C.	27 GEM 44	D.	28 GEM 10
	− 11 AQ 58		− 15 TAU 34		− 27 GEM 15		− 27 GEM 44
	1° 11′		17′		29′		26′

They could also all be performed both horizontally and as *addition*, illustrated in Figure 35. Once measurements are laid out side-by-side in this manner, they are much easier to visualize. There aren't any rules here, either, about what units one has to use; the key is the *type of mental process* by which the computation is made. In Example 35C, for instance, instead of 5′+10′+10′+4′, we could have just as easily moved by 10′ intervals, from 15′ to 25′ to 35′ to 45′, and then subtracted 1′ back to 44′ (i.e. 27 GEM 44). $3 \times 10′ = 30′ - 1′ = 29′$, giving exactly the same result.

With example 35D, all we have done is to think of all the figures on a sixty base, which requires no more than knowing what the 'complementary' number is for each number from 1 to 60: 1+59=60, 2+58=60, 3+57=60, and so on. Not all calculations take us from one degree into the next, such as 35B, from 15 TAU 34 to 15 TAU 51, in which case we would simply use a ten-base, as both 35B and 35C illustrate.

Some readers may already be working with mental arithmetic on a routine basis; others may not have, but will find it easier with practice. So long as the calculations are completed and done accurately, the work will get done. But this is one 'short-cut' which could be an invaluable time-saver.

Using the Chart's Positioning to Compute the Birth Time
When you make your initial assessment of the range of birth time

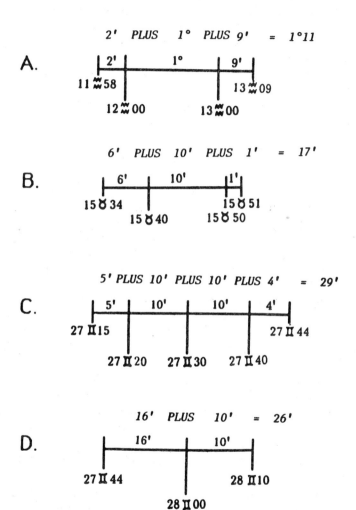

Figure 35. Horizontal Mathematics

based upon observation of the native, this will give you a likelihood for the spatial layout of the chart, not the birth *time*. You need to take those angles and figure out for what time that chart is cast. In fact, somewhere along the line in every rectification—unless the given birth time proves to be exact—you will need this particular skill.

There are two ways in which this can be done. The first, more common, is computing the time relative to your starting point. In other words, let's say you were told that a certain native was born at 7 a.m. and you began by computing the chart for that time. Then, upon rectifying the chart, you discover that the true midheaven falls approximately six degrees later than the chart you originally cast. Since each degree on the midheaven represents approximately four minutes, the native was born at approximately 7.24 a.m.

To check this out—since the true birth time might be 7.22 or 7.25—you can compute the chart for exactly 7.24 a.m., see if the final ST figure in the Table of Houses corresponds exactly to the rectified natal midheaven. If it does not, then compute the interval of adjustment, 1.30+, .55–, and so on.

You also have the option of computing the birth chart from the ST in the Table of Houses back to the time of birth. First calculate the difference between the Sidereal Time (ST) in the Table of Houses that corresponds to the chart's midheaven and the ST for the date of birth. Then do all the steps you would have done to arrive at the Table of Houses ST *in reverse*. If you would have added for Local Mean Time, subtract that figure. Subtract instead of add the correction for elapsed time. If you would have been adding the correction for longitude, subtract it instead; if you would have subtracted it, add it. Within a margin of just several seconds' time, you will arrive at the time of birth corresponding to the chart in front of you.

This method is invaluable for charts with no given birth time, or one that is quite inexact. After you have assessed some probable layout of the chart's wheel and planetary arrangement from observation of the native, you can take the midheaven of that chart that you plan to test and figure back to the time of birth, from which you can then calculate the planetary positions *exactly*. (Note: you would have been working with estimated planetary positions to assess the spatial layout of the chart, but such estimates would generally suffice for that stage of the rectification process.)

PART FOUR:
LOOKING AT THE NATIVE—
TRANSLATING OBSERVATIONS
INTO THEIR ASTROLOGICAL
ANALOGUES

INTRODUCTORY NOTE

The Relationship Between Native and Chart

This part of rectification—working with the native *live*—is a most exciting part, in that it gives 'living evidence' which, with a correct chart, will also confirm the chart's mathematical structure.

Rectification of the chart by observation of the physical native is based in the astrologer's perceptive skills—how acute are his/her observations and how accurate their correlation to astrological analogues in the native's chart. In Chapter 4, 'Your Signature in Space' (pp. 69-82), areas of the chart were highlighted that would be 'visible' in the native's appearance. Although all planets are present in each chart, obviously not all will be readily observable, only selected areas.

However, neither the information to come, nor 'Your Signature in Space' is more important than the other. They are always a unified consideration. Why the native appears to look like 'X' (same sign or planetary influence) will be directly related to where 'X' is found in the true natal chart. Conversely, a prominent 'X' in the natal chart ('X' rising, for example) will mean little until you learn to recognize what 'X' *looks like in the native*. It is this to which the present section of the book is addressed.

What Types of Observations Are Useful?

When we talk of observing someone, we are usually referring to what we can *see*. However, there are many other ways to observe. Often, when astrologers speak of 'picking up' information, they are referring to a *non*-visual process, not even necessarily a mental process, but some form of perception on an intuitive level. But even this often has a basis in what has been *observed*—an expression in the eye, a mannerism, the confidence of a walk, hesitation in the voice, the unspoken feelings someone conveys, and so on. Observation is a complex and multi-faceted process.

Visual observations are a very important part of the observational process. We want to make that as inclusive as possible, accompanied by its astrological analogues; but we also want to add in many non-visual components which will assist in identifying prominent planetary and sign influences in the chart.

Visually, we want to observe everything about the face, but expand our observations much further. The whole of the native's body will give just as many clues, as it is all part of the same birth chart.

In observing the face, all the features have their astrological analogues. That means the size, shape and set of the eyes, the shape and length of the nose, the set of the mouth, shape of the forehead and chin, the texture and colouring of the skin. Taking the head as a whole, the shape and size of the head, the set of the neck, and the colour and texture of the hair give additional clues.

Moving on to the body, the body build bears close observation, whether it is stocky or thin, square shoulders or sloping ones, the length of the limbs, length of the waist, the concentration of body weight. The bodily carriage alone is sometimes the key clue to the positioning of the chart. Does the native walk in slow, deliberate paces or with a spring, does he walk smoothly or awkwardly, does the head poke forwards, do the arms swing free—all have their astrological analogues.

The facial expressions and mannerisms vary from sign to sign, planet to planet. Do the eyes twinkle? Do the hands fly about? Does the native point? Do his eyes follow you about? Does he punctuate sentences with a sweet smile, or is the speech terse or clipped?

Once the native opens his mouth, a whole new set of clues pours forth. Is the voice high and harsh? Does he speak in a low, slow-paced voice? Does he speak in monosyllables? In long, rambling sentences? Do the words come out in a rush, or are they measured evenly?

It is easy to see that to call all these observations 'visual' undercuts the complete range of our perceptive faculties at work. Many areas of observation may have been activated of which we weren't consciously aware. Some areas of perception—such as listening to the timbre and pacing of the voice—are not visual at all, but auditory. Other areas—such as observation of bodily movements—are visual, but are also kinaesthetic, in that the body is no longer a two-dimensional graphic form but moves through space, like a dancer or an athlete.

Then there are the indefinable areas of emotional 'pick-up', or a general 'feeling tone' that seems to pervade a person which, however, is co-ordinated with physical characteristics as well, such as a Saturnine person of an emotionally insular character also being reserved in their physical expressions, with short, definite movements of a limited circumference. Maybe you 'picked up' Saturn because their voice was dead-pan and insistent; maybe you did it by observing the hard, bony body lines; maybe you observed tense or pointing fingers; maybe you noticed a flat, hard gaze. Maybe you did all this, or more, but none self-consciously and just said, 'I'm picking up Saturn here'.

However one approaches it, it is obvious that *the more ways you have to ascertain a sign or planetary influence, the more likely you are to succeed.* With the descriptions to come, many avenues of perception will be activated—visual, auditory, kinaesthetic, emotional, verbal, gestural, blending into characteristic composites of observations that will enable the astrologer to say with some certainty, 'There is a strongly-placed Mercury in this chart', or 'This native most likely has Cancer rising'.

In answer to the question, 'What types of observations are useful?', *any and all* types of observation are useful. This section of the book is organized so as to promote ready identification of specific qualities and traits observable in natives who prominently feature all the different planets and signs. But in actual practice, you will want to make note of virtually anything that is obvious to you, since if it is prominent, it will give you some key clue. Perhaps the key point of this endeavour is not just how to tell who has Pisces rising or who has a prominent Mars, but *how to observe*: how to observe *fully*, and to develop an easy access between your observations and their astrological analogues.

Emphasis Upon the Rising Sign

The rising sign will always be apparent in pervasive ways, whatever else is prominent in the chart, notwithstanding that its characteristics may be masked somewhat when planetary influences are also prominent (the so-called 'composite' picture).

Therefore, when we speak of 'sign' influence, be it Aries, Gemini, Scorpio or another sign, or consideration separately of elements, modes and planetary influences as expressed through signs, these will refer primarily to identification of the *rising sign* of the chart—not the Sun sign, or the sign of some other planet. So the section on

Taurus, for example, will not refer to Taurus Sun natives, but rather to Taurus rising sign natives.

The 'Component' Approach versus the 'Whole Sign' Approach
There are two equally effective and complementary ways of learning the identification of the rising sign. One is simply to learn the characteristics of each sign one by one, Aries through Pisces. The other is to learn how the *components* of each sign manifest, that is, the *mode* (Cardinal, Fixed or Mutable), the *element* (Fire, Earth, Air or Water), and the *planetary rulership* (any planet that is a ruler of the particular sign).

Identification of the rising sign by components will develop skills in identifying whole classes of people—such as Fixed sign rising people, or Water sign rising people—which will assist in narrowing down a possible twelve rising signs to four, three, or even less. The component approach is also highly effective in that one component may come the most strongly to the fore for any given native, such as the *Earthiness* of one Taurus rising native might be the salient quality, the *Fixity* of another, and the *Venus* rulership of yet another. Every human being is unique, so anything that is clearly apparent—be it mode, element, or planetary rulership—will assist in locating the sign rising at birth.

Sign and planetary rulerships may also 'resemble' each other in a chart, such as a prominent Venus 'resembling' Libra, which it rules, or a prominent Jupiter 'resembling' Sagittarius, which it rules, and the like. In terms of natal delineation, they are quite different, but in terms of apparent visible characteristics, it is useful to develop a flexible interchange between the many ways that sign characteristics register and that planetary characteristics register.

There is an equally strong advantage in learning rising signs on a sign-by-sign basis. The signs are not consistent in the appearance they produce throughout the entirety of a sign. Many early Cancer rising natives are heavy, but many late Cancer rising natives are thin. Many early Capricorn rising natives have goat-like eyes, but later in the sign, many eyes are triangular shaped. Respective components of signs can come to the fore differently in different degree areas within signs.

One of the most fascinating mysteries of astrology is this 'double truth': that a sign is both characteristically and identifiably itself (dead-ringer Virgo rising, for example), but is also a composite of its many components (mode, element, planetary rulership). This gives two useful overall ways to learn and use our identification skills.

It is also obvious that since there are many facets to identification, the greater the experience of the astrologer, the more rapidly the identification can be made. This is another reason to begin rectification work with charts you already believe are accurate, so you can study at first hand the many ways in which rising sign influences will register. Accurate charts and their real living owners will be your best teacher in this regard, to see how accurate correspondences register, before tackling more uncertain territory.

One small note before we begin, as there is conflicting literature on the subject: 'The 'cusp' theory—whereby the last few degrees of a sign and the first few degrees of the following sign are said to be somewhat alike—is a theory only, and certainly does not work in regard to ascendant identification. The latter degrees of one rising sign and the first few degrees of the following sign are astonishingly different.

Now, to begin, we will delineate the 'component' approach to rising signs: modes, elements, and planetary influences.

13.
THE MODES:
CARDINAL, FIXED, MUTABLE

CARDINAL—ARIES, CANCER, LIBRA, CAPRICORN

The Cardinal Temperament

Cardinal rising natives act, and re-act in direct, expedient ways. The hallmark of the Cardinal signs is spontaneity, directness, and acute response. Self-motivation and initiation come naturally to these people, even the sometimes shy Cancer rising native. These aren't always 'me first' types by any means; it is simply most natural to act, to do something, to respond, whether the response is emotional (Cancer), verbal (Libra), practical (Capricorn), or Aries straight-from-the-hip self.

Aries and Capricorn can be overtly aggressive, initiating, Aries to assert himself and Capricorn to organize others at his direction. Cancer and Libra are equally direct, but both gauge the responses of others to pace their own, Cancer via emotional rapport, and Libra by verbal and social interchange.

None of the Cardinal signs equivocate or get into a quandary (a Mutable quality), or excessively deliberate (a Fixed quality). Both Aries and Capricorn can be brusque and impatient, but Aries goes it alone, whereas Capricorn will manoeuvre and spar and defend its position. Cancer and Libra have *re*-active mechanisms that can stop on a dime. Give Cancerians an emotional response and they will shift their expression and tone accordingly. Challenge a Libran and you'll get your repartee post haste. Spontaneous redirection is a primarily Cardinal trait, whichever form of Cardinality it assumes.

The Cardinal Physiology

General Characteristics

The Cardinal rising native is often distinguishable by the body build as a whole. The Cardinal body tends towards evenly-distributed weight and proportioning, top to bottom, notwithstanding whether the native is thin or heavy. This corresponds to the Cardinal temperament, in that these people are poised for ready action, and one cannot move readily, rapidly and spontaneously physically if the body itself is top-weighted or bottom-weighted.

The Cardinal rising profile tends to move forward in a fairly direct line from the top of the forehead to the tip of the nose, and then straight down. The chin does not recede (as it does for some Mutable rising natives). The set of the head tends to be erect but mobile, not stiff like for some Fixed sign natives, or pressing forward like some of the more humanly-involved Mutables. The gaze tends to be direct, as are the hand and other bodily motions.

Characteristics of each sign

ARIES is characteristically tall and large-boned. The bones of the shoulder may be large and prominent, but are balanced by large feet and a long, march-like stride. The body frame tends to be spare with this rising sign, and the length of the Arian body also compensates for the large-boned, sometimes ungainly-looking Arian physiology.

Where symmetry is apparent in the Arian body at a glance is with the carriage. Aries rising leads with the head, and also with its large feet, which often point out. It is the proverbial 'Forward march!' with some, head charging forward and feet to match.

Aries' opposite, LIBRA, is just as Cardinal, but it *looks* softer. It moves into ready action like Aries (save the more laid-back, Venusian types in this sign), but on a reactive, responsive basis rather than as a loner. The shoulders are slightly rounded (not dropping straight down as with some Virgo and Pisces natives), and hips are slightly rounded as well. Even with a weight gain, the bodily curves don't expand out of proportion—the curves are gentle, even, not overly-pronounced, nor flat. The 'padding' of the hips and buttocks just all expands in a perfectly even way, *à la* Cardinal symmetry, while the top part of the body gains, too. These natives never look 'fat'— merely 'plump'!

Whereas with the Aries walk, the symmetry is starkly head-toe, Libra's symmetry is right-left, with the focal point in the hips. The walk gently 'sinks' into one side and then the other. These natives never rush, but retain their centreness, as the pelvis moves slightly sideways and then returns to centre position on each step—right, left, right, left.

With CANCER rising, the weight is still centred, even though some of these natives (usually early in the sign) are heavy and broad. The buttocks are flat with both women and men (Water), but the torso may be broad.

Where the weight gets centred (Cardinality) is in the stomach area (Cancer rulership), producing in the extreme instance, a kind of 'blimp' effect. But such natives are still light on their feet! The reason is the centred weight; it doesn't impede them physically because it is not weighing down either the top or bottom half of the body.

The walk tends to be soft and flat-footed, in a sinking motion, but some of these Cardinal natives can move exceptionally swiftly when they perceive their help or direction is needed.

Cancer's opposite, CAPRICORN, sports some heavy but many thin natives; and when Capricorn natives are thin, they may be 'skin and bones'.

The points of symmetry in the carriage are the knees, which lead the walk, and the shoulders, which are not infrequently high and hunched-up. Many Capricorn bodies are naturally structured so as to be poised for defence, the shoulders guarding the upper torso, while the knees provide the complementary curve in and upwards. The body carriage as a whole may look the opposite of some Cancerians, where the stomach area protrudes and the extremities 'hang back' in an open way. The hunched-over, protective-looking Capricornian may accentuate his stance with a proverbial point of the fingers. (Capricorn and Virgo rising are rivals as the 'pointers' of the zodiac.) But even at that, the tension pervades the whole upper half of the torso; the Cardinal body functions as a single unit.

To summarize, Aries and Libra rising builds and body carriage are opposites as follows: Aries is large-boned and spare, with a straightforward march of a walk, a real 'one-step'. Libra rising is softly-rounded and has a 'two-step' walk, sinking in on each side alternately. Aries has a head-toe symmetry; Libra a right-left symmetry.

Cancer and Capricorn are opposites as follows: Cancer hangs free with the stomach leading; Capricorn hunches over protectively. Cancer body lines are rounded and fleshy; Capricorn is hard and sharp. Cancer walks soft and flat-footed; Capricorn lifts the knee in a kind of 'prance', with a definite, measured rhythmic assertiveness, its legacy from Earth.

Aries is poised for offence; Capricorn for defence; Libra for exchange; Cancer for rapport. All are equally Cardinal.

FIXED—TAURUS, LEO, SCORPIO, AQUARIUS
The Fixed Temperament
The Fixed signs epitomize stability, reserve, determination, staying power, the capacity to plan. They are motivated by purpose, principle, the long-range outlook (and occasionally inertia!), as contrasted with the Cardinal penchant for action and expediency. These aren't improvisers, unless the chart is strongly offset by Cardinal planets. (A strong Mars can make for an activist, but they still might not function in an improvisory, expedient *manner*, which is the function of the mode.) They work from a base of security, and strengthen by consolidation, incorporation, and cumulative endeavours, rather than by shifting course or capitalizing on momentary opportunities. Some Fixed natives may manifest their Fixity in stubbornness or intransigence.

These people are slower to get to know and slower to extend trust, as contrasted with the Mutables, for example, who relate openly and flexibly on the surface level. The Fixed sign may offer a wall to the observer; however, once they are personally entrenched with persons or projects, they are much more liable to stay with them.

All things being equal, they might gravitate towards occupations which emphasize managerial or organizational skills. For instance, many Capricorn rising natives, being born pragmatists (Saturn-ruled) gravitate towards politics. But equally Saturn-ruled Aquarius rising, a Fixed sign, more often does not because they will put principle before expediency and find it difficult to bend—no comment on the respective integrity of the signs, but of their characteristic *functioning*. Likewise, you will find many people with Gemini and Libra rising (Air) in fields such as newscasting, interviewing and personal communications, but less Aquarius, which is better at overseeing others than with the shifting circumstances and personalities that communications work features.

The Fixed Physiology
General characteristics
The Fixed model of human nature is reflected physiologically through the Fixed signs rising. The body tends to be top-weighted, with the upper torso more massive and the hips narrower. (Note: even with the thinner Fixed natives, this is the basic type.) This body shape is not suited to quick movement, as is the 'streamlined' Cardinal form, but it *is* suited to solid, firm, broad bodily movements of a deliberate character, which corresponds to the Fixed temperament.

We might say that the Cardinal 'shape' is pointed, balanced, honed for action, whereas the Fixed 'shape' is square, solid, massive. The solidity of the temperament is thus expressed. The most intransigent of the Fixed signs, Scorpio, is also the most square! Oft-times you will see a large square head, square jaw, square torso, square hands, square everything.

Many other qualities of Fixity cut across all four signs. Bodily movements are, on the whole, *slower* than those of other signs. Aquarius can be an exception, but its definitive thrust can be such that you are still very sure the sign is Fixed. When Aquarius moves quickly, it is out of an inner imperative, not simply expediency, as with Cardinal signs, or accommodation, as with the Mutables.

Fixed sign natives use broad, sweeping gestures, and the voice quality has a more resonant timbre than other signs, giving many a gifted vocalist. The Fixed forehead tends to be large and flat, and the profile appears flat with a strong jaw-line cutting across on the horizontal (not to be confused with the long *slanting* jaw-line characteristic of Saturn rulership).

Characteristics of each sign
All four Fixed signs have many thick-necked natives (Aquarius less so, because its Air element gives long lines), but the first Fixed sign, TAURUS, is perhaps the most markedly so—Taurus rules the neck. The neck appears especially thick with many of these natives, as the head is characteristically set right into the neck, charging forward, as it were. The shoulders and upper arm feature pronounced muscular development which often make that part of the upper torso massive, even though the shoulder contour itself is not really square—it's a straight angle down from the neck to the end of the shoulder, which extends past the usual shoulder line of the body. But Fixed bodies have *definite* shapes and that shoulder line is straight, not sloped or rounded as one finds with other rising signs, most notably Pisces.

LEO rising natives often have a thick neck, too—especially towards the middle of the sign, featuring many stocky natives—but the set of the head is different from Taurus. Leo governs the spine, and the thrust of the body forwards generates from the middle of the spine, which elevates the characteristic Leonine head *up* from the chest, rather than *towards* it, as with Taurus. The back is rather square, and you find many 'carrot on end' builds with this rising sign (with both men and women) with the thinner natives. Leo rising is also one of the signs that sports naturally good posture (Aquarius is another). The proud, erect set of the spine is the 'central control' of the Leo rising body.

SCORPIO rising, the next Fixed sign, is the most square-shaped of all. The back is square, but the outer edges of the shoulders are *rounded* (a Water characteristic). The buttocks are flat—even when the body as a whole is heavy—so the top-weightedness can be more apparent with Scorpio. The head can be both square and large, a trademark of several of the latter degrees of this sign. The 'duplicate squares' of head and back reinforce this repeating Scorpionic shape, complemented by large, definitive gestures and bodily movements. The Scorpio body tends to move compactly as a single, undifferentiated unit, reinforcing the Fixed quality of stolidity.

The body lines of the last Fixed sign, AQUARIUS, are characteristically a modifed square, namely a *rectangle*. If you take a square and push it up into a rectangle, you have it. The back is angular—either absolutely straight from the Air rulership, or bony and hunched at the shoulders from the Saturn rulership of the sign— giving an overall rectangular shape from shoulders to waist. The back of the head (and the side view) may show a duplicate rectangle, and is characteristically held erect. Many Aquarius rising women accentuate this head shape with barrettes or hairpins high up on the sides of the head, giving a striking line, with the hair itself often straight and fine.

The rectangle is duplicated on the Aquarius rising leg as well, which is characteristically narrow, with smooth skin. The upper part of the leg is elongated, again giving a 'pushed up' look to the body. On the lower leg, the calf (which Aquarius governs) is placed unusually high, a special trademark of Aquarius rising. The hips are characteristically narrow, again accentuating the angularity and length of the upper back. (Note: these natives are not long-*waisted*, a trademark of Sagittarius and Gemini.)

MUTABLE—GEMINI, VIRGO, SAGITTARIUS, PISCES

The Mutable Temperament

Temperamentally, the Mutable signs will be the ones most likely to defer or adjust or make accommodations, often for the sake of interrelationship with other people, a keynote which Cardinality or Fixity may lack. If there are enough Mutable people around, everyone will inevitably get involved with everyone else *personally*.

All four signs have characteristic forms of 'scatter': both Gemini and Virgo tend towards 'word spill-overs' of different sorts, and Pisces and Sagittarius are *the* 'emotional spill-overs' of the zodiac. We might say that Pisces and Sagittarius tend to 'emotional overgeneralizations' (the Jupiter rulership) and Gemini and Virgo to 'verbal over-particularizations' (the Mercury rulership). But for all four, the *mode* of expression is Mutability—scatter it to the four winds. These people fulfil a basic function in human affairs, to specify, particularize, and make freely available to all the many facets of life—emotional (Pisces), intellectual (Gemini), practical (Virgo), and self-actualizing (Sagittarius).

There is a natural curiosity and inquisitiveness which also accompanies strong Mutability as well. It is natural to exchange ideas, share confidences, to distribute details about oneself and glean details from others. Other rising signs are inquisitive, though not for interpersonal reasons: Aquarius to discover how everything works, Scorpio to be in an emotionally-defensible position, Capricorn to have a handle on things so as to organize them better. The Mutables, by contrast, epitomize human interest in its most direct form.

Mutable rising natives are found less in leadership positions than others (though this isn't a hard-and-fast rule); they are better at co-ordination than leadership *per se*. Sagittarius, of course, may assume inspirational or enterprising roles, but some of that comes from the Fire element of self-confidence. The Mutables adjust, defer, bend and accommodate more easily than other signs, and cope continually with the fluctuating ramifications of human relations.

The Mutable Physiology

General Characteristics
The Mutable body expresses the adjustable, flexible, accomodating temperament of the Mutables in its *bottom-weightedness*. As we can imagine with our mind's eye, lightness of the upper part of the body allows the body to *sway*.

The Mutable head shape is characteristically oval, on the small side, and the face *convex* shaped, with the forehead slanting back, the jaw and chin de-emphasized and the features narrowing in towards the centre of the face—the features also look *pulled forwards* on the face. (Sagittarius can sport a firm, Jupiterian chin, but the mouth tends to protrude with an overbite and the nose juts out as well, so the profile as a whole is still seen as back/forward/back going down the face by profile.) The eyes are characteristically closer together than for other rising signs. The bite tends to be narrow in width, even though parts of the Mutables—namely Sagittarius and Pisces— feature an overbite.

Mutable hands are quite active as contrasted with other signs. With Gemini, the scattery hand motions keep pace with verbage; with Sagittarius, they keep pace with the fervour; with Pisces, emotionality can toss them into a flurry; and with Virgo, pointing takes over when the 'point' of a Virgoan message need to be driven across. (Virgo makes little, specific pointing gestures, and usually points *in*.)

Mutability registers through verbal pacing as well. Even cool, Airy Gemini can produce rushes of words under stress, though not necessarily betraying their emotional content (both Air and Mercury can mask emotionality). Sagittarius becomes verbally emphatic under stress, while with Pisces, the voice can slide, crack, or the feelings simply spill out verbally. Virgo also registers stress *verbally*, through reiteration of what has been unwanted or offensive in the life. Other signs, of course, react to stress as well—but the Mutables tend to do it verbally.

Characteristics of each sign

With GEMINI rising, the body lines tend to be long and sinewy, with part of the Mutability of the sign expressed in physical agility. The arms are in constant gesticular motion—the hands are as agile as the tongue! Gemini's 'hand language' seems a graphic, kinaesthetic expression of words, marking them off in short, co-ordinating hand motions, cutting vertically, diagonally, horizontally, fingers mobile, yet *structured*—in exact pace with the *words*.

The waist tends towards length, and the body sways out at the lower back with both women and men, the women tending to gain weight on the lower half of the body, though the sign as a whole tends to be thin.

The head shape will be rather long and oval (Mutable) or pert and bird-like from its ruler, Mercury. In either event, it is not a large head, and the forehead curves in towards the top, both at the top of the forehead itself, and at the temples, which look like the side of a cylinder.

Gemini's opposite, SAGITTARIUS, can be equally hand-motion oriented, but the thrust is emotional and exaggerative (Jupiter rulership). In terms of body balance, Sagittarius' Mutability shows up most clearly in both a characteristic off-centre pose resting on one hip, and in the lack of physical co-ordination when agitated. With the Mutables, physical co-ordination tends to be an *issue*, and

Sagittarius runs the gamut, producing the most graceful, elegant dancers as well as people who trip over their own feet.

Large hips, and especially, large thighs accompany this rising sign (the men aren't immune), which certainly bottom-weights the body. The waist is notably long, as is the neck for many Sagittarian natives. The curvature of the back is different for this sign to that of Gemini, however. The Gemini back is characteristically straight (Air), and the Sagittarian back stooped, with 'wings' apparent just below the shoulders. Some of these natives could win 'the bad posture award', though the body build naturally predisposes towards this particular problem.

With the two other Mutable signs, both sport many short-waisted natives, though with VIRGO, the Mercury rulership can offset this, giving a 'mixed' picture throughout the sign. The head shape for Virgo rising may be notably oval (a literal 'egghead'), and the features markedly pushing towards the centre of the face, with a very narrow, pursed-looking mouth. The face *looks* like it is oriented towards making fine distinctions, since all its own details are drawn to a central point, nose oft-times aquiline as well, thin, jutting and sharp.

When Virgo rising is thin, it is an asthenic thinness, with the limbs moving in a loose way, Mutable style. The bodily motions are slight, but very flexible, like the vulnerability of a tuning fork to exactly the right or wrong pitch.

The last Mutable sign, PISCES, can be the most severely bottom-weighted. It is as characteristically drop-shaped as Aquarius is characteristically rectangular, or Scorpio square. The drop shape is apparent in the face of many of these natives, giving a narrow head on top, eyes close together and wideness at the bottom of the face, with sometimes a notable double chin. (Note: with some Pisceans, a large forehead slopes amorphously back, but that roundness is the Water component.) The torso repeats the drop-shaped pattern: sloping shoulders on top, with a lot of weight in the buttocks and thighs. The calf is low on the leg, sometimes with very loose, watery flesh; and when the arms are heavy, the weight is more towards the elbow rather than the upper part of the arm, where weight concentration would be more commonly found with other signs.

14.
THE ELEMENTS:
FIRE, EARTH, AIR, WATER

FIRE—ARIES, LEO, SAGITTARIUS

The Fire element epitomizes self-adequacy. Strongly Fire people do not need the praise of others; they believe in themselves. In a sense, they instill confidence in others partly because it is apparent how easily they can be off and on their own.

With Aries and Leo rising, a sense of aloofness or apartness is sometimes apparent by lack of participation with others unless they feel personally important and in a position to project their input. This isn't necessarily unfriendliness or selfishness; there is simply little overt dependence upon others and they gravitate towards areas which will afford them independence. Sagittarius rising can be equally aloof (as well as gregarious and participatory, but from the Jupiter rulership and Mutability) if they feel the environment is not compatible. All three Fire signs will find ways to maintain their independence, even on friendly turf.

These natives are frequently self-possessed in their manner, and the voice quality carries authority because it sounds sure, it projects *self*—Aries clear and direct, Leo gravelly-sounding, Sagittarius earnest but equally sure once these shy-in-youth natives have hit their stride. Whether their projection of confidence elevates them or isolates them in the eyes of others depends upon many contributing factors.

The lines of the Fire rising body will tend to be long, but not fine-boned, which is the province of Air. There are some short natives with early Sagittarius rising and in mid-Leo, even occasionally in Aries, though all three signs characteristically sport some *very* tall natives.

One real giveaway for Fire is the eyes. The shapes of the three differ, but what they have in common is a glint, a light (literally 'fire'). That light perks up especially when they come on some area of self-motivation. The Fire eyes are often a lucid, clear-coloured shade.

You'll find both brown and blue, though Leo's natural ruddiness will give more than its share of bright blue and warm brown, while Aries has many natives who simply have dark hair and eyes from the Mars rulership.

The eyes for all the Fire signs are characteristically deep-set, sometimes accentuated by a forehead which looks like a bit of armour—helmet-shaped, from which the eyes are set *back*. Leo rising, with its massive, Fixed forehead accentuates this. Fire eyes are characteristically *tucked under the lids*.

For the Fire signs, look to the *back*. Some Arians and Sagittarians tend towards a stoop (especially apparent with the men); and although Leo doesn't stoop (probably wouldn't just on principle!), the thrust of the body's carriage is centred in the spine, so all three signs will tend to draw attention to the back.

These signs sport plentiful hair in youth, but for the men, the hairline tends to recede later on, sometimes to baldness. Aries rising hair can be coarse and wiry, Leo's bushy (manelike), and Sagittarius more often than not straight.

Fire rising feet tend to point out, sometimes at a full forty-five degree angle, and the feet also tend to be large.

Fire rising speech can be blunt. Sagittarius is said to have the corner on this, but this is probably because the Mutability of the sign gives a relatedness to *people*, and blunt comments directed at people personally can create problems. Actually, Aries and Leo can be equally blunt in their speech, but Aries simply speaks for himself (oft-times quite tersely), whereas Leo will tend more to detach and conceptualize. Leo rising can take personal offence, but the response is rarely a fight, rather *detachment*—you are henceforth excluded from their world. All the Fire signs put self-respect high on their list of valued personal qualities—Leo grandiose, Sagittarius exclamatory, Aries right-to-the-point, all variations of the same Fiery tune.

EARTH—TAURUS, VIRGO, CAPRICORN

Earth rising natives assume a pragmatic approach to life. Even if there is no other Earth in the chart (i.e. no *planets* in Earth), they will *act* like pragmatists. Capricorn addresses action, authority and organization; Virgo tangible particulars and fine differentiations and comparisons; Taurus concepts and principles as they take on material form, with conserving, amassing and building as a way of life. All the Earth signs tend to assume that most things in life can be counted, measured, calibrated, organized and/or ordered!

The Earth rising native also tends more than others to be on the serious side temperamentally. Sometimes you will find someone with Virgo or Capricorn rising who is exceptionally funny, but in a dead-pan kind of way (Earth) or by caricature (Capricorn, under Saturn rulership). Taurus rising sports a few cornballs, who very nearly can't pick up a fork or a spoon without making it a prop for a joke, but many other Taureans specialize in lifting people up by settling them *down*.

Earth, a 'solid' element, features shorter body lines and short waists. The fingers—which are tactile, and may be very magnetic with Taurus—may be quite stubby on a fleshy hand. Look for exceptions to this with some natives of Mercury-ruled Virgo. Also, some natives of Capricorn, usually later in the sign, will be inexplicably tall, though usually bony and thin as well.

Watch the way the hands touch things. With Air, the fingers are often literally shaped up and out and into the air; with Earth, the fingers are more often curved *in*, move in a tenacious way, and may be stubby. What is most tangible to Earth is what can be touched, and assessed in material terms, and the body responds to these incentives. Many Earth rising natives gravitate towards healing professions, both because they are touch-sensitive, and because Earth energies can be soothing to others.

Earth rising skin may be quite sallow-looking, nearly brown for some natives of Taurus and Virgo. Capricorn doesn't tend towards good colour, but the skin tends to be more pale. Some Taurus rising natives pick up a strong Venus rulership and their skin will look rosy, not sallow, and these will also have Venusian features to match—rounded cheeks and chin, a sweet expression around the mouth and sometimes dimples as well.

Wavy or curly hair is common with Earth rising, and warm shades such as chestnut brown. The hair tends to be thicker with Taurus (Venus) and thinner and darker with Capricorn (Saturn). Some Taurus rising natives have kinky hair, with notable ridges across the forehead.

Earth rising noses tend to have a high bridge, and will rarely be absolutely straight. Ridges, bumps, crooks and large sizes are featured (save the Venusian Taurus types), and even the narrow late Capricorn rising nose juts out sharply. Though I've never surveyed it, I would not be surprised if Earth rising natives had a more acute sense of smell as well—along with touch, this is an Earthy characteristic.

Earth eyes tend to be large, with a pronounced lid, and a sombre, literally 'down-to-earth' gaze. I call them 'dry' looking eyes. They are not detached-looking, like Air eyes; they take you very *seriously*. But they do not flash or fluctuate with emotion (as you find with Water). With the eye size, if the planetary rulership assumes dominance over the element rulership, the eyes may be smaller, as the separate sections on each sign will clarify. For eye colour, you won't find severe shades, like turquoise, brown-black or harsh blue. There is a lot of soft, medium brown for Taurus and Virgo, some light blue for Virgo, clear blue for Taurus, and muted, light, or murky blue, green or brown with Capricorn.

The upper part of the mouth can have a 'puffy' look for Earth rising, especially with Capricorn. With Virgo, there is often a greater space than usual between the bottom of the nose and the upper lip, with the narrow bite accentuated. Probably it is not surprising to find the nose area highlighted for Earth rising, which highlights the physical senses.

The voice timbre, in terms of pitch and resonance is not consistent between these three signs, but they all speak definitively (exceptions: there are some timid Virgo types, and some shy Capricorn types, but also some *excessively* definitive types with all three signs). Virgo rising can be quite light and higher-pitched due to the Mercury rulership, but the manner is most often dry and matter-of-fact. Capricorn features some of the most *insistent* speech in the zodiac (with no room for laughs), while Taurus is the most resonant and musical-sounding of the three.

If you have missed other, purely visual clues with these natives, listen to *what* they talk about. You will hear lots of comments about material things, what they look like, what they are worth, how comfortable something is or isn't and the like. The interest level perks up when the subject is down-to-earth.

The hand motions, for Earth, move *down* (as distinct from 'flyaway' Air gestures or the exclamatory gestures of Sagittarius or Leo). With Taurus, the hand movements are solid and expansive-looking—nearly like they are holding and managing the very weight of life in their hands (which some undoubtedly are).

AIR—GEMINI, LIBRA, AQUARIUS

The Air element is the channel for communication, conceptualization, exchange of thoughts and ideas. Air expression, in the pure sense is free, unhindered by pragmatic (Earth), emotional (Water) or idealistic or self-interested concerns (Fire). Of itself, the

Air element is *detached*; and the Air rising natives tend to be
detached in manner and speech, in effect rendering them freer to
serve as a conduit of common thought *per se.*

This can sometimes indicate natives who serve objective/descriptive
roles (Gemini), or mediating roles (Libra), or those based upon
principles rather than personalities (Aquarius); and thus forms a bulk
of the world's 'reporters' (not just in the news), interviewers,
spokespeople—living channels of thought. The very good side of
the quality of detachment is the ability to take diverse viewpoints
and differing and/or conflicting ideas without prejudice, and literally
'air' them for common consideration and clarification, building
bridges of understanding that would never have been facilitated
without the presence of natives strong in Air, especially Air rising.

The Airy temperament is—very logically—reflected in more
ethereal body forms than the other elements. Air features long body
lines, with many thin arms and tapering fingers. The body moves
lightly, as if through air on a float, even relatively stiffly-structured
Aquarius. Gemini features a bit of spring in the walk, Libra a gentle
sway, and Aquarius a head-held-high, above-it-all demeanour. All
three rising signs feature many natives with an erect carriage and
a perfectly level, unperturbed gaze.

The bone structure of Air bodies is characteristically fine and the
features notably small and even-looking. In other words, when
someone is thin (but not with prominent bones, which can be
Capricorn or Aries), fine-featured, has long arms and tapering fingers,
you have to consider that an Air sign might be rising.

The hair of Air rising natives tends to be straight and fine and—
if the genetics give a choice—not too dark. Aquarius rising is notably
blond, genetics permitting.

The eyes tell the tale here, too—in fact, they are sometimes the
chief clue. They are detached in their gaze, sometimes appearing
to look at you yet not be looking at you. If you watch a newscaster
giving you the day's grizzly fare of murders, hijackings and natural
disasters with an utterly detached gaze, perhaps Air is rising, probably
Gemini or Libra. It doesn't mean lack of feeling; it just doesn't tend
to surface when the rising element is Air.

Air eyelids, though not heavy (as with Earth or Water) are very
visible, the opposite of the Fire element, where the eye is tucked
under the lid.

Look for longish necks with Air rising, but also reserve space there
for Sagittarius, the 'swan' of the zodiac.

Look to the hand motions. Gemini is the most pronounced, but that is a combination of Air, Mutable scatter and active Mercury. The Libran movements are more leisurely, with its rhythms co-ordinated with the speech and also with the response patterns of others. Aquarius moves the hands a bit more rigidly. Remember with all the Air signs, that the hand motions are to express or punctuate communication *per se*, not an emotional or dramatic expression. If you see someone using their hands in some definitive, large-scale, dramatic kind of way, it is probably a Fixed sign, not Air. Air goes with free, relatively small motions.

The shape of the nose tends to be straight—with Libra, classically so—and small. Many Gemini rising noses will be upturned, and the Aquarius rising nose may have a sculptured look—not *too* small, and with a chiselled-looking 'cut' slightly upwards at the tip of a straight nose. You will not find hooks or crooks or large noses unless the rising sign is prominently modified.

The Air rising voice tends to a good, even timbre, with an unperturbed sound to it. It may sound a bit breathy (very literally 'air'), but without breaks or cracks or great variation in inflection. The Aquarius rising voice may sound harsh and rich, but that is partly a Fixed quality, giving resonant voice timbre. Some of these natives will brave operatic singing, but only more rarely improvisory or pop art.

Airy skin tends to be clear and fair, with more than its share of 'fresh-looking' types; when genetics permit, Aquarius can be porcelain white.

WATER—CANCER, SCORPIO, PISCES

Water rising people are geared towards emotional rapport above all. In this sense, the element is never wholly objective in its outlook. On the other hand, emotional involvement can sometimes make for *better* decision-making. In any case, you won't lack that involvement with Water rising.

The Water rising people have a good sense of how to fit in socially and what it is to 'belong', even somewhat aloof Scorpio rising. The personal sense of wholeness is a function of emotional relatedness to others. They also *notice* emotionally-charged things, as much as Earth rising notices material things. They notice and they react. These are the ones who pick up on people's relationships like a sponge; and emotional closeness is a most valued personal experience. Scorpio rising may not be overtly sentimental (the other two, yes), but can overcompensate for lack of outward display by being clannish or possessive, or simply staunchly loyal. They still need to know 'where they stand' emotionally as much as the emotionally-effusive Pisces rising native.

Any environment is more socially cohesive with the presence of Water rising people, who blend in with and share common emotional currents, are often amongst the most empathetic, and put emotional sensitivities to the fore.

The Water element is soft, and one of the first places you will want to look to confirm Water rising is the *flesh*, which can be quite jelly-like, the kind of flesh that retains water weight and may look chunky or lumpy. Scorpio flesh is harder, because of the fixity, but you will still find a greater-than-average share of obesity from water retention, especially later in the sign.

Water tends towards short-waistedness and short limbs. If you look at the arm's length in relation to the torso, you will get a broad clue. If the elbow only comes down to the breastline instead of the waistline, you might well be looking at Water rising (especially Cancer).

The shoulders are rounded—even for 'square' Scorpio—with a positive slope for Pisces. The flesh of the face does not fall perfectly evenly (as contrasted with Air), even with the thinner natives, but takes some curves and dips and creases (Cancer accentuates this with the lunar influence). Cancer and Pisces rising are often pale and Scorpio more dark and swarthy; whatever the exact tone, you don't often find 'good colour' from the Water influence *per se*.

Thick, sensual lips are common with all three, with Pisces fishlike, the Scorpionic mouth down turned, Cancer also down-turned but with the lips conspicuously rounded.

The voice is soft. With Cancer, you can hear a kind of 'slushy' edge to the voice quality (sometimes appealing with actors and actresses). The Pisces rising voice may crack or slide, but the voice timbre itself is rounded. The Scorpio voice can be quite projective (Fixity), but it isn't harsh, it's still round.

Watery eyes are large, liquid-looking and expressive. The emotions come directly into the eyes. The three eye types differ in their set, but there are many bulbous types within each Water sign. Sometimes the eye colour will clue you in to *which* Water sign is rising—Scorpio very dark, Cancer muted hazel, blue or grey, and Pisces pale blue, genetics permitting.

The Water feet tend to turn in, pigeon-toed, and they also tend to be small, even if the native himself is heavy. The hands may well be fleshy or stubby.

The hair may be wavy or kinky (exception: Martial Scorpio straight and dark); Cancer, and especially Pisces tend towards unruly hair that does not stay in place.

15.
THE PLANETS

The Sun

As a prominently-placed planet
A prominent Sun in the natal chart—either rising or culminating—produces a robust looking and acting native. The carriage is more erect and dignified; personal assertion and confidence comes naturally. These people stand up for themselves and can ably push their own case.

The rising Sun tends to give a high-energy personality with good powers of endurance. The culminating Sun may not be quite as apparent in its physical effects, but these natives naturally assume high-level positions and they carry them in style. Whether they are necessarily the most gifted or qualified rests with the individual chart; not infrequently, they 'make it' in the world *anyway*, because they carry an air of authority which commands respect.

The rising Sun will also tend to give a little more bulk or stockiness to the body. It stiffens the posture a bit and gives a more commanding tone to the voice. The face may be more open and broad. The Sun on the seventh cusp or into the seventh house can give rising Sun characteristics but in a muted form; the rising Sun tends to be a special case all its own.

With a birth near dawn, you might have a real aid to rectification with the rising Sun. The ascendant may be in the same sign as the Sun, it may be in a degree earlier than the Sun (giving a rising Sun), or it may be in a degree several degrees past the Sun (giving a twelfth house Sun). Or the ascendant may be in the sign preceding the Sun, giving a composite picture in the native's appearance.

The difference between adjacent rising signs tends to be notable. For instance, a late Cancer rising native will tend to be thin and soft-voiced with pale skin and full sensual lips, a model which does not fit early Leo rising. Tall, loose-limbed, terse late Aries rising would not be readily confused with a sweet-but-sturdy early Taurus rising type. Also note if the native seems 'double Fixed', for example, or a combination of Cardinal and Fixed, or another combination of modes, or of elements.

Even when the Sun and ascendant are the same sign, there are notable differences between a rising Sun native and a twelfth house native. Does the native seem to be confident, robust, even a trifle 'pushy'? A rising Sun fits. Retiring? Twelfth house Sun more likely.

In sign rulership (Leo)
The Sun rising and Leo rising may or may not appear similar. You need, first, to look at the build as a whole and watch the person walk. The Leo rising walk doesn't rush, and the toes may point out somewhat. Listen to the voice quality and its pacing. Leo voices are resonant, and the words tend to be self-conscious and distinct. The eyes are deep-set—sometimes 'cat-like'—with the face open and broad. A rising Sun will give greater assertiveness to the personality, but it may not physically resemble Leo at all!

Temperamentally, Leo features personal sensitivity to praise or criticism, which is not necessarily a feature of the rising Sun.

The Moon
As a prominently-placed planet
An angular Moon—especially rising or closely culminating—can be easy to spot. Look at the eyes. 'Moon eyes' are large, liquid and expressive, and they focus in a continually fluctuating way, moving here, there, there as its natural way of functioning.

Quick responsiveness and open emotional exclamations are common with a prominently-placed Moon. These are *reactive* people—there are 'oo's' and 'ah's' and the voice may 'catch' or give a slight squeal. The feelings come out visibly and audibly, with a soft-edged expressive voice common. You also get more sentimentality, and ability to offer ready comfort and support to others with a prominently-placed Moon.

You might also notice what I call 'Moon lines' on the outer edges of the eyes. They are radial lines, as though radiating from an imaginary half-circle at the edge of the eye, with an eye set that is deep and broad—almost like the eyes are set into a round 'pool' of space.

A strongly-placed Moon can also give round body lines—genuine rotundity at the extreme.

In sign rulership (Cancer)
Cancer rising may share the above qualities plus more. An angular Moon will not necessarily have a Watery-type build, with flesh prone to water retention, a broad, relatively undifferentiated shape, or the disproportion in the length of the limbs. For Cancer, the arms can be notably short in relation to the torso and hang in, crab-like, something not necessarily featured with a prominent Moon.

Cancer rising natives are exceptionally *observant*, and their own personal functioning is geared towards the emotional climate as a whole. An angular Moon often features open self-expression, but not necessarily that keen, subterranean sensitivity to others. The Cancerian voice is modulated, soft and often vibrant.

Mercury

As a prominently-placed planet
A prominent Mercury can give long limbs and a long waist. Sometimes the mouth will have a pursed look, with the lips thin and clearly defined. The eyes may be a little smaller and closer together, and very alert, like bright little triangles blinking at every new sensory input.

A prominently-placed Mercury can also alter the speech patterns, to produce clipped, finely-enuciated or nervous-sounding speech, or other distortions in the verbal *pacing*—rushes of words and then pauses, or syllables distended in odd ways. A rising Mercury can give a high, light voice *timbre* and a detached manner of delivery. Rising Mercury people may also seem more 'intellectual' because a lot of the personal energy is channelled into verbalizing and clarifying details.

A prominent Mercury gives agility of the limbs, which may also manifest in manual dexterity depending on aspecting. The body build may be slight, with quick, nervous, sensitive bodily motions or mannerisms. A detached but wordy manner can sometimes be tell-tale for a prominent Mercury.

Note: *whatever* sign Mercury tenants may influence the voice timbre and speech patterns.

In sign rulership (Gemini, Virgo)
Gemini and Virgo are both Mutable signs; the difference is the element, Gemini Air and Virgo Earth.

Both rising signs have many natives with longish faces and long, loose-moving limbs, but if the Mercury component of either sign seems strong, there are also many ways to distinguish between them. Virgo's eyes may be heavy-lidded and protrude, and the skin will tend to be more sallow. Gemini eyes will be deeper-set and triangular-shaped (see exact description under 'Gemini', p. 240). With Gemini, the nose is likely to be straight or (often) turned-up, not hooked or crooked like Virgo. Virgo's face may be pursed into a narrow line through the front of the face, but not Gemini, whose face is more open. Gemini is detached; Virgo homes in on specifics with great emphasis and will press heavily on points of personal concern. Both signs use gesturing (Mercury-ruled), but Gemini's hands fly *out* (Air 'scatter'), whereas Virgo's hands point *in* (Earth specificity). Virgo rising may be a 'pointer', while Gemini rising moves its hand in pace with concepts, not as intent upon emphasis (Earth) as upon description (Air).

Nervous energy/intensity tends to be high for both these signs, as does a mental/verbal approach to life.

Venus

As a prominently-placed planet

A prominently-placed Venus can give a sweetness to the temperament, a graciousness and polish—the personal manner lacks rough edges. These natives can look at you and respond to what they sense you want, to create at least a surface harmony. Listen to the speech and its pacing—you won't hear anything abrasive or sharp. Venusian speech isn't emotional *per se*—in fact, when associated with Libra, an Air sign, it can be quite cool—but it *is* concerned with one-to-one contact with people. The pacing is listen/respond, listen/respond. It's a focus and rhythm that makes it easy to relate. Nor do Venusian people ever rush.

Venus softens the body lines, evens out the proportions and may add some weight but in a gently rounded manner. The eyebrows, eyelashes, cheeks and edges of the lips all take on gentle curves. A bow-shaped mouth, dimples, rounded cheeks and chin and the look of a sweet perpetual smile around the mouth are all Venusian qualities that are visual. Venusian eyes are round, wondering and bright. The native's colouring tends towards fair.

Venus gives small, even features, and a small, classically straight nose. Note that part of the reason a Venusian face 'looks even' is also because the eyeline is characteristically low, nearly the centre of the face, so that when you look at the centre of the face, you are looking at the eyes—a more aesthetic centre than the nose!

In sign rulership (Taurus, Libra)

Venus rules Taurus and Libra, but the Venusian features cited above are set into very different facial shapes and bodily forms. What is in common is the low eyeline on the face, and clear, gently curved eyebrows which go straight across the face. The Venusian eyes are roundish but not too large and the nose straight, but the Taurean nose, even when straight, has a high bridge, which the 'classical' Libran nose, small and perfectly straight, does not. Taureans can also have coarse-looking noses, from another component of rulership, Earth.

The Libran face with its small features sometimes looks like the features are bunched up in the centre of the face. The Taurean face is characteristically broader, with real width along the cheekbone line, and a square jaw—not Libran features. The Taurean chest cavity is also expanded and thrust forwards, whereas the Libran proportioning and weight distribution is simply even across the body.

The Libran neck is thin and rather long, Taurus short and thick. The Taurean projects in a robust, involved way; the Libran sits back and observes, alternating with entering into repartee.

Regarding the tell-tale low eyeline, in one curious rectification, I looked at the native and suspected Cancer was rising, but something didn't fit. This man was very rotund—very nearly a perfect 'butterball', and with a button nose typical of some degrees in early Cancer. It was the eyes that were wrong—they weren't Moon-like and the set was wrong. When I looked up the man's birthdate and the approximate birth time, it turned out that the Moon was in early Cancer on the midheaven—strong by both sign and placement. But the rising sign was *Libra*, and the giveaway was the eyes halfway down the face. Then I noticed those curly Venusian eyelashes! Everything in the chart fell into place from then on in.

The speech is apt to be paced and measured for both Venusian signs, but the voice *timbre* is different—low and throaty for Taurus, cooler-sounding and lighter for Airy Libra. Watch the straight eyebrows as well. Should you see two 'squareheads', and be wavering between Taurus and its opposite, Scorpio, take the arching eyebrows as Scorpio and the straight eyebrows as Taurus and you will often be right.

So if the astrologer spots two natives both Venusian enough to consider a Venus-ruled sign, there is much to enable you to go beyond a sweet smile!

Mars

As a prominently-placed planet
Prominent Mars influence gives qualities of intensity, muscularity, drive, and directness of motion, both physically and temperamentally. Mars has one direction: forwards!

Mars eyes are piercing, small, close together, and sometimes very dark. Mars hair is dark brunette, black or red. The nose is pointed and sharp. A very prominent Mars can give arching eyebrows as much as can Scorpio rising.

Mars gives muscularity without necessarily giving weight—where there is excessive weight, it comes from other chart factors. In fact, the torso can be quite spare with the Martial native, even when the muscles are prominent. The bodily motions are rapid and aggressive and the reflexes are quick. All the physical movements are as economical as possible. The handshake is *firm*!

Mars-prominent natives don't hesitate—if they feel something should be done, they just *do* it. If that Mars should be facilitated by clever Mercury or careful Saturn, such people might be known as pragmatists. There is often impatience here; though there is also physical courage above the average because they enjoy physical challenge and want a pathway straight through, even at risk.

In sign rulership (Aries, Scorpio)
Mars rules Aries and Scorpio. The Martial muscularity is common for both signs, though Aries tends to have a spare frame and Scorpio can have a heavy one, from its Fixity and the element of Water.

Both Aries and Scorpio eyes tend to be direct in their gaze. Arians are just straightforwardly themselves, and will look you square in the eye as an expression of clear-cut independence; your response may not be their concern. With Scorpio, the eyes are equally direct, but the Water element establishes rapport and they are *keenly* aware of whether or not you respond. The eye *shape* is very dissimilar between the two signs; only the directness and intensity appears to be in common: Mars.

An ironic trait Aries and Scorpio rising natives may share is the tendency to be verbally taciturn. Each goes through 'monosyllabic' phases in human relations, even if from different motivations. Mars is a *doer*—it doesn't necessarily *talk*! Not infrequently, when these natives see no ready course of action, they stop communicating. When action is in the offing, however, both drive on and can be verbally *aggressive* (Cardinal Aries) or verbally *persistent* (Fixed Scorpio).

An aptitude the two rising signs share is the ability to *direct* others, a Martial trait, though it works differently for the two. Aries rising can get right out there and point, 'You go here, you go there', whereas Scorpio tends to be more subtle. They'll not budge if the group as a whole is not gravitating in some desired direction, but are expert at consolidation and mobilization if they are. With consensus of purpose, Scorpio rising shines. Both signs, however, go with economy—of physical motion, words, actions—and that economy of motivation and direction is *Mars*.

Jupiter

As a prominently-placed planet

With a prominent Jupiter, the body as a whole may be larger—not just *taller*, as Uranus can give. Other physical characteristics are: back swaying out at the bottom, large thighs, a long, pointed chin, and the head shape about to be described.

The head is long and narrow both down the length of the face and along the head from front to back. This is the so-called 'horse-shaped head'. (Note: this is common with Sagittarius rising, but modified with Pisces; and Jupiter prominence alone can give this characteristic.) The top of the head is rounded from one side to the other, i.e. not round-shaped as a whole but with the appearance of a circular cylinder put on its side. In fact, the head often protudes back longer than a usual head shape, and then the head shape cuts notably back in to the neckline. The corresponding facial shape may look 'horsy' as well.

Note: the natural way to *carry* such a head on the shoulders is by leaning forwards slightly, which corresponds to the particular brand of 'friendliness' for which Jupiter is notable. This is an overtly participatory, sharing kind of friendliness or kindliness—not just a receptivity, but more, 'let's do it *together*'.

The walk for a rising Jupiter may be ponderous, with large, free-moving advances into space—sometimes 'absent-minded' looking. Low-set ears that stick out from the head is also a Jupiterian characteristic.

Temperamentally, Jupiter rising especially tends to give a good disposition—generous, cheerful, optimistic. (Jupiter culminating also gives optimism, but not strictly personal; it is more that 'life circumstances will always turn out a right'.) Jupiter has bright eyes with a twinkle and looks for the good in life. These personalities certainly have a lot of 'give' to them.

An interesting way to focus upon the effects of a rising Jupiter is to find one chart that you know has Jupiter rising and another that you know has *Saturn* rising; these are quite opposite in effect. You get a slightly forbidding feeling approaching the Saturn rising person, even if they are very nice personally. You sense subtle barriers and preoccupations, with definite and structured concerns. With Jupiter rising, you feel a lift; this one is open to options, sometimes he is on a kind of 'float'. The Saturn person moves with more restrictive bodily motions; Jupiter wanders free. Saturn scrutinizes; Jupiter accepts. Incidentally, when in synastry, one person's Jupiter rises in the ascendant of another's, it can be a great buffer against other problems by way of openness and receptivity between the two.

With Jupiter angular in the seventh, the physical effects may not be as prominent as with Jupiter rising, but they usually have the capacity to put others at ease.

In sign rulership (Sagittarius, Pisces)
Jupiter rules Sagittarius and Pisces. Both head tops tend to be small—Sagittarius not so in terms of the space it spans, but the narrowness of the head cuts down on the total bulk. Sagittarius's head is long and narrow both up and down and from front to back, a typical Jupiterian shape. Pisces narrows in at the forehead, so sometimes you get a 'pin head'. Watery Pisces can have a very fleshy face from the eyeline moving down to the chin, but still watch for narrowing in at the top.

What the two Jupiterian signs have in common is emphasis upon the mouth, which protrudes in a 'horse mouth' for Sagittarius and a 'fish mouth' for Pisces. Both sets of teeth tend to protrude, if at slightly different angles. Large hips are common to the Jupiter rulership of both signs, although Pisces is divided there, because it is also a Water sign, and the Water build is flat all the way down the back.

Temperamentally, Sagittarius and Pisces are *the* two most likely rising signs to blurt things out, traceable to Jupiter rulership, which is open and general in its manner, sometimes to the neglect of discrimination. These two signs are also the most easily flustered (unless Fire takes over with Sagittarius), because they are open to impressions and options. Distress may be openly expressed, featuring exaggeration and overreactiveness, and sometimes large, chaotic hand motions. These tendencies can be most helpful to note, since each of these signs is sandwiched between two signs of far greater outer reserve, Sagittarius between Scorpio and Capricorn, Pisces between Aquarius and Aries. When the birth time is uncertain, and you spot this 'free' demeanour, you may be on your way to the correct rising sign.

Both these signs will, at times, bend over backwards to right things or reverse course if they feel responsible for causing offence, showing the giving qualities of Jupiter rulership.

Saturn

As a prominently-placed planet

Whereas Jupiter enlarges and rounds, Saturn flattens and constricts. Saturn may flatten the face—especially noticeable down the pancake-flat cheeks, top part of nose, and sometimes a notable flatness right above the mouth and pressing down on the upper lip. Saturn makes the skin pale and pasty, sometimes white, and the eyes, when blue, may be very pale with a dominant Saturn. Sometimes it will give 'goat eyes'—large, wide-set and bulging—traceable to nothing but a rising or culminating Saturn.

Saturn can make a person considerably shorter. The body size as a whole may shrink, but where you really see the shortening is in the *legs*. Ultra-thin, bony natives also tend to come under Saturn rulership. The jaw-line may be very long, slanting, and with the jawbone prominent, making the face look gaunt with some Saturnine charts.

Watch the body motions with Saturn, especially the hands. The body moves in a measured, structured way—not like the Fixed signs, where the movements are definite but sweeping and broad, but rather in short, restricted motions, hard in their thrust, and there is also a tendency to point. Not the Aries 'point', which is a full extension of the arm, but pointing of the finger, with motion only from the elbow down, and the rest of the hand firmly clenched.

The Saturnine head shape is long and thin as seen from the front, with an oval shape and hard, long jaw-line. Its set is rather rigid, and the back of the head may be somewhat flat. The lines down each side of the face are also quite flat. The teeth may be small, angular and crooked (a Saturnine feature Capricorn rising sometimes picks up *very* strongly, much less so Aquarius). Saturnine ears are small, and closely pinned against the side of the head.

A second type of 'Saturn eye', along with the 'goat eye', is a triangular eye with a sharp downward outer fold, with the eye's gaze often clear and hard. Thick, dark, bushy eyebrows also seem to be associated with a prominent Saturn in the chart.

Temperamentally, Saturn gives reserve and caution, sometimes sternness, and a focus upon hard facts and specifics. The speech features short, concise segments, with a 'push' in the tone but little inflection or emotional expression. The reactions are studied, and sometimes it is difficult for such natives to 'loosen up'.

In sign rulership (Capricorn, Aquarius)

Saturn rules Capricorn and Aquarius. Aquarius has a double-rulership of Saturn and Uranus, but I think it is a serious error to abandon traditional rulerships when taking on modern ones. Part of the *reason* it is apparently an error is that the traditional rulership is always clearly reflected—not just in abstract terms, but directly through the native's physiology, which the astrologer can observe.

Where you see Saturn rulership reflected in both Capricorn and Aquarius is in the back—high and bony. With much of Capricorn, it is hunched over as well, a Saturn trait; Aquarius splits on this, part absolutely straight (Uranus and Air) and part hunched (Saturn). Capricorn and Aquarius also share Saturnian definitiveness of manner, not infrequently harsh. These two rising signs jointly produce the 'authoritarians' of the zodiac—Capricorn from the stance of personal authority and control, and Aquarius from the stance of principle, Aquarius natives being the rule-bearers of the world. Capricorn is personal authority, Aquarius impersonal authority. It is the authoritarian element, common to both, that is *Saturn*.

The voice tones and timbres are different between these two Saturn-ruled signs as well. Capricorn, when harshly Saturnian, will drum things in in a relative monotone; in any event, the pitch of the voice is not in the high range. Aquarius' natural voice timbre is high and rich, and when harsh, it can go quite shrill. If you ever have the chance to line up several of each in a row, you can hear it for yourself.

Both rising signs feature hard body lines and the bones are prominent. The face of Aquarius rising tends to feature the prominent *cheekbone* (Uranus), whereas the Capricorn face is more likely to feature the prominent *jawbone* (Saturn).

Both Saturnian rising signs feature natives who may appear cold, formal or business-like, but Saturn rulership can also take other forms, such as simple reserve, aloofness, or a native who is considerate and sensitive to a fault. These are people who do not readily change, so on the positive side, these are frequently the ones you can count on, because they are consistent. Aquarius can be erratic, but still, if they think a principle is involved, they might hold stronger than anyone.

Uranus
As a prominently-placed planet
A prominent Uranus may be spotted in many ways physically. Uranus lengthens the body, but in specific areas. If you think of a square stretched up into a rectangle, with the tension in the upper part, this is the repeating shape and tension across the Uranian body.

The cheekbones will be high and clearly-defined, with the skin stretched smoothly over the bone, often accompanied by what appears as a slight puffiness under the eyebrow, giving an overall 'sculptured' or 'framed' look to the face. These natives are often very photogenic.

The rectangle shape is repeated in the upper back—that is, the area from the breastline to the shoulder is lengthened, with the shoulder bony and high. The lower back, note, is *not* lengthened— these natives are not long-waisted, as with Sagittarius and Gemini.

The upper leg is also elongated, with that bone sometimes quite prominent. On the narrow lower leg, the calf is placed unusually high and looks very smooth.

The posture is usually quite straight, sometimes even stiff for Uranus-prominent natives. There is a steely look across the eyes, which are nearly lidless and may look quite Asian. Uranian eyes may look at you hard; though this is not the hardness of Saturn, which is a flat, cold gaze. The Uranian gaze studies you in an unfaltering, detached way, betraying no emotion.

The Uranian bodily motions are sure, precise and abrupt. These natives are cool, and immersed in mental interest. Uranus of itself is free of emotional tones and shadings, but relates to structure and form in a pure way; the bodily motions are clear, stark, and sometimes sudden.

The Uranian voice is high, rich, and harsh, with its phrasing definitive.

In sign rulership (Aquarius)
Uranus co-rules Aquarius with Saturn. To distinguish between Aquarius rising and a rising or closely-culminating Uranus, look to the whole body build. For Aquarius, the norm is length across the shoulders (not necessarily 'big' shoulders, as the bone structure can be fine) and narrow hips, something Uranus influence alone will not give. See if the features are small and evenly-placed, an Airy

characteristic which a Uranus-prominent person may well not have.

Temperamentally, there are some key differences between the Uranus-dominant native and the Aquarius rising native. Uranus-dominant people don't want to be fenced in personally, and are risk-takers. Aquarius rising, even if individualistic, demands *structure*. Aquarius relates on *terms*—they may be unconventional ones, they may even give special latitude, but terms nevertheless. Uranus is prone to break pattern on purely personal impulse, detached from its relatedness to others.

Aquarius rising can also be very reserved in manner, from both the Saturn rulership and the Fixity. Uranus influence alone is anything but reserved.

Neptune

As a prominently-placed planet
Neptune gives some dreamy-looking natives who may appear insecure and vulnerable on the surface, even if the fibre underneath is tougher. The person who rambles, hesitates or is tentative in their speech, especially if that speech is low and soft, may be reflecting a prominent Neptune. Over-idealistic people who glamourize life are frequently Neptune-dominant.

Neptune can also give exceptionally sensitive natives, emotionally and/or artistically. Subtle things are sensed about others, and the native attuned in finely-grained ways. How this might be apparent to the astrologer is in the native for whom it seems natural to open up panoramas of meanings, ramifications, and interpretations, or who gravitates towards subtle, blended colours, or who reacts visibly to shifts in emotional context which others, perhaps, would take in their stride.

You do see some 'fish mouths' with a rising or culminating Neptune in charts which have no Pisces at all, and weak chins. You will also find pale eyes, especially of a 'chameleon' variety, i.e. they change colour readily in the light, perhaps shifting from green in dim light to pale blue in sunlight. The skin tone may also alter subtly with moods, and the native may seem to 'light up' around iridescent, sea-like or Neptunian shades, which are rich, subtle, and flicker in and out of view.

The eyes may also look wistful or glistening—a 'faraway' look. With children, shyness and acute emotional sensitivity is common with a prominent Neptune.

Sometimes a native with an angular Neptune will have what I

call a 'swivel walk'. The hips literally swivel about in rotation when the native walks—not side-to-side, but a genuine swivel.

In sign rulership (Pisces)
Neptune co-rules Pisces along with Jupiter. The quality of timidity or self-effacement found with some Piscean natives is traceable to Neptune, not Jupiter. Jupiter gives kindliness, but does not of itself retreat—in fact, many Pisceans are openly gregarious, a Jupiter characteristic. It is Neptune that retreats, is uncertain, vulnerable or easily hurt.

If you are not sure whether a person has Pisces rising or a prominent Neptune, look to the shape of the head. Does it curve in through the forehead area, widening into the lower part of the face? Is the skin fleshy and/or obese? Are the eyes set close together? These are Piscean traits that stem from Mutability and Water rather than from Neptune, and will assist in making the proper identification.

Pluto

As a prominently-placed planet
For a dominant Pluto, I often look at the *skin*. Genetics permitting, the skin will tend to be sallow-looking (yellowish-brown) and it will have a stretched-out look. If one thinks of a caricature of someone with a stocking mask over their head, this would be an exaggerated example of what is being described. That type of Plutonian individual may show extreme personal reserve, and you may sense someone struggling out from repressive influences in the life. But the feelings are *strong*; and that energy, once released, can be intense. The speech may be very low but then, at times erupt; and a strongly Plutonian person can be quite humourless (to say the least!).

Other types of Pluto-dominant people are ultra-intense, but not a single spurt at a time, as with Mars—more a pervasive quality which seems to cohere to the person. Pluto is the least *mobile* component of the personality. Like a huge, lumbering sea creature, it comes to the surface and recedes, but it doesn't get *dislodged* unless there is a major dredging job done. The eyes may be intense and staring, but opaque in their gaze.

Well-directed Plutonian types can stay with persons or projects for ever. Generally speaking, when Plutonian energy is turned outwards, it is with a totalistic thrust, and can release enormous power, sometimes very controlling, possessive, or involved with power drives. Rationality or its lack depends upon other chart factors—Pluto in and of itself isn't rooted in rationality.

In sign rulership (Scorpio)
Pluto co-rules Scorpio with Mars. The Pluto component of Scorpio rising is the stare-right-through-you eyes, for one. Sallow skin stretched across the face like a mask is not uncommonly found with early Scorpio rising.

The extreme tenacity of Scorpio rising is partly attributable to Pluto. It is not just a concentration (Fixed) of emotional energy (Water), but a very deep *entrenchment* in the world view (Pluto). Pluto is deeply instinctual—a link between primaeval emotions and biology—and many a Scorpionic propensity to feel threatened and retreat, or to consolidate and project power is Plutonian in its base, not just Fixed/Water/Mars, Scorpio's other components.

Chiron

As a prominently-placed planet
Newly-discovered Chiron (1977) may show visibly, and certainly bears further observation. I have found that when Chiron is very close on the ascendant or exactly on the Sun, it may show through the eyes, which may flare in intensity. 'Intensity' alone does not describe it, as there is Martial intensity, Plutonian intensity, Uranian intensity, and now Chironic intensity. All are different!

With Chiron, you get a steady gaze of the eye and then, at some point (often a point which indicates, 'Yes, I comprehend'), the eyes seem to have a literal 'flare' going through them—widening, brightening, sometimes eyebrows slightly raised. Chironic intensity is not 'aggressive' *per se*, as is, for instance, Mars. With Chiron, the motivating energy is 'connectedness' and comprehension. Chiron mediates and synchronizes emotional, intellectual and mental levels of comprehension to some unified 'meaning point' where the components are inseparable.

Chiron-prominent natives can be expected to be more inventive and resourceful than others, not fitting into a mould.

I believe that Chiron is the 'wild card' in the planetary deck, not to be assigned to sign rulership.

16.
RISING SIGNS

Aries

Mode: Cardinal   *Element*: Fire   *Ruler*: Mars

Aries, like other early signs of the zodiac, has a simplicity given by consistency of its several components. Its mode, Cardinal, its element, Fire, and its ruler, Mars all point towards direct personal initiative and drive.

Aries is a straight-from-the-hip, blunt, sometimes very aggressive sign—machine-gun style. This doesn't mean that everyone with Aries rising will be overtly aggressive—some are nearly taciturn—but the sign as a whole is *direct*. One Aries rising native may fire off rapid speech—concise, terse, rat-a-tat-tat—while another may be equally concise and terse but simply speak far less. The key quality is lack of embellishments, and a serious and straightforward demeanour.

Whatever the content of the speech may be, listen to its patterns of phrasing and inflection—short clauses, declamative, and a voice that drops decisively at the end of a thought. For example, you won't hear Aries rising say in a soft, persuasive tone, 'Do you think you could tell me about it?', which implies that there is a two-way street (i.e. if you're willing to tell, I'm willing to listen), and also implies that there are other options: 'telling' is just one. More likely, you'd hear, 'Tell me about it', period, with the voice cutting off at the end of this terse . . . well, *demand*. Aries rising isn't harsh, *per se*; it's just direct. It is a strength in that Aries rising natives don't try to manipulate responses, they just state their own case in the fewest possible words.

Aries can be aggressive, but the sign is still *controlled*. The body lines are straight-up-and-down: the long triangular head which holds its erect set; the walk which swings the leading foot straight ahead;

declamative speech. If you watch the speech/body co-ordination, you will find that with many Arians, the head makes clear, straight nods down as a 'punctuation' when the native speaks—quite dissimilar from the flexible, curving motions of the Mutables. Economy of motion characterizes the whole Arian expression and bodily lines.

The Arian body tends to be tall, and is often of a spare, rugged, large-boned type, even for women, and many of its natives—both men and women—are thin, even lanky. The women are sometimes 'built like a boy', partly because the body lacks curves and partly because the carriage is a straightforward 'one-step'—no curves or wiggles or extra movements sometimes considered 'feminine' in a stereotypical sense. Both men and women can be quite commanding and self-possessed.

Some Aries natives have their head set erect on their shoulders, giving a 'military' cast to the carriage, from the Mars rulership. Others stoop, with the arms swinging in a regular rhythm.

Many Arians have a typical facial shape. The face is long and triangular-shaped, from the sides of the two temples to the chin, with the eyeline high on the face. Watch that 'point' on the chin, however. It is not a Jupiterian, very *long* chin, in which the chin length is extended whatever else characterizes the facial shape. The Arian chin simply is part of a clear triangle with the two other points, a triangle pronounced because of cheeks that move straight down just as the long, blunt nose moves down the face.

A common Arian eye type is tucked directly under the lid, a so-called 'gimlet' eye, i.e. there is no visible space between the upper eyelid and the eye itself. The brow is also close to the eyes, which are fairly deep-set. The overall effect is that you see the eye and the brow as a single unit, conveying in spatial form the Arian economy. Note, these are not bushy eyebrows, more often thin; but the Arian forehead, as with other Fire signs, is substantial, and many a high Arian forehead also recedes back gradually. The eyes, whether blue or brown (not too many hazel, mottled or murky shades with this sign), tend to be of a clear shade and the gaze is usually direct. The mouth is well-formed but many are thin-lipped (not extremely so, which is reserved for Saturn), and there is often a wide space between the bottom of the blunt, straight, not overlarge nose, and the upper lip.

The hair texture is often coarse and wiry, tending towards the darker shades (Mars rulership), often thick and plentiful in youth, but some of the men go bald in later years. This is a sign where the women tend to wear their hair long and straight, or cropped in a simple, short cut—some 'no frills' style which might match the outer personality.

The walk can be quite Martial, head first, feet forward nearly straight, and the stride is generally long. The feet are characteristically large (as are the hands) and frequently point out.

Taurus

Mode: Fixed   *Element*: Earth   *Ruler*: Venus

Taurus, like Aries, is a model of consistency. Its Fixed mode, Earth element, and ruler Venus all point towards a disposition which is settled and steady. These natives tend to convey outward stability, whatever their respective inner realities may be. Taurus rising is genuinely 'down-to-earth', centred in material concerns, and can have a greatly soothing and calming effect upon others. Conversely, when angered (slowly) or intransigently stubborn, they can be formidable adversaries. The head and shoulders for many do indeed resemble a charging bull!

In keeping with Taurus rulership of the throat, the voice does tend to be fairly low-pitched and 'throaty', with good resonance. This expressive sign has far more than its share of exceptional vocalists, and the physical energy can be quite magnetic, sometimes centred in a reassuring, magnetic touch.

There are two visibly different types of Taureans—the Venusian-looking Taureans and the Fixed-looking Taureans, with some variations in between.

The sweet-but-sturdy Venusian Taureans, often found early in the sign, feature bow mouths, dimples, and a warm charm. They may be heavy or thin (Taurus, being a Fixed sign, has more than its share of stocky natives), but the upper musculature and shoulder width is still proportionally wide. The hair tends to be thick and wavy, often in warm, earthy shades, with large, wondering brown eyes that settle their gaze into yours.

Small, well-balanced features—a Venusian characteristic—are often found on the Taurean face, even though the nose is often not straight. The Taurean's cheekbones are fairly prominent but way to the side of the face. Then the face, moving down, expands yet a little further to a wide, square jaw. The neck is also thicker than average. Even when the nose is straight, the bridge tends to be high, from the Earth component of the sign. The Venusian-looking Taurean will tend to have rounded cheeks and chin; spaced across the wide

Taurean face, visibly you might see three neatly-spaced 'mounds' clustered round a sweet Taurean smile.

Other Taurus rising natives are notably stocky, with a mass of hard weight concentrated around the shoulders and chest. There are many big-breasted women with this sign, but that is partly because the chest area itself is large. (Large breasts because of a lot of water weight is more Cancerian.)

Taurus, when Venusian, is 'sweet-but-determined' (as distinct from the 'sweet-for-the-purpose-of-relating-to-others' which characterizes Venusian *Libra* types). They speak slowly and clearly in a low-pitched, steady, resonant voice. They walk slowly, sometimes in clearly-measured steps, and their back is generally straight unless the 'forward charge' set of the neck is accentuated. The hands move in large, definite gestures, characteristically used to describe concrete reality. It is easy to imagine some of these natives sitting in a garden, scooping down their fingers broadly into the soil with great tactile energy and personal involvement.

There is great willingness to relate, but these are not compliant people. They can be enormously stubborn, sometimes despite appearances.

The profile for Taurus rising, as with many Fixed natives, will often go straight down a broad forehead to a chin which is firm and a solid jaw-line. The top of the head tends to be squarish in shape, but the wide jaw breaks the pattern.

The shoulder line is important to check with many Taureans. Many have strongly-developed musculature around the shoulders. The shoulders slant down slightly but in a very straight line, and the shoulder line extends past where a shoulder would normally end, the extra length being the musculature of the upper arm. Some walk with a definite jaunt, right shoulder forward, left shoulder forward, and so on. When you see it once and identify it, you'll not miss it again; and this is also easy to spot when observing from behind. Many a jocular, earthy nature accompanies that jaunt as well.

Some Taurean eyes pick up the large, heavy-lidded quality of Earth more than others, and the eyes for these are most often brown, accompanied by an 'earth tone' skin—sallow, yellowish or brown. By contrast, the more overtly Venusian Taurean types may be quite fair with blue eyes—oft-times features, build and colouring 'matches', whether Earthy or Venusian. The Earth-like Taureans have largish noses, which may well feature a high bridge (Earth), but tend to be nicely, evenly shaped around the nostrils (Venus).

Watch the eyebrow moving straight across the face, which is often also thick. Some Taurus rising natives also have clear ridges across a broad, flat forehead which frequently, for some reason, seems to come with kinky hair.

Gemini

Mode: Mutable   *Element*: Air   *Ruler*: Mercury

Gemini's model of 'consistency' is a quixotic one at best! Mode Mutable, element Air and ruler Mercury all point to activity, mobility, scatter. These are physically agile natives, often with long limbs. The neck is long, fingers often tapering, with long thin arms and wrists and the walk light-footed.

Although Gemini is ruled by verbal Mercury, don't judge whether Gemini is rising by how *many* words come out of the mouth—listen to their flow and pacing. Gemini can give a rush of words, nearly 'words for words' sake'. They may be paced unevenly, may be nervous or breathy for some, polished, with a clever twist for others. The tone is light, but very clear and slightly incisive. The syllables of words may be distorted oddly, rushing some words together and stretching others out. It has nothing to do with the *emotional* emphasis of words. In fact, a keynote of Gemini is that it does not readily verbalize emotions. Some may talk *about* anything, even the most intimate details of life, but they do not naturally express their *feelings*.

This rising sign can make for an excellent teacher or salesperson, for its explicit verbage. The hands are very active, with a built-in voice-hand co-ordination that 'spells out concepts' with hand motions. It would be very believable to discover that the graphic, explicit hand language used by the deaf had been developed by an inventive Gemini rising native! There is also a lot of extra gestural communication with this sign, a Mercurial trait. The eyes may squint, or the head jerk slightly to the side, the eyebrows may raise, or there may be slight shoulder movements—again, co-ordinated with *words*, a kind of 'gestural punctuation'. The dart-like eyes have an alert focus, and the physical movements are light and quick. Some Gemini rising natives have a quizzical, scrunched-up look about the face.

Less articulate Gemini types (certainly not all are 'intellectual', plus the latter degrees may be rather taciturn) can spill things out in rushes and spurts of words when under stress, even if they have (apparently) little to verbalize. The voice timbre is light, though when angry, it can jump *low* in pitch, low and breathy.

Gemini is one of the long-waisted signs (Sagittarius the other). With women, the breasts are small but the buttocks well-curved. Even with men, you will often see a sway back at the end of a long waist. Gemini rising frequently walks with a spring and swinging arms.

There are two types of Gemini rising face. One is a longish oval (Mutable), with the features convex, with long nose and a long neck which moves freely. The other type is 'bird-like' with small, alert eyes, a pert, turned-up nose, and the upper lip upturned as well. If you see in profile a parallel curve from a turned-up nose and turned-up upper lip, you can be sure you are looking at either Gemini rising or a prominently-placed Mercury. These crisp, somewhat cool Gemini types frequently have very good carriage (Air), and though not assertive in an overtly aggressive way, may always seem to be 'there'. Inquisitiveness and running commentary characterizes some.

The Gemini forehead also has a characteristic shape. It looks like a smooth cylinder (standing upright) going across the forehead. The smooth skin rounds in evenly around the temples (the 'cylinder' impression). This forehead gets very slightly broader moving from the eyeline to the top of the head—perhaps the mark of a 'well-developed brain', at least so it would appear visually! The face below the eyeline gets narrower, so the head as a whole is somewhat 'balloon-shaped'.

A characteristic eye shape repeats in many parts of the sign (a prominent Mercury can give this, too). It is triangular but of a special shape. The lower line of the eye is slightly curved. The top part of the eye is divided at a point about two-thirds of the way from the outer edge to the inner edge of the eyelid. These small eyes are often ultra-alert, perceptive, and quick to alter focus, but they are also detached in their gaze, an Airy trait. Gemini eyes are close-set.

The Gemini rising men with the pert, Mercurial faces have a nearly predictable penchant for *moustaches*. Not beards—just moustaches. Watch for them!

Cancer

Mode: Cardinal   *Element*: Water   *Ruler*: The Moon

Cancer is a sensitive, emotional sign, but being a Cardinal sign, too, its natives may not be shrinking violets despite some appearances. Cancer rising runs a wide gamut, with body types and temperaments which respectively emphasize Cardinality, Water, and the Moon, but also with many characteristics that cut across the entire sign.

This is an observant, responsive nature. Much as Libra, another Cardinal but responsive sign functions in a pacing of (verbal) listen/respond, listen/respond, Cancer rising functions by way of (emotional) observe/respond, observe/respond. These natives soak up their environment like a sponge and are assertive or recessive depending upon how their emotional compass assesses the climate.

The temperament, even when not expressing immediate emotion, has an emotional flow running through its expression: the voice timbre is soft, the inflections change fluently, the emotions come through readily in the eyes and the sympathies are apparent. The touch is sensitive.

The colouring throughout the sign, given genetic choice, is pale skin and 'Moon shade' eyes—this might be blue-green, hazel, light mottled shades or pale blue. The eyes are large, liquid and expressive. The flesh is soft. The skin across the face—whether for thin or heavy natives—has a 'creased' appearance, and the moulding of the face is amorphous—forehead rounding away, no clear jaw-line, cheekbones that cannot be pinpointed with exactitude. The lips are full and sensual, but with a slight downturn at the corners of the mouth, and the nose is never straight—there is often a slight hump or curve, and the end rounds off, is never pointed. The lips are also notably *rounded*.

Throughout the sign, the body as seen all the way down the back and buttocks is flat, whatever the native's weight. You do find some 'hour glass' shapes with mid or late Cancer rising women, along with 'wiggly' walks, but those curves will be in the hips, not the buttocks. A 'chunky', undifferentiated shape characterizes the Water element generally.

Cancerian hair is fine, sometimes wispy, often with a wave, and brown or blond rather than dark. The Cancerian men with large round heads who tend to bald will begin to do so from the *middle* of the head, rather than by way of a receding hairline as with the Fire signs.

Cancer rising shortens the limbs, which is especially noticeable in the arms. When you see an elbow which comes down only to the breastline instead of the waistline, carries some jelly-like weight and hangs in, crab-like, Cancer rising is a good bet. This is common with early Cancer rising (the first ten degrees), which features many broad, heavy natives, with broad, pale, fleshy faces, very short arms, short waists, small-sized feet that point in, and sometimes a 'button' nose. The head size tends to be large and round, but with a marked flattening right in the back. The head pokes forwards slightly, because it is set that way on the neck, and the lines between shoulder, neck and jaw are soft and blurred. The shoulders round; the arms are exceptionally short.

These natives sometimes look like a big, soft bear, and pot bellies are not uncommon with the men. The walk is flat-footed, but these natives are not heavy on their feet. The voice is soft, slushy, and persuasive. These people are sometimes adept salespeople—they go right for personal appeal and it works. Sometimes they are excellent at uniting people around common concerns.

The eyes are wide-set and also deep-set in a characteristic way. The whole area surrounding the eye is spacious, in a broad face, so the eye looks set into a 'pool' of space. The eyes themselves tend to be pale, and are liquid and large, usually with Moon lines on the outer edge.

Late in the sign, another type of eye is featured. This is a rather bulbous eye, very expressive, and rapidly fluctuating in its focus. Mid-Cancer eyes also look like they have what looks like a cylindrical casing across an almond-shaped eye with a band narrowing across the eye on the top. Watch for it, and you will always find Cancer emphasis in the chart—sometimes it is a Cancer Sun.

Later Cancer rising features many thin natives, with small feet and a mincing walk, but large eyes, creased skin, nose with a rounded tip and full, downturned lips. The voice is still round in timbre, but you also find natives who are openly exclamatory, sometimes gushing. Deliver a bit of good news and when you hear a torrential, 'Ah! Oh! Oo-oo-oo-ooh!', you will know that either someone has just been attacked, or that a Cancer rising native has just discovered something wonderful!

Cancer rising can be a positively *aggressive* sign as well, when it has successfully discovered the 'wavelength' on which it can operate effectively. Watch for the Cardinal profile and body build for this Cancerian type.

Leo

Mode: Fixed   *Element*: Fire   *Ruler*: The Sun

The keynote of Leo rising is *personal confidence*, spelled out by the Sun (the personal identity), Fire (self-actualization) and Fixity as well, as Fixed natives share a common forté of standing firm. If they have personal confidence, they'll exude it in a broad, sunny smile, big personal plans, a positivist outlook, flamboyance or other forms of self-assertion which are not necessarily *active* at all (that's Cardinality, this is Fixity), but convey a confident position, demeanour or outlook. They can also inspire confidence in others.

If they *don't* have a high level of personal confidence, it will still be an issue. Having the Sun's sign on the ascendant puts the personal identity, self-worth and self-respect in a perennial spotlight, which the astrologer will be able to recognize through the native's speech and personal projection. If they do not project self-confidence, they might pretend to have it, be seeking it, or bemoan whatever slights, obstacles, or hurts seem to have kept it from their grasp. The pride is keen with this rising sign. (Note: this is sometimes where rising Sun natives are freer to be themselves than Leo rising natives—they simply have extra energy, without feeling an 'image' might be at stake.)

Leo rising certainly *looks* confident in its bodily form. These natives tend to be robust and sturdy, with high personal energy, and the carriage is erect and sure. Leo governs the spine, and the carriage is generated from the spine, which pushes up straight, throwing the chest forward and head up high. This sign certainly has a sprinkling of commanding, imperious types, both amongst men and women.

The colouring is good, sometimes ruddy, and the face is usually open and broad. The forehead can be flat, and it is massive for many areas of the sign, with eyes that are deep-set. Sometimes the forehead looks like a bit of armour for the men, with the 'crown' part of the head literally graced with thick, coarse hair, sometimes wavy, with more than its share of red and gold. The men often sport beards.

The eyes may or may not be 'cat eyes'. These are very deep-set eyes in which there is a sharp fold down onto the part of the lid closest to the nose, giving a 'cat-like' expression to the face. This folded-over lid is a Fiery characteristic, as with the Arian 'gimlet eye'.

Other Leo rising natives, however, have large, round eyes which project authority, from the influence of the Sun.

The chin is firm, as is the jaw-line, though a puffiness in the face from the cheeks down can blur that line. The neck can be very thick, especially for the middle degrees which feature many stocky natives. Parts of this sign are tall and thin (even some of this sign's amply-built women can be *very* tall), but when this is the case, they feature a 'carrot-on-end' build, broader and somewhat stiff across the shoulders, narrow at the hips.

The Leo voice timbre has good resonance and projection, and often has a low, *gravelly* sound or a *brassy* sound which is unmistakable. The tone can be commanding, it can be definitive, with some it can sound smug, but it can also be reassuring coming from many a confident, sunny, self-possessed native of this sign. Very typical for this sign are cheekbones that fall directly in front of the eyes with slightly puffy cheeks giving, very literally, a 'front and centre' thrust to the Leonine face!

Leo rising natives often speak slowly, clearly and with care, with a 'This is the way it is' delivery. They may resent being interrupted more than other signs. The hand gestures tend to be broad and expansive, and are used to describe 'scenarios' rather than minor details, as characterizes the Mutables. The sign is naturally dramatic, with a sprinkling of overbearing or brassy types.

This is not a sign to be rushed (Fixity), or to change course on without both warning and consultation. If they don't get respect, they may pull out rather than suffer loss of face. But they may also work harder than anyone else to prove themselves, the sign featuring many hard-driving, overworking types who'd rather do anything than not do their best.

The feet may point out with the walk, which is characteristically slow, ponderous and sure-footed.

Give especial consideration to the natal Sun when Leo is rising—it will assume a double importance, as you see what type of identity is 'on the line'. Watch for that glint in the Leo rising eye, however. So long as you take *them* seriously, they are quite willing to have fun!

Virgo

Mode: Mutable   *Element*: Earth   *Ruler*: Mercury

Everything about Virgo is geared towards *specifics*: Earth (tangible), Mutable (relatedness), Mercury (details). The keynote of Virgo is not only the oft-touted penchant for exact, tangible details but their *relatedness*—comparisons and differentiations, what is better, worse, more helpful, more irritating, more suitable, not suitable at all. Virgo rising people, however, make not only adept critics, but also excellent craftspeople and discriminating perfectionists in whatever area they focus their interest.

Virgo rising natives are usually only of medium, or medium-short height, and its natives alternate between a slight, asthenic, Mercurial build, on the long-waisted side, and a more chunk-like, solid Earth build, on the short-waisted side. You do find a few very tall natives occasionally, more often late in the sign, whose extra length comes from long Mercury limbs and a long waist.

Many Virgoans have an earth-tone coloured skin—brownish or sallow—which is often accompanied by heavy-lidded Earth eyes, with their dry, sombre gaze. The nose is high-bridged for some, as an Earthy characteristic, with some bump or ridge or crook. Even if not high-bridged, the nose will most often be *pointed*, a Mercurial characteristic, but not turned-up like Gemini—just a good solid point. The thrust of the nose tends to be accentuated on the Virgoan face, as the bite is often narrow with the upper lip clearly-defined and slightly protruding, so the eye has to take the nose and mouth 'in one package', as it were. Perhaps an apt physiological signature for being both 'nosy' and taking the liberty to *say* something about it!

The eyes are mild in their gaze; when intense, it is out of perceptual quickness and nervous intensity, rather than a burning Martial intensity, or a hard Uranian one. For those Virgoans with heavy-lidded Earth eyes, they are most often brown—you do see blue, Mercury-type eyes with this rising sign, but the Earthy eyes will usually be brown. When large, heavy-lidded eyes are in the blue family (usually pale blue or clouded blue), you are much more likely to be looking at Capricorn, Cancer, or Pisces, from their respective planetary rulerships of Saturn, the Moon, and Neptune. For some reason, the genetics of signs seem to cluster in such 'matching' packages of traits.

Very typical for this sign is a strongly convex face, pulling in towards a centre line, against which you discover the close-set eyes, long nose, and prominent if narrow mouth. This can give some faces nearly a 'chipmunk' look about them. The shape of the face as a whole, including the heads, tends to be oval—sometimes, for the men, a real 'egghead' appearance—and the cheekbones low on the face. A high, receding forehead with baldness later in life is not uncommon for the men. Capricorn's head can also be conspicuously oval in shape, but the emphasis there is on a hard, long jaw-line—not a Virgoan feature—so these two need not be confused.

The hair may be curly (Earth) or straight (Mercury), and sometimes it is positively kinky. The shoulders slope. The hand gestures are small, precise, pointing and take on a definite 'downbeat' kind of rhythm, as distinct from the more chaotic-looking scatter of Mercurial Gemini.

The voice is often middle-range or on the high-pitched side, often light and mild, very undramatic, if one will, and they speak readily about tangible things. Leaving things to the imagination is not Virgo's forté. However, many of these observant natives will also be kind and considerate to a fault, hence *easier* to be around than others. Those types are normally very industrious, can work hours on prized, highly-specialized projects, and take pride in small details. This is a reasoned, well-considered, serious temperament, which treats everything alike with a kind of matter-of-fact dispassion. This expression of the Virgoan temperament is centred in concern for facts (Earth) as they relate to people (Mutable), and includes some extraordinarily helpful individuals.

Other Virgoans may have a raspy or scratchy-sounding voice, rather a 'cutting edge'. But the voice is still not genuinely resonant, like the Fixed signs, nor modulated into interlinking waves of sound, as with Air.

You will also note that with *all* the rising signs, both that there is an emphasis upon the part of the body that the sign rules, and that that part of the body tends to lead when the native walks. With Virgo, it is the intestinal area, which is the most prone to weight gain; and this 'middle-centred' walk is light, close-to-the-ground and not especially graceful, lacking the Gemini agility and spring.

Virgo rising lips are characteristically thin. Not so the tongue— yet without these reflective natives, the world would undoubtedly be a far less ordered place.

Libra

Mode: Cardinal   *Element*: Air   *Ruler*: Venus

Libra rising is basically cool and detached—relating *to* someone presupposes a *separation* between the two—though it features a wide range of sweet, beautiful types (Venus), aggressive types (Cardinal), and people who seem to function much on an ethereal plane (Air).

What is common across the sign is small features and an evenly-proportioned body. The lines are basically long for an Air sign, and you will see many of the 'same' long willowy arms that characterized Gemini rising. You do see a lot of open fingers when the hands are in motion, which is characteristic for Air, as are *long* fingers. But the Libra rising hands stay fairly close to the body, and behave in a more mannered way; it's part of an overall model where the poise doesn't get ruffled too easily.

There are two distinct eye types to watch for. One is fairly round and bright, sometimes with curly lashes, and this eye isn't overemotional but it does sparkle. The other eye type is very detached in its gaze and fits the following pattern. If you remember the *Arian* eye, close to the thin brow, with the eye tucked right under the lid, the Libran eye is the *opposite* of that. That is, the brow is rather thick, by contrast, and space between the brow and the eye is wide, and quite a bit of the eyelid is *showing*. This isn't a heavy lid, as with many Earth and Water rising natives—it is simply *visible*.

For all Librans, also watch for the low eyeline on the face, often nearly halfway down the face. The eyebrows are pronounced and move straight across the face, perhaps just curving down slightly at the ends. This makes the forehead quite high for some, but you won't get the impression of a high forehead since the eye gravitates towards the face's evenly-shaped centre, so you simply look right in the middle of the face and see the eyes. This eyeline-in-the-middle look seems suitably to accompany an even disposition as well.

The hair tends to be straight and fine for the Airy types, and may have a bit of a wave where the Venusian component is prominent. The 'Venus model' of Libra rising also often includes long curly eyelashes, a bow mouth, dimples, and a small, classically straight nose. Sometimes the small, even features look 'bunched up' in the centre of the face.

The voice for Libra is clear and medium-high for the women and never too low for the men. Many Librans fix gently on their words and never sound casual or rushed. They are easy to talk with in that they lay sentences out neatly, listen, then respond; though sometimes—just as one hesitates to mess up physical surroundings with Virgo rising near—you might feel inclined to watch your own speech more carefully lest you 'mess up' some Libran native's perfectly even and cultured flow of words.

Other Libra rising natives are quite direct (Cardinal) and inquisitive. This model is a great rising sign for chat show interviewers, because they'll get you quickly to the point, even by subtle provocation, without ever seeming to offend or push, and they develop a rhythm of verbal interchange. More aggressive Cardinally-oriented Libra rising natives can be mediators, diplomats, or even generals! Librans are adept at staying out of the foray *personally*, while keenly observing the thrust of polar opposites.

There is a slightly different model of Libra rising physically, which features curved eyebrows and a mouth which is more rounded and dips gently down on each side, giving the mouth a rather blasé look. These natives have backs that are not absolutely straight (as are the more Airy Libran natives) but curve gently. In the women, the hips and buttocks are gentle curves as well—like one general, even padding from shoulders to thighs which increases or decreases as a whole when the body gains or loses weight.

This sign does feature more than its share of *charming* natives, and they are quick to notice and act upon people's *social* needs. As a class of people, however, they do seem to be relatively unkeen on physical work. It may be that social skills are just a greater area of aptitude, but physical manipulation of objects doesn't seem to come naturally. Where the Cardinal component is strong, however, you'll find exceptions.

Scorpio

Mode: Fixed   *Element*: Water   *Rulers*: Mars, Pluto

Whether manifested in emotional (Water) reserve (Fixed), concentrated (Fixed) drive (Mars), intensity (Mars, Pluto) or intransigence (Fixed, Pluto), Scorpio is undoubtedly one of the 'heavier' signs of the zodiac. This is sometimes—though not always by any means—reflected in sheer physical weight, but Scorpio also makes its presence felt temperamentally as well, whether through forceful projection or even extreme reserve. It's a 'feeling presence'.

Scorpio does have more than its share of stocky natives, since Fixed bodies tend to be more massive, and Watery bodies both retain water weight and have shorter limbs and a shorter waist, which makes weight more noticeable.

Commonly found (though not usually early in the sign) is a fleshy, square face with large, intense, liquid eyes, and thick eyebrows that begin at the top of the nose and arch way up on each side. The eyes are wide-set throughout Scorpio and the nose often ample (and hooked), so you will often see a space between the eyebrows that looks like a flat ridge (parts of Cancer feature this as well).

The heavier Scorpio rising native tends to have a massive forehead, with skin that is not completely smooth, but shares an amorphous appearance with the other Water signs. The hair tends to be massive and thick, and grows up in a straight line from the top of the forehead, which features a 'widow's peak' more than other signs. Where genetics permit a choice, the Scorpio rising native will be dark-complexioned with dark hair and eyes. With natives with blue eyes, you will still find more than their share of *intense* blue shades. You see fewer warm, rich browns and you will see many eyes that look rather murky— you have to look at close range to determine whether it is a dark muted green or some shade of brown.

As with Taurus, when the Scorpio rising native is stocky, the head size tends to be quite large and the neck thick.

Many Scorpio rising natives walk with a kind of silent slink, leading from the pelvis area, leaving the top part of the body motionless as they walk in one compact unit. Indeed, Scorpio's 'silent shoulders' may be tangibly contrasted with its opposite, Taurus' overt emphasis on shoulder movement.

The voice timbre is soft, rounded and tends to be low-pitched, even though with Scorpio's Fixity, this is a voice that can *project*. Some Scorpio natives have a soft, low-pitched but very *husky* voice (for both men and women), which is unmistakable and projects with self-possessed command.

The term 'soft' for voice timbre calls for clarification. It does not mean talking softly as opposed to loudly. 'Soft' is a rounded edge to the timbre. A Gemini rising native, for example, may speak at a softer pitch than a Scorpio rising native, but the words themselves are clipped and cutting and chopped into phrases, while the timbre itself has a cutting edge because Mercury constricts the timbre in a concentrated way. If you think of an oboe, for example, it is a light tone but is not 'round' or 'soft'—it is cutting. When, by contrast, you think of a bass drum, it is not soft in pitch, but the sound is 'rounded' or 'soft'. Note that 'rounded' voice tones often accompany lower-pitched voices as well, though Taurus and Leo have many natives with low-pitched but rich voices.

Scorpio rising natives do not look the same throughout the sign. Some towards the middle of the sign have a 'bald eagle' look about them—intense, bulbous eyes, brownish skin with amorphous facial lines, a beak-like nose, downturned mouth, square jaw and a solidly muscular build. Some natives in late Scorpio can be excessively heavy, and have a marvellous ability to hold back and skillfully observe others. Scorpio rising throughout the sign are strategists and rarely give anything away—they have to know exactly who and what they are relating to first. Second-guessing and bargaining can be Scorpio rising's greatest skill. Slowly-gained trust is the watchword in personal relations.

In the early degrees of the sign are many fairly *thin* natives, but with a specific type build. The body is definitely top-weighted, with visible muscles on the arm, even with the women. The hands are square and have a firm grip. The waist is *short*, but below the waist are narrow hips and long, spindly legs, giving the impression of 'a body on stilts', because of the disproportion of upper and lower halves of the body. That native tends to have swarthy-looking skin which has a smooth, stretched-out look (Pluto), and the features are fairly small but the nose never completely straight. The voice is firm and tight as if guarding energy, but these natives can be very plain and definitive. These people often have tons of excess drive, but are careful where they expend it. The body, which can be quite athletic, moves with little excess motion.

A certain percentage of Scorpio rising natives are taciturn, and will speak at length only with people with whom they feel close emotional rapport and trust. Every now and then you will meet a coarser Scorpio type who is a bully and very verbal about it, with massive bodily weight to 'throw around'. One can be in for an emotional battle with such types—pure reason will never do.

Don't forget the Scorpio rising mouth. It may be full and sensual, but downturned into a kind of 'grimace' at the edges, topping off a firm, squarish chin. Combine it with the more extreme examples of thick flaring eyebrows, glaring eyes, black hair and the widow's peak, and Mephistopheles here we come!

Sagittarius

Mode: Mutable   *Element*: Fire   *Ruler*: Jupiter

The so-called 'split' signs are traditionally Gemini, Sagittarius and Pisces, but temperamentally, Sagittarius probably fits the bill best of all. Mutability and Jupiter rulership both incline towards a gregarious, outgoing temperament, but Fire reserve and self-command may contraindicate. These natives are often shy and self-contained in youth, gaining their gregarious, expansive, projective side only in the more confident adult years; vulnerable in youth, only to assert a fiery independence when grown up. This temperament is personal (Mutable), incorporative (Jupiter) and impassioned (Fire) in its projection to the world, giving not surprising penchants for oratory (Jupiter/Fire), self-aggrandizement (Jupiter/Fire) and also much down-to-earth frank talk (Jupiter/Mutable).

Sagittarius aims for the long leap—philosophically (an incorporative world view), pragmatically (take the 'big deal'), physically (through athletics), and emotionally, through extending trust to others, at least 'on credit'. Physiologically, these temperamental bents parallel not just the characteristic long body lines of this rising sign, but its extra strength and muscular development in the legs.

The head is long and narrow, both as seen in profile and as seen from front to back from a top view. The neck is often exceptionally long for the taller natives, 'swan-like', with the arms long and thin. The legs are long, though the body is definitely bottom-weighted, too, with heavier hips, buttocks and thighs, and a broad, large calf on the leg. Even the men, many of them, are not exempt from this disproportion.

A word about the set of the head. It is very mobile, and leans forward in a characteristic Jupiterian outreach. The hands of an involved Sagittarian are continually in motion, and when flustered, can go into a regular swirl. The Sagittarian mouth tends to protrude into a 'horse mouth', with the laugh also sometimes a 'nei-ei-ei-eigh' (which, incidentally, photographs just *terribly*!). The eyes often have an intense fiery glisten, and the voice quality may glisten, too: a combination of slight breathiness, earnestness, and declamatory fervour when the interest is keenly aroused. Nor will an angry Sagittarian hesitate to 'preach'!

Many Sagittarian eyes are almond-shaped but not too close-set. The lids are folded-over across the middle of the eye, leaving the lids showing on each side. Others have eyes which *are* close-set (often towards the beginning of the sign), with a Mutable cast to the face generally, both the features and the head itself coming *forwards*. These are the overtly friendly types who say 'hello', and 'how is everyone doing?' just to kick off the day in good spirits.

All across the sign, you will see many high, receding foreheads, as with the other Fire signs, but with a different cast. Aries gradually slopes back. Leo's forehead is broad and doesn't slope back too much, though the hairline does tend to recede. With Sagittarius, the forehead goes up a ways, and then suddenly slopes back. When you examine the forehead, you can see a clear 'break point' in the curve upwards.

Sagittarian cheekbones can be prominent and high, but not so high nor far apart as the Uranus-dominant native. Part of the reason Sagittarian cheekbones *look* so high is the characteristic 'hollowing in' beneath the cheekbones, which also contributes to the 'horsy' look.

The nose may or may not be large, but it does tend to be long, and it may hook down towards a protuding mouth. In profile, you can see this nose going way out front and down, and the mouth—in a parallel line—also going out (the protruding bite) and down.

It is the *opposite* of the profile of a bird-like Gemini rising face, in which the nose and upper lip both tilt *up*, also in unison!

There are many tall, spare natives and also many stooped natives in this sign, who have prominent 'wings' in their back. There are also many graceful 'swan-like' natives, the sign having an ample share of models and dancers, which latter is favoured by development of the thighs. For better or worse, this sign also sports natives who trip over their own rather large feet in a flustered rush to get here or there. The body propels forwards from the thigh area (which Sagittarius rules), while the feet tend to turn out. Do try it out. You might gain a sympathetic understanding of how this sign can inadvertently destroy a lovely pair of new shoes in a week flat!

Sagittarian hands are often used expressively and dramatically for the adept, while no-one is more awkward about hand placement than an ill-at-ease Sagittarian. The body leans forward on listening, which its opposite, Gemini, does not, should the two be momentarily confused.

Some early Sagittarius rising natives are stocky and short, and may be on the jolly side. Often, this type can talk you into anything, or will at least try. The pragmatically oriented Sagittarians, with good material and acquisitive instincts also seem strong in the early part of the sign. The speech-making visionaries seem to gravitate more towards later degrees.

The temperament tends to be 'live and let live', and Sagittarians are pretty good about making external adjustments. In fact, staying put is not considered very appealing. Challenge these people to a race—they'll love it!

Capricorn

Mode: Cardinal   *Element*: Earth   *Ruler*: Saturn

Capricorn includes many of the ultra-pragmatic activists of the world: realistic (Saturn), materially-minded (Earth) initiators (Cardinal). These natives take life in their hands and organize it, direct it, control it, manage it, use it—do everything but leave it alone! These are *the* realists of life, perhaps more so than the Capricorn Sun because of the ascendant's outward thrust which sets one's own personal stage in life. Politicians, managers and organizers of all sorts fall readily into this group.

Even those Capricorn rising natives who back away from the social arena are precise, definite, and very *serious* about how they approach life. They are generally a heavy, insistent, driving lot, with an occasional native here and there who appears unusually calm and unperturbed but has notable qualities of reserve, discrimination and personal caution. We need remember that *all* the rising signs have both extroverts and introverts, even Aries, even Leo—and certainly even Capricorn, where Saturnian shyness may predominate.

The cheeks are notably flat throughout this sign. The body is bony and sometimes very thin, sometimes also very short, though tall natives in the latter part of the sign are not uncommon. Those tall natives tend to be hard-looking, with high, hunched-up shoulders which seem to 'guard' the body, and many prominent kneebones as well. Some of these natives have an odd, dry sense of humour, sharp and pointed which seems to match the definite but oddly-jutting bodily lines. These are also amongst the large-nosed natives of the zodiac, with a high bridge, often a big 'hook', then a long, narrow nose coming to a definite point. Small, angular, crooked teeth is very nearly a trademark for this type.

A typical set of the head for Capricorn is as follows. The jaw-line is long and slanting and the head shape oval. The total head shape slices in *diagonally* into the neck, with the shoulders hunched up *around* the area of the jaw. Men with this physiology often like goatees, but not full beards, which are a little too unruly for the Saturnine image.

The Capricorn eyes are of two different types. The first type, which seems more common for those natives with a 'chunk-like' build (and sometimes a weight problem) is a 'goat eye'—large, bulbous and wide-set. These eyes are often pale blue or murky blue-green, sometimes medium brown—rarely any intense shade. Corresponding with this eye type is pale and pasty skin tone. The hair tends to be dark rather than light, often with a curl. The lips may be thick and puffy-looking around the upper lip. When these natives have a problem with excess weight, the Saturn rulership of the ascendant seems to make it peculiarly difficult to manage.

The other Capricorn rising eye is small and triangular, a clear colour (often clear blue), and has a flat, hard gaze, like the eye has no 'light'. The triangular shape differs from the Gemini triangle eye, which is open, alert, and the 'point' of the triangle falls two-thirds across the eye. The Capricornian eye features a heavy fold down across the outer side of the eye, seeming to slant the whole eye downwards, giving a sad or mournful expression to the face.

The Capricorn rising walk can be a clipped 'trot' in its sound down an echoing hallway. Physically, it looks a bit like a prance, with the knee leading the body and lifting up clearly before the foot steps down. Natives with this type of walk are frequently as businesslike, organized and intent on overt control of life circumstances as the brisk, sharp clip of the walk implies—never mind that it may be attached to a pint-sized woman, all of seven stone.

All throughout this sign are natives who are definite, emphatic and ultra-pragmatic. Some can drum in points incessantly. There are also shyer, softer, more sensitive Capricorn rising types, ultra-responsible, who are quite Saturnine in their own way—shy, nearly silent, soft-spoken when they do speak, and serious in demeanour.

Capricorn rising is one of the zodiac's 'pointers'. The 'points' move repeatedly down, down, down to tick off points in their speech at a rat-a-tat-tat pace. The voice may have a hard, dry edge and can sometimes go monotone. The speech can carry conviction, but does not feature emotional inflection.

Every now and then, a Capricorn rising native has a true comic gift, which is often accomplished by caricature or mime, where sharp, definite movements are a plus (Saturn) and the body is well-equipped for the task. Saturn also figures in strongly with dead-pan humour and with one-liners marathon style. Serious or all for fun, with these natives, you'll always get the point!

Aquarius

Mode: Fixed   *Element*: Air   *Rulers*: Saturn, Uranus

In an ironic twist of astrological reputation-building, Aquarius, probably the most *impersonal* of all the signs—detached Air, cool Saturn and the reserve of Fixity—is known as the most 'friendly'. It is true, however, that the sign lacks bias against individuals for personal reasons, and provides an impersonality, or true *impartiality* in human concerns.

Aquarius rising is both the individualist and the group participant *par excellence*. Its forte is principle (Fixed air), and it is perennially in the 'testing' mode of existence. These 'question shooters' accept little at face value. They are admirably suited to some areas of science, are the 'rule bearers' in social settings, and the sign runs the full gamut from fascinating experimenters to people who will make friends with (reasonably) anyone, to reactionary dogmatists. Their key concern in whatever context, is what is 'fair' and what is 'right'. Even if the native is not particularly intellectual, reason and rational explanation are Aquarius rising's bread and butter. Ironically—to complete the loop—they do actually wind up 'friendlier', in that they don't allow emotional partialities to cloud their perspective on matters of common interest.

Crisp, clear-minded Aquarius often comes across as the most 'together' looking sign of the zodiac. Its natives almost always carry themselves well. The body lines are long for Air, and Uranus rulership gives severe, clean-cut angles to the body. The upright Aquarian walk leads from the calf (which Aquarius rules) like the clean, clear sweep of a broom—Aquarius walking down the street can look very much 'above it all'. The complexion tends to be clear (sometimes porcelain fair), and the straight, fine hair falls evenly over the angular, erect head. Many of its natives are thin, and even those with high Saturnian shoulders are balanced by narrow hips.

The 'shoulder pads' look was designed for an Aquarian woman's build to accentuate its height and erect carriage, and some Aquarian women wear their hair pinned high and straight on each side to further accentuate the angular lines.

The Uranian component of Aquarius rising is often dominant in the build: the square stretched up to a rectangle with the tension at the top. The sculptured-looking head is neither too large nor small, with a prominent angle near the back, and a flat forehead. The upper back is elongated (from the breastline to the shoulder), with a tension (sometimes rigidity) holding the body erect. The very high, wide-set Aquarian (Uranian) cheekbones gives the face a sculptured cast as well.

The calf tends to be placed high on the smooth, narrow lower leg. These natives move with surety, and the arms swing in a brisk, clear, definite motion, controlled in pace, with a straight-legged rhythmic walk.

The nose looks sculptured as well: medium-sized, straight down, and then 'chiselled in' slightly on a diagonal. The eyes not infrequently look Asian, and may crinkle when the native smiles. They are more often than not blue as is the hair sandy or blond if genetics permit the choice.

The voice timbre is high and rich, and the voice carries authority. Early Aquarius can be a bit *loud*, and they are sometimes delegated the job of keeping order just by that virtue! Some Aquarius rising women have beautiful singing voices—usually a rich soprano. (Lower-pitched, throaty Taurus sports more pop singers, as well as classical and other vocalists.) Aquarius rising may be too structured for pop art, in any case, perhaps with a few exceptions. The Aquarius rising speaking voice can go quite shrill under pressure.

Aquarius may appear brusque or stiff, especially on first contact. But if you give these people a good opening and a break, they are more than likely to respond in kind! Sometimes their altruism— rugged, detached, individualistic in style— exceeds anyone's.

Pisces

Mode: Mutable   *Element*: Water   *Rulers*: Jupiter, Neptune

Pisces is the most people-oriented of all the signs, both because Mutability accommodates to shifting human concerns, and because the Water element facilitates people blending in with one another emotionally and socially. The Jupiter rulership of Pisces gives the sign compassion, tolerance, receptivity and a gregarious nature.

This doesn't mean that every Pisces rising native will be friendly, but when they feel constrained to relate emotionally, it is more keenly frustrating to them than to any other rising sign. Many Pisces rising natives feel they very nearly cannot function without companion- ship—that even problem-ridden companionship is better than no companionship at all.

These natives are rarely tall, and they tend to retain water weight. The body is often drop-shaped, a shape that is repeated many times over the body. The forehead narrows in, sometimes also sloping back in a very amorphous, watery way. The relatively narrow forehead widens below the eyeline, into an amorphous jaw, wide bite, and sometimes a double chin. The head size can be very large for this type Pisces rising, even though the top of the head is 'narrow' within the overall proportions.

The torso features sloping shoulders on top, with concentrations of jelly-like weight on different parts of the body which seem to hang low, so one can find distortions like a weight concentration near the native's *elbow* in an obese native, weight low in the buttocks, or a heavy calf very low on the leg. Speaking of calves, the basic bodily 'shapes' for Aquarius and Pisces is so utterly different (one 'pushed up', the other 'sinking down'), that frequently it is very easy to dis- tinguish between these two adjacent signs for an uncertain birth time.

Some Pisces natives will be flat all the down the back and buttocks—a Watery characteristic—but they will tend to have a broadness across the buttocks (Mutability) which even heavy Cancer or Scorpio rising natives will lack.

You sometimes find a 'pin-shaped' head leaning slightly forwards. The hair tends to be wavy and is definitely a candidate for 'the most unruly hair in the zodiac'. The skin may be pasty pale, with very light eyes, the favoured colours being pale blue, bluish green, or colours that change readily in the light (Neptune rulership). The eyes are set close together, even when the face is quite large as a whole, with a nose that may be quite large but it starts with a narrow bridge and swoops down towards and over the mouth, commonly enough the proverbial 'fish mouth'. You find many large 'fish eyes' as well, despite the closeness of the set.

You also find some fine-featured natives with this sign, usually in the latter part, but they still have the Mutable characteristic of the features being drawn towards the centre of the face.

Some speech patterns are characteristic. First, they are often very talkative, especially about people and subjects of human interest. The emotions readily surface, and you see a lot of reactiveness, sometimes overreactiveness. The voice may be very inflective, sliding up and down, and words may be stretched out into extra syllables. For example, an Aries rising native (the greatest contrast) might say declaratively, 'You can go if you want', period. Pisces would say, 'You can go-o if you want too-oo', with the 'go-o' and the 'want too-oo' beginning on a high pitch and descending down in tones. The voice timbre itself is not even, but features 'cracks' in the voice, partly due to continual fluctuation in emphasis and inflection.

Other Pisces rising natives are very soft-spoken (Water), careful in how they approach others, sometimes hesistant, always aware of the response, always aware if there is any offence given or taken.

These natives are, on the whole, not decisive, and they may endlessly weigh various ramifications before arriving at decisions. Even then, they are more likely to be led by emotional reasons rather than pragmatic ones. The emotional impressions are strong and stay with the native, even though the memory for hard facts may suffer.

The hand motions get scattery under stress, as does the whole person. Many issues become emotionalized that had not begun that way. The two most overtly overreactive signs are Pisces and Sagittarius, but Sagittarius goes into speech-making to let out emotional stress, whereas Pisces just lets loose with a free-for-all emotional binge (with some, an eating binge as well). But being openly emotional is natural and healthy for this sign, and it is especially sad to see a Pisces rising person who has clammed up because they feel that there is no-one left that they can trust.

Common with Pisces rising is low-set 'stick-out' ears, and double chins for the heavier natives. The hands may be pudgy, and the feet are generally quite small. The walk is flat-footed, sometimes toddling, sometimes mincing or swivelled.

17.
WORKING WITH COMPOSITES

This is the most interesting and challenging part of ascendant identification. It is helpful when the native is stereotypical enough of one ascendant to determine that with relative certainty and then figure out the modifications. But that might not be immediately apparent, because sign and planetary identifications may resemble one another, such as a prominent Jupiter and Jupiter-ruled Sagittarius rising. However, when you work with the chart as a whole, and locate the effects of a *composite* of prominent visible factors in the chart, all the pieces will 'fit'.

There are endless possible combinations, making every chart a learning experience.

Adjusting by Prominent Planets

One native seemed an apparent case of Pisces rising, at least apparent enough to prefer it over any other sign. She had a pursed mouth, convex face and low cheekbones, which could be either Pisces or Virgo. But the jaw-line was undefined, there was weight concentration in the hips, the head tended towards a pin-head shape and, especially, the voice and emotional temperament were stereotypical. This was an emotionally-deferring person, who overtly weighed ramifications and responses from others, was kindly unless pushed too far, and had a voice with sliding inflections up and down the scale.

I still suspected there was a Virgo planet in the works, though, and when I looked up the birth date, was not surprised to find *Saturn* in Virgo, expressed physiologically in very flat cheeks and lack of colour in the face and temperamentally, by a serious demeanour. Unfortunately, however, this wasn't all that helpful in narrowing down the birth time, since the Virgo planet, Saturn, was at 29 degrees of the sign, i.e. any ascendant from 0–29 Pisces will put the Saturn

solidly in the seventh house, since the seventh house with Pisces rising
will be wide—in the native's case, a sign-and-a-half wide.

However, other modifications in the native's appearance had to
be accounted for. I looked at the feet. *Large*. That isn't Pisces at all,
but it *could* be the next successive sign, Aries. (It might have been
a Sagittarian planet on the MC as well—not as likely as a rising planet,
but both Aries and Sagittarius sport large feet.) The ephemeris showed
Jupiter at 14 Aries.

The rising Jupiter did show up by its placement by *sign*, note.
The feet were Arian, large and pointed out, and the walk took on
an Arian modification as well, a touch of a straightforward march.
But the Jupiter also showed up as a *planetary* influence.

The way Jupiterian influence showed up was in a modification
of the head shape, narrow up and down and narrow from front to
back. It wasn't a 'perfect' case, in that the head was still somewhat
pin-head shaped, but such 'crosses' are expectable. The composite
of Pisces and Jupiter told the story.

Now with the wide first house of Pisces rising (in the northern
latitudes; Virgo rising gives a wide first house in the southern
latitudes), perhaps anything could have been rising from 0 to 29 Pisces!
Any setting along the way would give both Jupiter rising and Saturn
in the seventh with these particular planetary placements. I would
caution that if the effect of the angular planets is as obvious as it
was with this native, they are probably *not* a whole sign away from
the ascendant, even with a wide first house. But in principle, we
still have quite a wide range left.

Luckily, there were other Virgo planets, Mercury at 10 Virgo and
Venus at nearly 18 Virgo. So we begin moving the seventh cusp
backwards from 29 Virgo, the location of the visible Saturn, to see
how far back we can go before 'bumping into' another Virgo planet,
which will be Venus at 18 Virgo. If that Venus is visible, it should
be within three degrees of the seventh cusp—to be on the safe side,
five, since judgements are relative. If it is *at least as* visible as Saturn
in a later degree in the sign, then the Venus would be into the seventh
house.

Upon observing the native, Venus was not visible at all—not in
features, not in build, not in manner or voice or bodily motions.
The chart was thus narrowed down to between 23 and 29 Pisces rising,
with very satisfactory final results. The given birth time had been
very approximate—'6 p.m.'—landing the astrologer into a rising sign
of Capricorn, which the native, despite a couple of subsidiary

Saturnine traits, positively did not fit.
Figure 36 illustrates the adjustment.

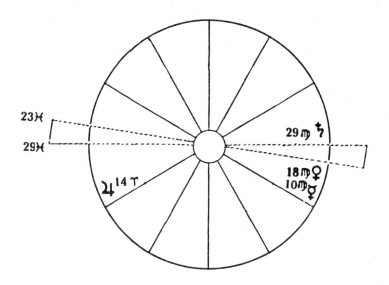

Figure 36.   Adjusting by a Composite

Birth Times an Hour Apart
The second example is clarification of the differences between the
two hypothetical chart settings used for 'The Many Types of Spatial
Difference', Figure 6A and B, p. 50.

    The most obvious difference between the charts is that chart A
has Scorpio rising and chart B has Sagittarius rising. The chart A
native is likely heavier, with a compact build, square jaw, large intense
eyes, slow, definite hand motions, a rounded voice, and so on. The
chart B native is likely loose-limbed with a long waist, perhaps an
off-centre stance when at ease, a thinner face with a wide bite, a
narrower head, a more offhand manner than the chart A native, and
so on. These may not be the exact differences between the natives,
or there may be others not mentioned; in any case, you are likely
to have enough 'clues' to make some initial determination if the
choice is between two adjacent rising signs.

    With these *particular* two charts, the job is simplified, since the
respective *composite* pictures between the two charts gives an even

wider margin for discrimination than the two different rising signs alone.

First, chart A features Jupiter rising in Scorpio *and* an exact trine from the ascendant at 19 Scorpio to the Moon at 19 Cancer. This is a feeling, expressive, responsive person, notwithstanding the Scorpionic reserve, probably quite 'Watery' in build—fleshy; large, expressive eyes; short limbs; pudgy hands—and the native is much more likely to be heavy, with Jupiter tending to expand the body size, and the Watery Moon trining the ascendant increasing the tendency towards water retention.

This native is also likely to be sure of himself emotionally. He relates from his feelings, his instincts, and is a keen observer of human nature. This person submerges himself into living, readily establishes rapport with others and, likely, gives reassurance to all with whom he is emotionally close.

Note now that Uranus is also nearly culminating. The native is likely to have striking body lines—angular shoulders or high cheekbones and, with the expansive/dramatic composite of Leo/Scorpio/Jupiter/Uranus perhaps a sweeping, overbearing manner. This is an 'imposing presence'.

Chart B's planets, note, are in the same zodiacal locations as chart A's, but are positioned differently within the chart. For example, this may still be a deep-feeling, compassionate human being, with the Moon/Jupiter trine in Water signs, but that is not what surfaces to the observer. His chart picks up a rising Saturn rather than a rising Jupiter—in many ways, an 'opposite' influence. Harsh, sudden, electric Uranus is replaced by unemotional, matter-of-fact Mercury on the midheaven of the chart. The Fixity of chart A—Fixed sign rising, and rising and culminating planets in Fixed signs—is supplanted by Mutability on all counts for chart B.

Chart B shows someone outwardly more structured than chart A. A uses large, broad, spacious hand motions to project great thrusts of emotional energy. Chart B shows someone less intense emotionally (even muted, from the rising Saturn), and more scrutinizing and reserved in manner. The bodily movements will be definite and controlled from the rising Saturn, with culminating Mercury in ultra-particular Virgo focusing in on the dominance of details—their descriptions, their ordering, their priority. You can talk brass tacks with the chart B native without much emotional rapport at all and he may still be very involved. With the chart A native, you would be likely to feel swept into the native's presence and approach

WORKING WITH COMPOSITES   263

everything from a much more subjective context. This native functions on a broad scale (Jupiter/Uranus/Fixed signs) in close attunement and receptivity with the emotional environment (Water/Moon/Jupiter). This native may bank on making a major impression before a thought is even formulated, much less uttered.

Chart B's outer orientation, by contrast, is mental/intellectual (Mercury in Virgo culminating square scrutinizing rising Saturn): 'Meet me, meet my mind.' This chart approaches life as a specialist (Mutability to the fore, Mercury in Virgo square fact-oriented Saturn).

Chart B will also reflect the angular planets and their mode (the same as the rising sign, Sagittarius) in the physiology. The face is likely to be quite Mutable-looking: features drawn closely towards the centre of the face; a long but not very large head; short, descriptive hand motions; a loose-limbed physical co-ordination; and, combining a prominent Mercury with Sagittarian influence, a long-waisted build. Although Sagittarius ascends, this native is likely to be of only average height, since Saturn is rising in the first house (plus *early* Sagittarius doesn't tend towards great height); but the shortness might well come because of shortness in the legs, and this may accentuate the long-waistedness that the Mercury/Sagittarius composite is likely to give. The native will probably not be heavy, either; early Sagittarius is sometimes rotund, but both the rising Saturn and culminating Mercury contraindicate.

This native is a little self-conscious in his demeanour (native A, no!) with the rising Saturn (Mercury in Virgo takes care as well), dressing with care, speaking with care, relating to life with a structured caution. This native wants to know *exactly* what he is getting into before proceeding ahead.

The chart B native may show other rising Saturn characteristics: flattened-down cheeks, wide-set bulbous eyes, pale skin, and so on. The culminating Mercury might offset by drawing the eyes closer together, or it may restore some of Sagittarius' loose-limbed agility that Saturn might have restricted. But every movement will still be *directed*—the open, sometimes chaotic gesturing of other Sagittarians is probably out.

Note the aspecting of the two charts internally is the *same*. Chart A still has the Mercury/Saturn square, for instance; and with Saturn in the second house, squared by Mercury and quincunx Pluto, this native might be known to pinch a penny. But that does not come into the bodily form, nor into the outward projection of the person.

These two hypothetical natives, born just an hour apart, are genuinely 'two completely different people'—physically, in their emotional and intellectual expression, in their anchors of functioning, in how they look, in the impression they make, in what they seek from others. Working with composites will guarantee that two so dissimilar as this may never be confused!

PART FIVE:
LISTENING TO THE NATIVE—
A GUIDE TO SKILLED
INFORMATION-GATHERING

18.
THE ASTROLOGER AS TRANSLATOR

Translating Biographical Information into Astrological Analogues
It is harder to 'see' a chart's timing at a glance than it is to see its
space (as perhaps the many lists and diagrams of the METHODS
section were sufficient to convince). But we do have skills available
to clarify timing that parallel the visual and other observational skills
detailed in Part Four. They entail *learning how to listen*. The following
will detail information-gathering skills, in the conversational context
which characterizes much astrological work.

There is considerable current emphasis upon counselling. However,
although some newer books focus upon establishing rapport with
the native and conveying our findings in language that 'he can
understand', there is little guidance on how to listen to the native;
and moreover, how to translate his input into its astrological
analogues. The implicit assumption is that *we* have something to
tell *him*. What of what *he* has to tell *us*? If we don't know how to
'read' both his physical person and his own recounting of his life,
we might just as well counsel from an isolation booth as in a one-to-
one session.

Astrologers are translators. Just as we have begun translating
between the native's physical person and the space of his natal chart,
we will begin translating between his own life story and the timing
of his chart.

Astrologers usually relate to clients and friends *conversationally*.
Now someone isn't going to tell you, 'Listen to this piece of
information about my life; it describes a certain *transit*. Now this
next bit of detail is about how *progressions* happened to me . . .,'
and so on. He just talks about 'my life'. The astrologer has to make
the appropriate translations as he speaks, based upon whatever
information is offered.

We have already examined structural models giving a unitary

framework within which natal, progressed and transiting positions co-function, and practised reading them (the partials and sequences) as if out of a book, or as a script reads line by line from a movie. When we looked at several patterns taken together for one event, it was like the finished movie of parts of the life story, each partial or continuing sequence filling in further details. We could use those methods for a sophisticated astrological rendition of the native's life because we made rather thorough use of our technical tools. We worked with an already-rectified chart, so everything worked.

But where we might have actually begun, of course, is in some kind of conversation with the native about his life, to glean 'pointers' towards that true timing. In fact, we could have begun learning rectification at this point, rather than through technical considerations; it would have been an interesting approach and not lead us astray. However, we would have then gleaned information without tools to make use of what we found. Now we are in a position to glean information conversationally from the native, and have working models of how that would show up in graphic representations, enabling us to make 'running translations' in some depth, even initially.

In any case, the approach to come is as important as any technical piecing-together of figures. Your contact point is always the *native*; the chart without the native is meaningless. Astrology is no more than life itself; its structure, based in natural law, can do no more nor less than define the current and directions of real life experience. A rendition of experience from anyone (be it only accurate) is as valuable as any figure from an ephemeris. The fact is, that neither those figures nor the life's details make astrological sense at all until we piece together that synchronization point—the birth moment— which makes sense out of the two (i.e. life itself and 'the mathematics of life', astrology) inseparably.

We have already explored the technical, graphic end of the translation process which 'spells out' life. Now we will explore the face-to-face encounters with the native, its many forms and expressions of spoken language within which we will trustfully find the *astrology* spelled out therein.

Life Itself Happens Whole
A most frustrating facet of information-gathering is that no matter how skillfully the astrologer has broken down the assorted progressions, transits, aspects, cusps and so on, the native will simply

tell you *what happened to him*! Somehow, amidst the bewildering continuum of all the transits, all the progressions and their continuously-shifting interrelationships with the natal chart, they have all congealed together *somehow*, or nothing definite would have happened at all. So we hear about when he married, when he left school, when he got his current job, when he purchased a new home and so on through the many definite circumstantial changes of the life. The astrologer may be awash in computer print-outs or struggling with diverse philosophical and psychological ramifications of some transit or progression not to mention having to locate which of the many, many planetary and cuspal figures at hand are relevant to all this. Meanwhile, the native's life still apparently . . . well, it just 'happens'. Doesn't this tell us something?

What it tells us foremost is that sometimes we approach astrology from the wrong end, so to speak. Perhaps we are not here to 'break astrology down' and paste it onto the bits and pieces of a human life. Perhaps our job is to discover life's *natural* structure, sequence and priorities (as related by the native), and simultaneously discover that same unified reality in the astrological chart, i.e. to use real life experience—not an arbitrary layout of planetary positions—as the springboard into the 'translation' process. For alas, that reality is apparently *already* whole, so must contain the keys to the structural unity we seek.

There is something to be said about the pacing of the rectification process as well. If you don't allow yourself to acquire a grasp of a person's characteristic patterns, in speech, in mannerisms, in characteristic types of experience, you are more liable to have difficulty zeroing in on the chart's correct setting. It is like the simple experience that the better you know someone, the better position you are in to know the meaning of their experience, its context, the patterns of reality that are its substructure. Your initial information-gathering time is prime time to absorb the whole native, and to allow the connections between your observations, what the native says and your examination of the chart's possible settings to congeal into plausible, viable patterning.

Life in Capsule Form: Astrology versus Speech

We will begin by assuming that somehow the structure of life—its highlights, directedness, intensities, emphases, relative priorities and sequences—is *already described by the astrology of the accurate chart*. We have but to discover it.

Our discovery process in relation to the *astrology* happens in many diverse (however interrelated) parts. We have now had some practice in capsulizing them and organizing their syntax graphically, without sacrificing any of the component parts. Specifically at the time of major junctures in the life, multiple convergence with its many different orders of aspects enabled us to put 'what happened to me' into a capsule form. Usually some longer progression 'sets the tone' for an entire period, and the transits set off something specific of that character, defining its exact details, something like a bit of kindling igniting an entire bonfire. The result may have been a few partials, to 'spell out' the lead-in, the context, the framework within which an event was 'lined up to happen', as it were.

However, when people talk about their lives, they will most often convey the surface reality, not the gradual, subtle or pervasive ways in which they got there. You may see a couple of graphic partials at a glance, but take a while to sort out their ten or twelve components, some immediate (the rapid transits), some a while in coming (the longer progressions), some a matter of predisposition (natal planets and cusps). When people talk about their lives, many of these pieces are unstated, or assumed by the native but not expressed in his speech.

For instance, you might hear, 'That's the month I met Sally, and we were married'. That kind of statement, a simple 'what happened' kind of statement usually leaves a lot of 'background' out from the astrologer's point of view. What the native might have said, as a more complete picture of 'what happened' is something like 'I was in a state of receptivity to relate, which attracted harmonious ties of a romantic character and then, right about that time I met Sally and we were married'.

The astrologer looking at the native's natal and progressed chart, along with the transits of the meeting date, might be looking at, let's say, progressed seventh cusp conjunct natal Venus, which describes the unstated *basis* of the experience, which was, 'I was in a state of receptivity to attract a romance', without necessarily adding, 'I met Sally' at all.

For the native, 'I met Sally' sums it up. For the astrologer, the capsule has to include the underlying preparation, or time period within which 'I met Sally' was free to happen. A few free-floating transits won't bring a meeting that leads to marriage. The native did tell you 'what happened', and, as is common, you were told about the transits and their effect, with the rest assumed or submerged— in effect, 'missing'. Yet if those other components were *really* missing (i.e. the major progression involving the seventh cusp), then meeting Sally and its leading to marriage would have been an *unlikely* event rather than a *likely* one. Rule 7, 'Different Orders of Aspects Simultaneously' isn't just a rule; it is part of the way time coheres to make material changes possible. We move into a general state, then into a more specific state, and then whatever transits hit the chart, they are genuinely 'effective' because the pathway has been defined. It is something like having to be in England before you can go to London, or in the United States before you are able to visit New York.

The native is our main compass, being the only one who can lead us right to the mark: 'It happened *then*, 9 August 1974'. Yet that exact point in time is often also like the proverbial tip of the iceberg. You're not getting all the ready information you need; you find out the surface, the 'what happened' part without any clue as to the background astrology that facilitated and more fully described that happening.

When this happens, you can often refer to the astrology you see against the chart you are testing and say, 'The astrology suggests that. . .,' or 'Would you characterize it as. . .,' and see if the native agrees with what the astrology of that time spells out. That is one excellent way to elicit information, especially in regard to the effects of *transits*, which are immediate in their impact.

In this section, however, we will focus upon just listening to the native, and how many probable astrological correlations may be drawn before one even refers to the ephemeris or the chart. Indeed, without astute listening as a matter of course, tons of invaluable information strewn in the astrologer's path could be inadvertently disregarded. So let us put aside our 'working tools' for a while, for the purpose of strengthening equally vital working tools: our own faculties of perception.

The Structure of Time as Expressed in Ordinary Speech

The many examples of life experience about to be described in conversational context will all be familiar, even if they bear unfamiliar labels: Time Levels, Co-existent Time, Quantitative Time, Contextual Time, Qualitative Time, Objective Time. Labels are simply a way of clueing you in to the tangible astrological structure which underlies some statement about what has happened in the life. 'Contextual Time', for example, simply refers to what the native is telling you being embedded in a larger context of events, which have their own respective astrological markers. If you know the timing of what came before and what came after, it will assist you in 'finding your place'.

The key purpose of this section is to master information-gathering skills in the context of face-to-face contact. The more ways you have to match up descriptions of life events with exact astrological positions that you can measure and manipulate, the easier it will be to locate the true chart rapidly and accurately. We all experience reality in structured, patterned forms that correlate with astrological configurations. Though everyone's manner of expression may vary, the structural components of astrology's workings in the life tend to be embedded in the speech, and we want to have as many means as possible to draw them out.

In a sense, we are about to play 'astrological detective' with our aural observations much as we did with our visual ones, such as 'She's talking about *depression*—I'm looking for *Saturn*—Yes, there's transiting Saturn exactly conjunct the progressed ascendant'. Every such clue can bring us closer to confirmation of the birth chart.

Working with Equivalencies
Much of skilled information-gathering rests in knowing how to draw simple translative equivalencies between what is said and its astrological analogues. It is true that no life situation is exactly like any other, nor are its astrological representations exactly the same, but there are 'classes' of experience (cataclysms or opportunities, disappointments or breakthroughs), areas of experience (relationships, family matters, education or self-expression), the consideration of *how* something happens (rapidly, gradually, shockingly or gently), and its effects upon the native (startling, taken in stride, encouraging or hurtful), all of which enable the astrologer to gain a plausible, sometimes surprisingly exact idea of what to look for in the astrology as the native speaks.

Not everyone will convey the details of their life with equal depth or equal objectivity. The mind may 'edit' past events, or 'forget' their more important components. Some people will emphasize the emotional effects of events and be vague about what actually happened. Others will be crystal-clear about dates and details, but volunteer little about surrounding circumstances or contexts. (The astrologer should also never underestimate how much can be learned about the *natal* chart by these various predilections!) For the moment, we will disregard individual differences, and practise drawing equivalencies from many simple, common examples of how information might be conveyed from native to astrologer via speech.

There are three primary, ready means to draw rapid and plausible equivalencies between information given and its corresponding astrology. They correspond to house cusps, planets and aspects.

House cusps show the circumstances of life, or the areas of life in which an event occurs. For instance, if you are told of a change in career, it will necessarily involve the midheaven (tenth house cusp). A change of residence will involve the fourth cusp. An illness will involve the sixth cusp of health, but it will also involve the ascendant because the native is personally affected. It could involve the eighth if the native is talking about surgery, certainly the twelfth for hospitalization, and the fourth if life-threatening.

Planets show the character of what happens, impacting, of course, upon whatever house cusp is affected. For instance, if you are told about injury, anger, haste, aggressive new starts or feverish illness, you would be 'hearing the native talk about Mars'. Jupiter would be spelled out by opportunities, friendships, monetary gain, good times. When hearing of hardship or denial, discipline, responsibility, or stable, pragmatic endeavours, Saturn will not be far off.

We can already experiment with rudimentary combinations of house cusps and planets: an injury (Mars) to the body (ascendant); an opportunity (Jupiter) for the career (tenth cusp); a foreclosure (Saturn) on a home (fourth cusp), and so on.

Aspects show the energy form in which the event arrives. If the native is relating a cut-off (of funds, of employment, of a human life, and so on), look for one or more prominently-placed squares. Periods of stress will be marked by quincunxes, as will illnesses. Conjunctions intensify and bring matters to a head. Oppositions block off or polarize. Trines and sextiles ease and facilitate.

We are omitting *time* equivalencies (how *long* each action or circumstance is in effect), but as we will see, we can pick much of this up in context.

Let's begin with a few simple happenings in the life, and the kinds of astrological associations that could be useful.

'The illness developed gradually, and I thought I was holding my own, but suddenly found myself landed in hospital.'
    The illness probably registered in one or more prominently-placed *quincunxes*, perhaps involving the natal or progressed *sixth cusp*, but possibly also the *ascendant*. Find out what 'gradually' means—

two months, six months, a year. That could clue you in to some *slow-moving progression* at work. The sudden turn for the worse might well feature transiting *Uranus*. Also, an illness of a chronic nature might prominently feature *Saturn*.

'A couple of years after my daughter left home, I took a class and discovered I could paint. To my amazement and delight, it began a new career for me. I felt like I could express myself freely for the first time in my life.'

This glowing commentary could well be marked by a major progression involving an angle and natal or progressed *Sun*, as the whole sense of identity and life work was affected. The ascendant has to be strongly involved; possibly the fifth cusp for creative endeavours as well, but most certainly the ascendant. The 'freedom' the native described could be marked by Jupiter, possibly Uranus in very harmonious aspect, or it could be *Chiron* as well, which brings novel, alternative twists to the life and new understanding of one's capabilities.

Note, an underlying assumption in this *may* be that it was the first opportunity for the native to establish a career outside the home after many years at home raising children, though don't assume that. If there were strong career opportunities earlier in life, you might have some parallel astrological configurations to work with.

For specific involvement as an *artist*, and the great self-fulfilment to the native, check Venus. Check Neptune as well for artistic pursuits and idealistic/spiritual endeavours of all types.

'We didn't have any money when we married, so it was hard, but otherwise we were happy.'

Find out if 'not having money' was a usual circumstance for this native, or if it was perceived as a special hardship at the time of marriage. It may be reflected in a Saturn affliction at the time of marriage. If things were generally circumstantially inconvenient, it might show in an aspect of the progressed Moon. 'Happiness' is frequently shown through Jupiter or Venus, but don't rule out the Moon (comfort, security) or even Mars (enthusiasm, motivation).

'London wasn't that far away, but I had never lived away from home before and came from a small village, so it was a very big change all round'.

With someone else's chart, a trip to London might be an everyday third house matter. But for this native, it was a relocation, coming under ninth house rulership. Check the natal and progressed ninth cusp, but also check the ascendant for personal changes. The progressed Moon is likely involved as well, since the entire climate of life changed at once. Other changes in the life (job, relationships, money and so on) can be specified.

'I was extremely discouraged at that point. . .'

Sometimes this means that difficult afflictions have been hanging on for some time, such as transits from the outer planets in long-range affliction to angles. Discouragement *per se* can be Saturn, when persistent effort is unproductive or things never seem to get off the ground. Neptune can discourage as well, out of confusion, unfair treatment, being ill-suited to one's life circumstances, or the feeling that life is going in circles. Pluto in affliction or by conjunction can be discouraging in an oppressive kind of way, feeling there is too much going against one and it may be impossible to burrow out.

'There was a period of a year or so there when I had to make several trips overseas for business. That really disrupted my home life.'

Since both business (tenth cusp) and the home (fourth cusp) are involved, you would have to find strong aspecting involving the meridian, natal and/or progressed. A square might be a good bet, because 'disruption' was cited, and a major progression since the time period of a year was cited. The ninth cusp would be integrally involved for the trips. Get as many dates of departure as possible; but also remember that there might have been seven or eight of them, and maybe it was *one* that was significantly 'disruptive'. Also check *Uranus* when 'disruption' is cited.

What is also possible here, depending upon the native's age at the time, is the ninth house cusp might have progressed to the tenth, meaning that any affliction would simultaneously involve the natal tenth and the progressed ninth.

'I won a scholarship I didn't expect to get. It opened up a whole new world for me.'

Uranus might well be involved with an unexpected occurrence, but be sure that's in harmonious aspect in this case. Check the third/ninth axis for education, the ascendant for its happy effect upon the native, and the tenth for overall improvement in life standing. Jupiter might well show up for both money and the boost in morale, and even Saturn in harmonious aspect if it had the effect of stabilizing the life and making long-range goals possible. Also look for *Chiron*, which opens many a special door in the life.

Also note that there will usually be a time gap between when the scholarship was received and when the native actually began schooling, so this might be 'an event that happened in stages'.

'I don't think I was ever told the truth about . . .'

If this statement refers to a specific *event* in the life, get the date of the event and look for the position of *Neptune*. If it refers to a permanent situation (such as, 'I don't think I was ever told the truth about my parents'), check the position of Neptune in the natal chart. Also check the aspecting for the time when it occurred to the native he was being kept in the dark, if that happened at some specific point.

19.
THE MANY GUISES OF TIME

Time Levels

The remainder of this section will explore how time is spontaneously portrayed in many 'modes': by its context; by its various modes of action; by its objective and subjective components; by its exact designation by date; by its emotional colouring; by its technical components.

'Time', for our purposes here, is a general equivalent for *experience*. Experience happens in time; the astrologer gauges that experience through the timing of the chart, much as we have been gauging the physical native through the chart's space.

'Time levels' means concurrent levels of experience at some specific time, usually a date in the life which marked major change. The levels are often marked off by different orders of aspects—natal, progressed, transiting—though this guide is only general, since most aspects will be *between* orders of planets and cusps, such as a progressed or transiting planet to a natal cusp.

'Levels' also implies a stacking-up, something like a double-decker (or triple-decker) bus, where different things may be happening on each level, yet all are part of the same unit in transit at the same location. The tri-circled model, used for partials, conveyed that stacking-up in a circular format. Whatever were the many parts of that three-tiered picture, in the native's perception, it happened all-at-once, like, 'That's the day my big brother left home'. Whatever progressions and transits, with their differing time frames contributed to that event, the experience was, to the native, unitary. Oddly enough, ordinary speech can reflect that remarkably directly, as in, 'There were many "aspects" to that (one) experience'!

A few examples with dramatic contrast will accentuate the point. We have all at times experienced conflicting emotions: sadness and depression along with acute pain, or shock side-by-side with relief. With the former, we might find Saturn (depression or sadness) in some prominently-placed aspect concurrent with a prominently-placed aspect of Mars (acute pain). Let's say now that both the Saturn aspect and the Mars aspect become partile at the same time; thus one experiences *both*.

With the example of shock side-by-side with relief, we might well find a Uranus affliction (shock) coming partile concurrent with Jupiter in harmonious aspect (relief).

Such concurrences—even when the character of the two 'levels' is apparently conflicting, such as 'shock' and 'relief'—happen repeatedly in our lives, hence have corresponding astrological analogues. We perceive it as simply complex or conflicting levels of experience. Astrology facilitates specific identification of the separate (though co-functioning) *components* of our experience, and to read its referential meaning as out of a book: 'Here is where you were depressed' (pointing perhaps to a transiting *Saturn* square progressed ascendant); 'here is where you were angry' (pointing perhaps to a progressed *Mars* quincunx the natal ascendant).

Note here that Saturn was transiting and Mars was progressed, i.e. the transit showed some *current* situation, whereas the progression inferred a situation which was of course 'current' as well, but covering a longer time period, since the duration of the progression would be considerably longer than that of the transit.

So we have an immediate, Saturnine experience within the context of a larger, Martial framework. On one 'level', we experienced Saturn; on another 'level', we experienced Mars.

Understanding that time happens on different 'levels' can make it possible to work with astrology selectively *as the native speaks*. For example, say someone tells you, 'That whole year was nothing but upheaval, some of it good, some of it bad'. Ignore for the moment that you may be 'enlightened' and don't like the words 'good' and 'bad'; perhaps even be grateful that your client is simply being definitive, because that will make it easier for you to find the corresponding astrology!

'The whole year was upheaval' tells you that some major progression was in play, and anything strong enough to badly upset the life will be registered through the chart's *angles*. Don't neglect the *fourth* cusp here—that isn't just the home, it's the basis of one's life, and major upsets frequently register against it. In any case look for some progression that takes at least a year—a progressed angle to a natal planet, progressed planet to natal angle.

That takes care of the 'whole year' part. For 'upheaval', most often one is talking about *Uranus*. (Pluto can be enormously disturbing, and Chiron thrust one into very unfamiliar straits; but most frequently, 'upheaval' has a Uranus component.) Uranus moves so slowly by progression, it probably was not that. It may have been an angle progressed to affliction natal Uranus, though don't rule out a sextile or trine to the Uranus *in combination with* various concurrent afflictions which link all the points together. You do need to find a major affliction involving an angle, most likely the meridian, and you need to find prominent involvement of Uranus. There may be more than one way in which that can occur with the chart in question.

Uranus also moves slowly by transit, so possibly the native is referring to two different Uranus *stations* within a year (each station would be intense in its effect and last for many weeks), both afflicting key points in the chart. Yet that *alone* would be unlikely to produce, 'The whole year was nothing but upheaval'; you also want to find support with a major progression.

With 'some of it was good, some bad,' of course find out what happened specifically. But as a general model, 'good' (or easeful) will bring in sextiles and trines, and 'bad' (or stressful) will bring in squares, oppositions, conjunctions with malefics, or quincunxes. (Remember that quincunxes alone do not make for clean breaks.) The 'some of it good, some of it bad' may also clue you in to the major progression being a *conjunction* involving an angle, which would both intensify a transiting square ('bad') and also intensify the effects of a transiting trine ('good'). Try to obtain exact dates of some specific things of a dramatic character that happened during that period, which will test out with transits if you are looking at the correct major progression to describe that period of time.

Incidentally, don't have the slightest hesitation to use the older, so-called 'traditional' approach of 'good equals trines and sextiles' and 'bad equals squares, oppositions and malefics'. Whatever may be one's *attitudes* towards life experience, you will never specify its *character* without clear-cut application of specific aspects, specific planets and their time-proven effects.

This also means that if you are told philosophically, 'That was the most difficult year of my life, but I look back and I'm glad it all happened because I changed and grew so much', do give priority to locating '*the most difficult year*' part of the native's statement.

(Also note that if the native has a Saturn-ruled sign ascending, or Saturn or another reservation-prone influence is strong in the chart, the native may be very literal in his assessment of 'the most difficult' even if he conveys little emotion in the telling.) If that assessment is an accurate one, you will probably find *many* afflictions, including afflictions from transiting malefics—also check slow-moving Uranus, Neptune and Pluto. The very fact that an unusual amount of 'change and growth' occurred during a 'most difficult' period indicates that the chart was probably being walloped rather severely, since it knocked the native out of accustomed patterns.

In fact, you will do well, when you take any statement involving 'the most . . .' ('the most happy', 'the most challenging', 'the most exciting' and so on) as literally meaning that you might find 'the most' number of confirming appropriate aspects!

Co-existent Time

Time levels alone (transiting 'versus' progressed 'versus' natal) often do not tell the whole story. We often perceive life in what seems like separate if simultaneous ways. A common expression of this is 'feeling two different ways at once', without necessarily getting the feelings 'together'. There isn't necessarily conflict, but different types of response just seem to 'coexist' through the same circumstantial change in life.

An example might be, 'I felt very relieved when the divorce came through' (transiting Jupiter at 12 Scorpio trine the natal seventh at 12 Pisces), 'even though during that time period I felt personally shattered (progressed ascendant/seventh at 8 Leo-Aquarius square the natal Uranus at 8 Taurus). Note that the difference is defined through *degree numbers*. Also note that the astrology lines up two parallel responses within the same native, one for the *natal* seventh and one for the *progressed* seventh. Both factors are important to watch when you come on what seems like 'mixed reactions'.

The native has experienced one reaction, in effect, 'apart from' the other. The way major events are characteristically laid out, involving *many* major aspects (ten or twelve is not uncommon), this is found often enough. When the astrologer can separate out whole configurations at different degree numbers, let's say one at degree '15' and one at degree '21', clarifying their respective effects can be most helpful. A simple conversional approach will do, such as, 'The astrology seems to be saying two different things: both that you felt very shattered through that general period, but that at the specific time the divorce came through, you experienced personal relief.'

This particular technique has extended ramifications. Awareness of *degree numbers* enhances all rectification work. When you see many transits and progressions at degree '8' for some event, for example, look to see if there are also natal planets or cusps at '8' of whatever sign. Or if you see three natal planets at degree '16', then any year a progressed angle comes to that degree (in whatever sign) is likely to be a year of major change that you will want to enquire about. You may find that some charts are geared more than others to 'coexistent time' experiences because there are three planets all at degree '9' and two planets and a natal angle all at degree '14'.

When we consider that only very narrow orbs are effective in the *timing* of a chart, this will also make *very close* natal aspects far more important in terms of one's characteristic experience of life than those of, let's say, four degrees' orb.

Quantitative Time

Time levels and coexistent time both involve simultaneity of experience within the native. Other modes of time perception are simply an identification of where we are 'time-wise'. This includes *quantitative time* and *contextual time*.

Let's return to our old line, 'Where were you when . . .' If you are asked that, do you respond, 'Oh yes, that happened 22 July 1962 at 5.34 p.m. British Summer Time in London, didn't it?' How convenient that would be for your lucky astrologer! It is not too likely a response; but that rare gem is a *quantitative* assessment of time.

Some natives will be much more forthcoming in this respect than others. Some Pisces rising natives might remember every possible ramification of something that happened, for example, and then blank out totally on the date! Perhaps another native who has Mercury in Capricorn in the third trine Saturn (i.e. a retentive memory) and Scorpio rising (i.e. reticent) might meticulously provide all the requested dates from memory, but little else unless you ask. It is astonishing the range of responses one receives from the simple request to list the dates of major events along with descriptions of what happened. The rectifying astrologer, incidentally, should assess those responses in view of what they might indicate about the natal chart. The time spent gleaning information initially cannot be overestimated in terms of its value in observing both the physical native and the patterns of response. No-one, whoever they be, just gives the astrologer 'hard facts' about themselves. The living presence, the gestures, the gaze, the manner of speech, the type of information volunteered all become 'part of the job'.

Now, if you've come on a native where the particular problem seems to be recalling exact dates, there are many ways to gently jog the memory. 'Do you remember how *old* you were at the time?' is one, and often used for childhood events. 'Do you remember what *grade* you were going into?' 'What *time of year* was it?' 'You said you made *two* trips overseas—did this happen on the first trip or the second?'

Often, when you look at the requested list of dates, they are not only inexact, but there are (what turn out to be) key dates *missing*, such as a solar arc direction to conjunction an angle, or some other major progression involving ascendant or meridian. If the chart is quite close to exact, it is easier to uncover these 'missing events', which often occur in childhood and are either (1) blocked out due to trauma; (2) the event happened to a family member, yet it affected the native strongly; (3) it was too far back to remember; or (4) (very common), 'I didn't realize it was important'.

Once in a single day, I came upon two different charts that had a Uranus solar arc direction to the seventh cusp (i.e. opposition ascendant) in childhood. In both instances, the native was sent away to boarding school that year and found it very alienating! It had occurred to neither to mention it until they were asked what happened to them at that specific age.

In another instance, a Uranus direction came to the fourth cusp at a very young age and on being questioned, the native still drew a blank, but then reflected that that was the year a younger sister was born. I asked if that disrupted (Uranus) the family (fourth cusp) in any way. The native responded that the mother had almost lost the baby and 'was supposed to have been very upset'. That could adequately account for such a direction—the chart being in order otherwise—because it describes upheaval (Uranus) in the home (fourth), as well as an upset (Uranus) mother (opposition tenth).

Rectifying the chart of a child can be difficult and uncertain since relatively so little may have happened yet; or the chart of someone with apparently very limited life experience. But still you can work with the most important things that have happened. If they assess it as 'most important', it will probably register in some clear way. Even moving house can change the life circumstances relatively decisively.

The section entitled EVENT GUIDE (pp. 306-312) will provide

a more comprehensive look at what are amongst the most important dates to obtain if they are within the native's experience.

Contextual Time

When you are not provided with a ready stream of exact dates, some may be gleaned by exploring the *context* of those dates within the native's memory. Dates are sometimes remembered because they fall near someone's birthday, or it was close to Chrismas, or just before the end of the school year.

Even more commonly, dates are embedded in a sea of other temporal references: before you met Johnny, after your mother died, the period during which you discovered a new religion, and so on. This may or may not jog the *exact* memory, but it jogs the *relative* memory and whole segments of life history that at first did not seem available may be brought to the surface.

Even questioning the *sequence* in which events happened, tends to bring other details to the surface, and the more information you have, the more entry points you have to pin-pointing dates to exactitude.

The method of sequencing is also invaluable in filling in pieces of the life history. If you see something that likely marks off the native's appointment as vice-president, for example, and see some major aspect one year earlier or two years later, you can enquire what happened one year before the appointment or two years following it. Sequencing is so distinctive from chart to chart, the context of many years surrounding a specific event can assist in finding exactly the right positioning of the natal angles.

Qualitative Time

In your eagerness to obtain exact dates of events in the life, be careful of an overbalance of surface information to the neglect of other facets of the native's life history. Some people, after you've told them you want a listing of major events in the life, will give you mainly dates and a terse description of what happened. Other people, however, may get very involved with the tenor or feeling of what happened to them, such as that the horse threw Jimmy and 'it was absolutely dreadful', while the date itself is foggy.

The 'absolutely dreadful' part of the description is *important*. For one thing, a person who offers that first and more 'technical' things such as dates later on, shows certain personal characteristics of a more subjectively-oriented or emotional temperament that may assist in the rectification. Plus that very reaction itself—'absolutely dreadful'—will show in the aspects of the date when the event happened, likely as an affliction involving the natal and/or progressed ascendant, since the native had such a strong personal response.

Attention needs be given to all inflections of experience. This is a *qualitative* renditioning of time. The 'Oh yes, wasn't it terrible!' and the 'That was the happiest moment of my life!' show up *astrologically*. And it is a subtlety, but probably true, that when you make note of the native's own strongest responses, you are synchronizing with them personally, hence are better attuned to give a reading which will be meaningful for *them*. Not everyone wants the same thing out of a reading. Your only clue may be the chart itself, in absence of the living native. If it is accurate, that is a lot to go on, by all means. But if the native is right there personally, you have a living directional guide to assist you in reading that chart, even if the native says little verbally.

In any case, what we are calling 'qualitative time' relates to feelings and surrounding memories, and the astrologer needs to know about *that* kind of 'when', too. It is part and parcel of life experience, and as much a part of the astrology as any so-called 'objective' occurrence in the life.

Objective Time

This brings us to the last parameter of time travel, which is time as it is demarcated—thank goodness—*objectively*. 'Objective time' is shown by the exact layout of the planets and house cusps (natal, progressed and transiting inclusive) at the date of some event in the life: marriage, hit-and-run accident, relocation, a scholarship, career choice, hospitalization, and so on.

Why is this any more 'objective' than anything else that has been described? Think back to our imaginary house, and remember that a distinction was drawn between the native's preference or different functioning in some one 'room' of that house (representing some house in the natal chart). But then we noted that each room of the imaginary house also signified something that was *the same for everyone*, such as the meridian (the 'master bedroom') is always the parental axis, whatever is the contents of any particular chart.

This entirely objective area of astrology is termed 'event astrology', and it is the bedrock of sound astrological practice, notwithstanding its tattered reputation. It is a hopeless prospect attempting to adjust a birth chart to exactitude without it.

Objective correspondences between astrology and what happens in the life have to be monitored and verified in three major ways when rectifying a chart: house cusps, planets, and types of aspects. (The signs, which are so important with the natal chart and its spatial layout and natal delineation, are of lesser significance in relation to the chart's *timing*.)

A BOOK OF REFERENCES (pp. 287-312) includes delineation guides for identification of house, planetary and aspect correspondences, along with a guide to what is commonly found in the chart for several kinds of major events in the life.

The Many Different 'Times' in Context

The identification of many different types of 'time' is primarily a means to facilitate translation of life experience into its astrological analogues. The distinctions between the timing categories are artificial in that the categories inevitably overlap, being many ways of viewing the same indicators. But their different foci give the astrologer a pragmatic, flexible approach to information-gathering. If one approach isn't working, try another. If you are getting insufficient feedback, move your information-gathering into some area that will round the picture out.

In practice, problems most often arise in relation to sorting out 'objective' versus 'subjective' factors. Some types of information are quite 'objective', such as the exact date when something happens; others are more 'subjective', such as how a person *felt* during the experience in question.

This presents no real contradiction, and in many instances is an aid. Often, they are flip sides of the same coin. For example, a sudden event for which one is unprepared will be marked by a prominent Uranus, as indicator of the event *objectively*; but your reaction of shock—a *subjective* response—is also marked by Uranus!

It is not always this clear-cut, because not every indicator in the whole astrological picture will show a direct effect upon the native. But the objective/subjective overlap is invariably found in some form in most happenings in the life. Psychologists would call it an 'appropriate response', meaning that the subjective response is an appropriate reaction to objective circumstances. The astrology of an accurate chart will give you the tools to verify both ends of the objective/subjective polarity, as well as to recognize their natural integration in the process of living.

It is undoubtedly most efficient and time-saving to give priority to the more objective aspects of rectification work until the timing seems to be plausibly descriptive. This includes what has been termed 'quantitative time' (the exact date something happens) and 'objective time' (what the corresponding astrology looks like on that date, inclusive of natal, progressed and transiting positions). However, bear in mind that any timing designation can be a springboard into the others in the hands of a skilled interviewer.

PART SIX:
A BOOK OF REFERENCES—
A GUIDE TO ASTROLOGICAL
COMPONENTS OF EVENT ANALYSIS

INTRODUCTORY NOTE

What follows are guides to interpretation. They do not prescribe any specific application for any particular chart, but rather the types of changes that aspects involving specific planets will bring about in the life. For instance, afflictions involving the ascendant/seventh house axis could refer to personal frustrations, marital problems, a medical problem, injury, some break-off in personal affairs or simply a period of personal struggle. Exactly *how* afflictions manifest depends upon many factors, such as other concurrent aspects, the house(s) the planet rules natally, and the strength of its positioning in context.

Aspects also arrive into a matrix of past history, conditioning, and at wherever the native is poised in life at the time of the aspect: his age, current life standing, current health, stability, mobility, level of character and breadth of involvement in the world.

With rectification, however, you do not have to cope with *predictive* work, for which consideration of all of the above would be central. Your initial determinations will be of what is *plausible*, and what aspects, planets and house cusp involvements *account for* various major happenings in the life.

The section to come is divided into the three major components of event analysis, house cusps, planets and aspects, and finally an 'Event Guide' to several of the major events commonly offered for chart rectification work.

20.
HOUSE GUIDE

House cusps show the circumstances of life, and the areas of life affected.

The Angles

The most important house cusps are always the *angles*. They signify the structure of the life. The ascendant (first cusp) shows the native personally, his physiology, physiognomy, outer personality, his responses to life; the seventh cusp shows his relationships, partnerships, capacity to co-operate, to compete, to be at ease with or spurred into action by others.

The midheaven (tenth cusp) shows the career, the life-path, the worldly status, the perspective on life, the mother; the fourth cusp shows the home, the family, the roots in life, one's inner convictions, the father. The fourth cusp traditionally governs the end of life, but it also governs the very basis of life in the human form, and you will find it afflicted in life-threatening crises, such as accidents, injuries and serious illnesses.

Whenever anything that is governed by an angle happens in the life, aspecting will highlight that particular angle, natally and/or by progression. However, anything that is 'major' in its impact on the life as a whole is likely to register against one or both angles. The event *per se*, might not be strictly a first, tenth, seventh, or fourth cusp matter, such as an inheritance (eighth cusp) or a creative debut (fifth house). But nearly everything in life has components that register through the angles: the direct impact upon the native through the ascendant, the impact upon the course or direction of life through the midheaven.

Several types of specific effects upon the angles are as follows.

The Ascendant Axis

Sense of personal well-being: Examples are Jupiter trine the ascendant, native feels uplifted and relaxed, morale bolstered; Saturn square ascendant, native feels debilitated, depressed or constricted; Neptune quincunx ascendant, native feels in a quandary or confusion, with no satisfactory resolution.

Actual physical impact: If the body is injured or ill, you will find afflictions involving the natal and/or progressed ascendant. For example, when the body is cut, bleeding, burned or in pain, look for Mars; state of shock, electrical injuries and gunfire come under Uranus. (See *Encyclopaedia of Medical Astrology*, by H. L. Cornell, Samuel Weiser Inc., New York for a wealth of astrological signatures for medical conditions and other conditions affecting the body.)

Personal response to any situation: The immediate personal response to what is happening in the life, in whatever area, will nevertheless register through the ascendant. This shows the overt reactions, whatever might be the inner ramifications or levels of change.

Relationships: Aspects conjunct the ascendant (i.e. opposition the seventh cusp) and aspects conjunct the seventh cusp are different in their effect. For instance, if transiting Uranus is conjunct the seventh cusp and a marriage is already unstable, that could be the signal for separation. In the native's experience, it is the end of the *marriage*, however painful the shattering. But if the Uranus is on the *ascendant*, the impact is specifically *personally* shattering, with surface personal upset greater. Neptune on the seventh may cloud the circumstances and conditions of relating to others, and bring people of a Neptunian cast into one's life. Neptune on the ascendant will bring a personal sense of confusion, or others will view the native as an uncertain entity. Trines, sextiles and squares to the first/seventh axis of course register about the same at both ends, but with the *quincunx*, the effects are very different. With one native, a year was spent with various personal casualties—accidents, injuries, assaults, debilitated health—under two major quincunxes to the ascendant, but the major relationship of the life was very strong during that period, the seventh cusp being unaffected.

The seventh cusp is not only one-to-one romantic relationships, of course, but is an index of one's capacity to relate to others generally. Also note that events directly affecting a spouse or partner will register through the seventh cusp.

The Meridian

Career: Major career changes invariably register strongly through the tenth cusp. This can be changes of occupation, or changes of position or status within the same occupation. The aspecting involving the midheaven spells out how the change arrives: by cut-off, a square; easefully, sextile or trine; as a fork in the road or an uncomfortable choice, a quincunx. The planets involved describe its character: the Sun carrying (or cutting off) prestige; Venus, what the native personally wants; Mars, allowing for (or cutting off) personal initiative, and so forth.

Major change in life direction: The career may not change, *per se*, for the direction in life to be altered. This is part of why major relocation registers through the meridian, not only the ninth cusp. The fourth house is obviously the home, but tenth house alterations are also often involved, in that the native has a different leverage in the new environment, his place in the community and overall status is different.

Whatever happens that alters the direction or overriding purpose of the life will be likely to register through the meridian of the chart. It is also helpful to realize that not everyone has a 'career', *per se*, but everyone has a life outlook and some position in his or her 'world'. The meridian, like the ascendant, is a backbone of life, and may be simply transposed into whatever context or life orientation is relevant to the native.

Relocation: Major relocation comes strongly through the fourth cusp, but the tenth as well, and the ninth cusp for a move far away.

Events affecting the parents: In a child's chart, the meridian registers changes in the parent's lives, which of course bear upon the native's position in his or her young world. Later in life, illness or death of the parent still registers through the meridian.

Life-threatening situations: Circumstances that threaten the physical life will register through the fourth cusp of the chart.

Other House Cusps

The following is a guide to the types of circumstantial changes in the life which will register through the intermediary cusps:

Second/eighth axis: Monetary loss or gain of income or capacity to earn (second), loss or gain of fixed assets, trusts, inheritances (eighth), partner's assets (eighth), surgery (eighth), deaths (eighth).

Third/ninth axis: Higher education (ninth), relocation (ninth), mental disturbances (third/ninth), publication of work (ninth), events affecting siblings (third), neighbourhood environment (third), travel (ninth).

Fifth/eleventh axis: Birth of children (fifth), creative endeavours (fifth), organizational involvement (eleventh), events affecting friends and associates (eleventh), love affairs (fifth).

Sixth/twelfth axis: Illness (sixth), high stress situations (sixth), hospitalization or other institutionalization (twelfth), self-improvement and development.

21.
PLANETARY GUIDE

Planets show the character and quality of what happens in the life.

The Sun

Major progressions involving the natal or progressed Sun will be liable to affect either: the self-esteem and sense of well-being/accomplishment; enhanced or debilitated physical strength and vitality; the career; the sense of purpose and morale.

Major progressed aspects involving the Sun in relation to the midheaven relate to the prestige and accomplishment in the world, harmonious aspecting enhancing it or boosting one to either a high, or a personally coveted position, perhaps giving personal authority, or some position that will *last*. Afflictions involving the Sun and midheaven also make prestige and standing an *issue*, but can be damaging. Be it the Sun, this is likely to be a 'high profile' situation, affecting how one is centred and projects to the world. Quincunxes involving midheaven and Sun can give quandaries about either career choice or maintaining a viable position in life in the face of mitigating or hindering circumstances.

Major progressions of ascendant/Sun give boosts to the self-esteem, feelings of accomplishment, and a boost to the physical vitality. Personal success and self-satisfaction is the hallmark. Afflictions involving ascendant/Sun make achieving one's goals and self-esteem an issue, but block it from coming to fruition. Quincunxes show high personal stress, and the need to prove oneself; being a quincunx, it can also be debilitating to the physical energy.

Issues involving stability and longevity of the career, personal recognition, personal disgrace or discreditation, identity crises or affirmations, or periods of enhanced or diminished vitality (sometimes involving the heart) may show involvement of natal or progressed Sun in aspect to the chart's angles.

The Moon

Whereas with the Sun, both a progressed angle in aspect to the Sun and the progressed Sun in aspect to a natal angle are both in orb for approximately a year, with the Moon, its progression through a single degree takes only about a month or a little less. Therefore, a progressed Moon aspect would show a momentary wave of favour (harmonious aspect) or disfavour (inharmonious aspect), comfort (harmonious) or discomfort (inharmonious), a period when the climate seems natural (harmonious) or unnatural (inharmonious) to make personal (ascendant) or career/life course (meridian) progress.

Of course, a square (for example) from the progressed ascendant to the *natal* Moon, is an aspect lasting a year or more, marking an entire period of not quite 'gelling' with the environment, a proneness to emotional disappointment, where responding freely and naturally does not bring what one wants, and—if in life circumstances where public approval or popularity is central, such as for an entertainer or politican—this is a time when popularity is an *issue*, but one tends to fall into disfavour or publicity goes awry.

The Moon and Mercury are the arbiters of routine, in their respective spheres. The Moon shows emotional routines (as in, 'I've grown accustomed to her face'), while Mercury governs life's schedules, details, verbal and written communications. The Moon is also associated with the physical functioning and how the emotions affect the physiological functioning (as in, 'I don't *feel* well'). Thus harmonious Moon/ascendant aspects can mark times where one 'sails' through life, and afflictions can mark times of physical and/or social discomfort. Travel also comes under the Moon.

Progressed midheaven afflicting the natal Moon might deny one what is 'usually expected' in the career area, and mark a year in which it is difficult to gain ground socially or in public contact; though the very fact that the Moon is involved would make it an issue. A progressed quincunx to natal Moon from the ascendant would certainly predispose towards emotional stress, whereas a quincunx from the midheaven could give a period of quandary, not settling readily into anything without much inconvenience and necessity for adjustments.

The progressed Moon is important to watch for virtually *any* event in the life, timing the native's emotional orientation at the time, and showing how the environment facilitates/highlights or impedes the native's functioning in relation to whatever cusp the Moon aspects.

Not infrequently, important new people, or those with whom one has good emotional rapport come into the life when the progressed Moon harmoniously aspects the ascendant/seventh axis.

Regarding the *transiting* Moon, you will not be able to obtain that unless the native provides the time of day for the event in question. It is interesting to look into and helpful, though with all the other information available, not having it should not impede achieving a correct rectification.

Mercury

Mercury, like the Moon, is an arbiter of change, but this is mobility, *per se*, and does not of itself have emotional connotations. Life's details, schedules, habits, programmed routines, decisions, written and verbal communications all come under Mercury rulership.

Progressed major aspects involving Mercury/angles could show studies, journeys (especially if related to business), changes in the formats of living. For those so involved, papers, books, classes, documents and/or mental improvement could be key. With Mercury/ascendant aspects come active, restless times, inquisitive, where communication and learning activities come to the fore. With Mercury/midheaven aspects, Mercurial pursuits to the fore—this may be legal or clerical matters, deals, business on many fronts, or life as a student even in the adult years.

In affliction, Mercury aspects can show miscalculations, poor deals, being cheated or misdirected. With ascendant or sixth house involvement, this could be part of configurations of mental or nervous overactivity or stress when in affliction. The onset of any serious kind of mental problem is apt to involve Mercury in affliction (third/ninth axis might also be consulted).

Transiting Mercury is a *timer*, notably for making decisions, signing of documents, reaching agreements, altering the handling of details, initiating communications, hatching new ideas, entering a new state of mind. In affliction, it can be involved with signatures for slander, libel, misunderstanding, miscommunication, and various types of 'having one's wires crossed'.

Venus

Venus governs what one wants personally, what one values, how one harmonizes with others, and pursuits of a Venusian character: art, clothing, luxury, social contacts and romance.

Major progressed aspects involving the ascendant and/or seventh cusp are a prime time for entering into relationships. This is not ruled out by a square, incidentally, but you often find a broken engagement or the equivalent under such an aspect. Whatever is the range of social contacts at the time of such aspects, they are highlighted with trines and sextiles facilitating, and squares obstructing. Quincunxes give stress and sometimes breaks, but with the native not being entirely sure what is desired or if it is being achieved, should be held onto or left alone. Perhaps the native is trying too hard to please (Venus), or putting out too much effort to be satisfied with mixed results.

Progressed aspects involving the meridian sometimes describe one's state of pleasure or dissatisfaction with the course of the life at present. Harmonious aspects could show the achievement of some personally-cherished goal, afflictions could focus attention on lack of personal fulfilment.

Transiting Venus will tend to show whether a situation is convenient or not, peaceful or not, whether or not it brings people together, whether it is assimilated as welcome or not.

Watch Venus, both in progression and transit with births, as harmonious aspecting with the mother's chart is common. Venus is also almost invariably involved with *deaths*. It seems to have something to do with passing between planes, and curiously, the expression 'being laid to rest' might well be an expression of the action of *Venus*.

Mars

Mars is prominently involved in accidents, quarrels, anger, rash decisions and actions, feverish illness, sudden losses, haste and impetuosity, bold new starts, independent enterprise, personal courage, danger, passionate involvements of all sorts, fires, involvement with the military, competition and/or enmity, athletics.

Life tends to proceed rapidly and directly under Mars influence. Thus Mars *squares* can be especially acute in their action, potentially causing much disruption in the life when in major progressed aspects involving the angles. Sextiles and trines show periods when things are *expedited*, and personal initiative is maximized. Quincunxes show *acute* frustration, because the urge to action is strong but there is no clear way through.

Transiting Mars is decisive in its action. If you are evicted or lose a job under a Mars affliction to the meridian, you are probably out and that's it! Mars catapults one decisively out of one situation into another, or on one's own for good or ill. Mars transits are found where there is high, fast-paced action, things come to a head, or zoom off in a new direction.

In terms of its action—rapid, expediting, a sudden force—Mars and Saturn are antitheses.

Pain, being cut and bleeding, and dangerous activities have a strong Mars component. Almost every injury shows Mars involvement. It is also involved with fires, explosions, thefts and personal assault.

A prominently-placed Mars transit also shows the readiness and willingness to act, so if someone describes being tentative, cautious or controlled, it would contraindicate prominent Mars involvement with the ascendant.

Jupiter

Jupiter is involved with money, enterprise, expansion, extravagance, religion, altruism, friendly contacts, and anything in life that gives an uplift, be it business, personal, religious, organizational, scholarly. It shows the open mind and the giving heart at best, and a wastrel, profligate or hedonist at the other end of the spectrum.

Harmonious aspects with the meridian give success, prosperity, ease of circumstances, things on the upswing, a good deal, help and/or co-operation in managing one's life—of course, dependent upon one's current circumstances at the time the aspect becomes partile. Inharmonious aspects with the meridian can be overexpenditure of energy or funds, discreditation, or even legal problems, but bear in mind that Jupiter is still a benefic, and for serious problems to be involved, you would need to find significant supporting aspecting.

Harmonious aspects with the ascendant can show good fortune, contentment, birth of children, special opportunities and advantages. Jupiter can also be involved with travelling, broadening the mind, being open to new options. Inharmonious aspects can show overexpenditures of energy and money, dissolute behaviour (if otherwise so inclined), careless, overblown actions, extravagance, or poor judgement in the exercise of liberty. Medically, Jupiter can be involved at the onset of liver problems, haemorrhages, and conditions of the blood.

Saturn

Saturn constricts, consolidates, organizes, disciplines, makes responsible, reins in, hardens, manages, conserves; also makes more stable, secure and enduring in harmonious aspect. It governs falls, bruises, disappointments, depression, personal loss, delays, blocks and hindrances.

Harmonious major aspects of Saturn/meridian may show hard-won gains, well-assumed responsibility, consolidation of assets or position, ventures that will last, stability and security of a post. Affecting the fourth cusp, it would stabilize home conditions and also tend to keep one put during that period, i.e if there is a move (any major aspect involving the fourth cusp could be part of a signature for a move), it will be of a stable, secure character.

In inharmonious aspect to the meridian, it could show professional discreditation or down-grading, being treated shabbily, being blamed for loss, having to face hard facts, or buckle under with no way out. In aspect to the fourth cusp, this could be a foreclosure, or constricting home circumstances, or a time of problems making ends meet.

In harmonious progressed aspect with the ascendant, this could stabilize some long-range tie, stabilize the native personally, give him more responsibility, also slow him down. Inharmonious aspects could show times of depression, disappointments or hurts, the stress of material circumstances, indebtedness to others, being bound in by restrictive codes or circumstances.

In medical matters, Saturn involvement will be found with chronic ailments, ailments that have come on slowly, problems with the bones, teeth or skin, and depression.

Saturn by transit delays or slows, blocks or makes progress tedious, measured or slow.

Uranus

Uranus is involved with sudden breaks, shocks, sudden gains, risk-taking, or sudden shifts in comprehension or circumstance. 'Expect the unexpected' is the watchword for Uranus transits over the angles, especially when by planetary station. However, Uranus will not break what is not already unstable—it is like an earthquake erupting where there was already a fault. Uranus works in apparently eccentric or erratic ways, and brings into the life people and circumstances of a different or reversed character from the norm.

Aspects from a progressed angle afflicting the natal Uranus can have quite drastic effects upon the life. Whatever damage, cut-offs, or reversals the career or the person sustains during such a period, there is no way back; though this sometimes serves the constructive purpose of allowing the native to build on a new foundation, free and clear of unstable or ambiguous elements. Money can be lost, relationships lost, prestige lost, there can be scandal, unexpected breaks, high risk ventures backfire. Uranus involved by either progression or transit with the seventh cusp may be involved in a divorce configuration. Unusual, erratic or eccentric people may enter the life under ascendant aspects, there can be a high level of nervous stress, overexcitement and emotional explosions and, on the physical level, killing fires, gunshot and electrical accidents also show Uranus involvement. Shock and trauma come under Uranus, though for psychological trauma, the asteroid Psyche should always be consulted.

Harmonious Uranus involvements or conjunctions can bring sudden gain, sudden romance and unusual turns in the life patterns, sometimes thrusting one into an iconoclastic, ground-breaking or innovative role. Dynamic, exciting, dramatic events come under Uranus rulership, as do adventure and risk.

Neptune

Neptune works in a diffuse way, clouding barriers, involved in misunderstandings, doubts, uncertainties, manipulation, deception, subtle forms of ruin, slander and malicious gossip. With Neptune, you cannot easily find the source of difficulty or correct it in a clear-cut way.

On the positive side, romance and both spiritual and artistic inspiration come under Neptune rulership, as do idealism, unsuspecting trust and self-sacrifice. Neptune in harmonious involvement with the ascendant/seventh can bring romantic, mystical or poetical attachments to people, which may be motivated by altruism or, in some instances, by rose-coloured glasses, which may later come off. Circumstances may sneak up as if by stealth, with unknown motivation or outcome, and even with harmonious aspecting (including the conjunction), judgement may be impaired by seeing what one ideally wants to see rather than what is there.

Progressed ascendant in affliction to the natal Neptune can give a period of confused motivation, where effective action seems elusive. Any Neptune afflictions to the ascendant could be part of a signature for peculiar experiences, untrustworthy people in the life, being deceived or spied upon, suspicious circumstances, hidden motives, unpleasant cut-offs that are difficult to either understand or remedy.

Neptune in inharmonious aspect with the midheaven can give uncertain prospects for the future, not being credited at one's true worth, denial of opportunities to function in areas of capability, problems in making headway in any step-by-step coherent kind of way. Neptune in harmonious aspect with the midheaven isn't necessarily that great a help. Neptune especially depends upon context—it is something like a rare orchid of delicate beauty under exactly the right climatic conditions, but worse for the wear in many of the ordinary affairs of life.

Neptune is involved with drugs, poisonings, comas, addictions, or illnesses that elude proper diagnosis.

Pluto

Pluto works by dredging, oft-times with very pervasive, difficult ramifications, circumstantially, materially and emotionally. Excessively bureaucratic, complicated, totalistic skeins of circumstances will often feature Pluto. Pluto transits across or square angles can pressure one to conform to social norms, sometimes with heavy emotional penalties incurred by free self-expression. Pluto raises the stakes on everything—all your finances are at stake, or all your emotions, or all your personal influence, whether you wanted to risk all or not. Physically, it is not infrequently found as part of a life-threatening configuration.

Pluto can be prominently involved with power struggles, obsessive commitments to persons or projects. You may find yourself 'in very deep with no way out', and, if the overall aspecting is severe, Pluto can obliterate and make the native an anonymous entity.

Even the harmonious directions of Pluto can be an intensive experience. The native is brought into touch with deeper levels of instinct or socially-conditioned behaviour. If it does bring benefits, it can be *great* benefits—big money, power, relationships of an enduring, even obsessive character.

The inharmonious aspects can be very stressful. 'Gruelling' is the watchword. A major progression is a year's worth, and even a Pluto transit can, in effect, be prolonged that much or a little more with the slow zigzagging of this outer planet. One may feel snowed under, immobile, caught in oppressive circumstances, which are sometimes internal ones. It drives one inwards and one may make invaluable self-discoveries, but at a cost. With Pluto, I would have to define the conjunction as an affliction.

A Pluto component is common for murder, sabotage, sex crimes and mass deaths.

Chiron

Chiron relates to alternative perspectives, situations that are resynchronized into new contexts, unique learning opportunities, novel solutions, new openings in the doors of life, families relating at new angles to one another, challenges to act and respond in new modes and from a different framework of motivation.

Harmonious aspects with the angles can give new chances at life, and breakthroughs that don't shatter the life—like Uranus—but open new vistas of perception and functioning. Creative windows of ingenuity may become apparent, new ways to relate to others (ascendant), new capabilities and perspective on life (midheaven). Specific learning experiences may give new tools for coping with life, or the native has to discover new resources within himself to cope with unfamiliar settings.

Inharmonious aspects of Chiron are still a challenge. A Chiron square, though stressful, is nothing like a Uranus or Pluto square, for example. This aspect can jolt one out of ruts, or redefine the terms of one's life.

Psyche and Sappho
(See 'Extra Information: The Asteroids' p. 173)

22.
ASPECT GUIDE

Aspects show the energy form in which an event arrives.

Conjunctions

Conjunctions have a strong, direct impact; the character of what happens is dependent upon the character of the conjunction and its surrounding aspecting.

The context of conjunctions is important to their delineation. For a natal or progressed angular degree affected by a planetary conjunction, the conjunction will simply show the character of the planet in the circumstance of life shown by the angle, e.g. Mars conjunction ascendant could show high-spirited energy, or it could be a new start marked by aggressive initiative. But let's say that the progressed ascendant has reached conjunction natal Saturn, and then the transiting Mars comes along and is conjunct both progressed ascendant and natal Saturn. The Saturn-Mars *combination* rebounding upon the ascendant is frustrating and unpleasant at best, as the Mars is bridled by Saturn, and the Saturnian sensitivities are aggravated by Mars. So it is not the 'same' conjunction at all.

When, let's say, the progressed Moon is conjunct natal ascendant, that is a time for personal change—of attitudes, or directions, or contacts. Now if, let's say, transiting Uranus is square the ascendant/Moon conjunction, the change could be quite disruptive and painful. If, on the other hand, the conjunction is graced by lovely harmonious Venus aspects, the 'same' progressed Moon conjunct ascendant could mark the birth of a child with its attendant devotion and happiness.

Squares

A square can show a cut-off or break in circumstances, sometimes surmountable but with effort. Squares can also simply be very energizing and a challenge, but a square is never easy to labour under. What is helpful about progressed squares is that it enables the native to make clean breaks, which we all need from time to time. But don't expect that something new undertaken under a major progressed square will result in a smooth time, and oft-times the seeds of a later break-off are apparent within the aspecting itself.

It is important to distinguish between squares in natal delineation and squares in rectification work. Squares in a natal chart give tools to cope with living, strengthen skills, build character. Progressed squares in effect do the same, but what actually *happens* is stressful, obstructive or conflictive.

Sextiles and Trines

This frees energy into the life. Things happens easily and naturally in the house cusp areas involved with sextiles and trines.

There are a couple of qualifiers one needs to watch, however. Most major events have some kind of a mix of harmonious and inharmonious aspects. See which aspects set the basic tone for what happens in the life—usually the major aspects involving the angles. A strong progressed trine from the midheaven qualified by squares from transits is different from a progressed square qualified by transiting trines. Consider the progressed aspects first.

Another qualifier is sextiles and trines to outer planets. Sometimes a trine to Neptune, for example, can show a skittish, cloudy situation, more than *no* aspect from Neptune.

Oppositions

This can show alienation, which can, in effect, promote breaks, but it is *not the same as* a square, where the action is harsh, sharp and overt. Oppositions demand perspective and the ability to see contrasting sides. Sometimes you will see violent swings of energy (the Mars/Jupiter opposition natally is probably the most notable for that), but its action is shifting or oscillating or blocking. Oppositions block the native from 'getting life together', whereas the square brings about an overt split.

With oppositions involving the angles, remember that any planet opposition one angle is conjunction another!

Quincunxes

This is very important in rectification work. It is found with illness, death of loved ones, high-stress situations, forced choices where no alternative is a good one, decisions which have mixed ramifications or result in continuing dissatisfaction. Reconciliations are problematical, because adjustments can of themselves create additional problems. To quote a colleague, it's 'damned if you do, damned if you don't'. The quincunx can be gruelling in its effects, and the aftermath slow to resolve.

It is good to note, however, that sometimes people with strongly-placed quincunxes *natally* can become quite strong personally, because they have learned to take the bad with the good and vice versa and have learned how to compromise life circumstances without compromising their integrity.

23.
EVENT GUIDE

Introductory Note

Once life circumstances are altered to the extent they can be termed an 'event', many astrological components have come into play. One aspect alone may show a predisposition or climate for change, or a period during which certain kinds of things are likely to happen. But definitive changes do not materialize without sufficient support in the aspecting structurally.

The following guidelines are extracted from the astrology of many common types of events in the life, citing what might be likely to be found and suggesting interpretation.

Naturally, every event will be somewhat different in its aspecting, not only the different types of events, but the 'same event' from chart to chart, such as leaving home for the charts of three different natives. Remember that the astrology reflects *exactly what happened*, and past the basic structural design (Blueprint 3: The Structure of Events), the specifics will vary as much as any two lives do in character, range, and patterns of response.

Career Changes

This is a tenth house (midheaven) matter. Harmonious aspects generally show change for the better, promotions, new opportunities, coming into one's own. Prominent aspects involving the natal or progressed Sun give prestige, an enhanced sense of personal identity, tenure, status in the community and the like. Jupiter gives more money, ease of functioning, and friendly relations with others. Mars gives the opportunity for personal initiative. With one chart, when the Mars solar arc hit the midheaven by conjunction, the native started her own business. It lasted a year, the approximate length of the aspect, and it was the *only* year in her life she undertook such an endeavour. Harmonious Moon aspects (such as from the progressed Moon) during major career changes make them high-profile, with attention and support from others.

Afflictions involving the natal or progressed midheaven make for difficult years career-wise. One has to hang on tight the year progressed midheaven squares Uranus or Mars, or make frustrating choices if the progressed midheaven is quincunx one's Saturn.

When the native is a child, the midheaven most often signifies the parent's career and overall status in life. But I have seen exceptions with precocious and gifted children—for one, progressed midheaven conjunct natal Moon marked the native's young debut as a concert pianist and its attendant publicity.

Termination of a job is frequently marked by a planet hitting the fourth cusp of the chart, i.e. opposing the midheaven. This seems to mark a natural time for leaving—even if the break is unpleasant or harsh—as distinct from a square where there are interfering or conflicting factors at work. Mars is often involved in a signature for 'You're fired!' or 'I quit!', Uranus for departure under crisis. Neptune over the fourth, however, probably would not mark taking one's leave because it has no definitive punch, while planets like Venus and Jupiter are benefics and unless there is aspecting otherwise of a harsh nature, it might well mark a favourable fourth house circumstance rather than something like termination of a job.

Deaths

What is offered most commonly is the death of a parent. This registers in explicit ways, frequently with heavy aspecting.

Three house cusps are invariably involved. The meridian (tenth/fourth house axis) signifies the parent in question, usually the mother for the tenth and the father for the fourth. Aspects to that axis show how the parent died. For example, if there is an affliction from Mars in Leo involving the natal or progressed fourth cusp at the time of the father's death, enquire if he went with a heart (Leo) attack (Mars) and you will often be right. A quincunx (gruelling) from Saturn (long-range or debilitating affliction), especially by progression will generally indicate that the parent had been chronically ill for a long time so that, in effect, death came slowly (Saturn). Any affliction from Saturn to the appropriate parental cusp will show suffering and conditions of stress surrounding the parent at the time of death.

The aspects to the ascendant of the chart show the effect upon the native personally. An affliction from Saturn would show depression and/or grief; from Uranus, shock; from the progressed Moon, an openly emotional response, and immediate emotional involvement in the event.

Some major aspect(s) involving the natal and/or progressed eighth cusp is also mandatory. This shows how death, *per se*, has touched the native's life and how his consciousness was affected. A Saturn affliction, for example, would show a native slow to spring back from the experience; Chiron might show a more comprehensive understanding of life arising from death; a harmonious aspect from Saturn might show that the native was prepared for the situation. Delineating such aspects can be subtle; the most important thing is to be sure a major aspect is located concurrent with the event.

With Chiron in death situations, it frequently shows how the environment and the native's own drives and capabilities are resynchronized in the absence of the loved one—an index of a newly-constituted personal reality.

Marriage and Relationships
You will invariably find seventh cusp involvement, though don't rule out fifth cusp involvement for a love affair that is not geared towards marriage. Very frequently, the progressed seventh cusp will be in exact, most likely harmonious aspect to a natal planet, often Venus, the Moon, Jupiter, or ruler of the seventh cusp. There is no hard-and-fast rule about which planets have to be involved, but the reason that the norm is a major, harmonious aspect, be it conjunction, sextile or trine, is that marriage is most frequently by personal choice and sextiles and trines facilitate things happening. Presumably, there are feelings of love and expectations of happiness, so naturally aspects such as Venus trines and Jupiter conjunctions frequently turn up. If you see the progressed seventh cusp approaching conjunction natal Venus, for example, the likelihood (given reasonable personal circumstances) for a major romantic involvement is high. But you need to enquire to confirm the character of what you are reading from the chart.

Also, some do marry under awkward or pressured circumstances, which the astrology will reflect. If the native had to buck opposition from others, or is 'marrying on the rebound', you might find the seventh cusp progressed to a quincunx. A marriage caused by pregnancy, for which the couple is basically unprepared will show in Uranus aspects—stress aspects if the marriage is really reluctant, but I've seen trines where the couple was going to marry anyway a little later on. If you find something as drastic as progressed seventh square natal Uranus, most likely the marriage will not take place at all.

In many charts, you might find some likely 'marriage aspect'—like progressed seventh conjunct natal Jupiter—when the native is obviously too young to marry; but general relations with everyone will be improved under such an aspect.

It is also most helpful to obtain the date when the couple first *met*, which is the initial 'stage' of the relationship which leads to marriage. Meeting someone whom one will later marry frequently registers strongly on the seventh cusp, especially if the attraction is immediate.

Watch the progressed Moon at the time of marriage for some gauge as to the initial adjustment period and for where the emotional energy will be focused.

Divorce

Divorce comes under Uranus more often than any other planetary influence, but can sometimes come under a Neptune square (a Neptune *conjunction* would be unlikely to split up a marriage, just create confusion and ambiguity in the relationship, and the concommittant alienation). Neptunian divorces almost invariably leave a lot of loose ends hanging, emotionally and even circumstantially.

Divorces obtained under conjunctions, squares and quincunxes also differ from one another. Squares make a clean break. Conjunctions make for intensity. Quincunxes require give-and-take in the midst of a break that can be very painful. Sometimes the native isn't sure what has been traded off in return for freedom.

Note that Pluto afflictions do *not* tend to produce divorce, though it can give a native who feels pressurized, or even trapped by the expectations of a relationship.

Accidents

People do not have accidents without some major affliction involving the ascendant. For a major accident, look for a major progression involving the natal or progressed ascendant. But also check that the character of the planet corresponds with the character of the accident. Most common, of course, is Mars, which governs bleeding, pain, assaults upon the body and/or a rash or careless manner that preceded the accident. Very nearly any accident will have a Mars *component*.

Several afflictions involving the ascendant (natal/progressed) is common for major accidents, with the twelfth cusp for hospitalization the eighth cusp for surgery, and involvement of the fourth cusp for life-threatening situations.

Saturn governs falls, bruises and suffocation; Uranus gunfire, electrical accidents and fires that kill; Neptune drownings, poisonings, drug-related deaths, or death where the circumstances are open to question; Pluto, in conjunction with other indicators could be involved in murder, sabotage, mass deaths, and sex crimes.

If there is a Venus component in the astrology of an accident, it is probably not an accident component, *per se*, but rather an index of inconvenience or distaste with the circumstances. (Note: with illness, any planet can potentially be involved, since even 'benefics' rule various types of ailments.)

Illness
Look to the ascendant (the physical body) and both the natal and progressed sixth cusp (how the body either adjusts to stress or falls ill).

The character of the illness will be described by the planets involved with afflictions to the sixth cusp. Saturn chronic, hard-to-shake, perhaps affecting the bones, teeth, or skin. Uranus can be a critical illness, Mars a feverish one, Jupiter involving the blood, Venus involving the sugar metabolism and, with women, the female system. (For an excellent guide to astrological signatures of illnesses, see *Encyclopaedia of Medical Astrology* by H. L. Cornell, Samuel Weiser Inc., New York.)

The sixth cusp will generally show what is wrong, but you will also find overt symptoms coming through the ascendant.

Travel and Relocation
The ninth cusp shows long trips, but also watch the ascendant and the progressed Moon. The reason for travelling might also register, such as the tenth house for business reasons, the fifth/eleventh house axis for social ones, Mercury to facilitate communication, Jupiter to broaden the outlook or exercise personal freedom.

Permanent relocation will invariably involve the ninth and fourth cusps. In one instance, a decision was made about a major relocation when the progressed ninth and fourth cusps reached the same degree number as the ascendant, and many planetary stations (including the decision-maker, Mercury) hit that same degree number at once.

Birth of Children

For a woman's chart this will usually register strongly, and sometimes with a man, but not with the same regularity. For a woman's chart, look to the natal and progressed fifth cusp and its aspecting, also the ascendant, which may receive aspecting from the Moon or Venus. Afflictions from transiting Uranus to the natal or progressed fifth can indicate Caesarian (or abortion), and Neptune involved with the fifth may indicate an out-of-wedlock birth.

Every now and then a woman will claim nothing of import happened in the life but marriage and birth of children. This usually is not true, as further questioning might reveal, but you can work with it, especially if there were some distinguishing features of the births, like complications or great joy. One mother said she didn't understand why with one particular child (she had several) she didn't feel maternal, right from the start. The progressed Moon was found squaring Saturn and not in aspect with first or fifth cusp at all. More commonly, the progressed Moon will be involved with one of those cusps, especially for a first birth.

Dramatic Personal Changes

An unexpected boon, or a change marked by great excitement or fast-paced action is often marked by Uranus, often involving the angles. With Uranus, part of the life may be shattered, which can be painful and/or constructive, but always has a quality of shock, suddenness, upset or electric excitement.

Very sudden major changes can also come under Chiron. If over an angle, this can sometimes signal an instantaneous transformation, like you were suddenly 'beamed' to another point on the planet Earth. Suddenly things are possible that were not possible before. Perhaps your life is more sedate, but Chiron will still tend to open new perspectives.

Neptune can add a touch of mystery or glamour to life, but will not be the mainstay of major change. Pluto does not bring 'upbeat' changes in the life, though one may *emerge* from Pluto transits with major changes intact—gained 'the hard way'.

Learning Pursuits

Education, *per se*, comes under third/ninth house rulership. But any new study or philosophy, therapy, or even group educational pursuits (which might come under the eleventh house) can show their effects on the ascendant.

Learning skills which will further the career may well involve a major progression involving the natal and/or progressed midheaven.

Self-knowledge and self-improvement in the health areas, whether physical or mental health, would have a sub-rulership of the sixth/twelfth house axis.

Mercury will tend to register with communication, computer or clerical skills, Venus with artistic skills, Mercury/Mars for manual skills, Mercury/Uranus for mathematical skills, Jupiter for philosophy, Mercury and the outer planets for psychology (though this study is so often related to personal motivations that the immediate planetary impulse may vary from chart to chart), Neptune for spiritual studies. The Sun can also be integrally involved with any efforts at self-improvement and enhanced capabilities.

Don't neglect Chiron for learning experiences, even if you are not familiar with this planet on a routine basis. This may or may not be involved with school learning configurations, but can be a quintessential component of what we loosely call, 'learning about life'. Chiron opens new perspectives mentally, shows specific usefulness of previously-untapped resources, and can give life a whole new compass and design, sometimes with astounding rapidity. Views of the meaning of life may be radically altered under Chiron influence.

PART SEVEN:
ADDENDUM—SPECIAL USES
OF THE RECTIFIED CHART

INTRODUCTORY NOTE

When we speak of a rectified chart, we are now speaking of a chart with exact-to-the-minute accuracy or very nearly so. Even two minutes' discrepancy in the birth time would create a difference of ½° on the midheaven, and over a degree on the ascendant with some charts, which makes a substantial difference in the chart's timing, certainly substantial enough to violate the one-degree orb stricture, without which we could not have successfully rectified the chart at all.

The exacting rectification process has also been a *dynamic* process, breaking the static natal chart out of its insulated shell into the fluidity of passing time.

Traditionally, the natal chart, often cast for an approximate time, has been used for delineation of character traits, aptitudes and characteristic life patterns and experiences. For some, this is the *sole* function of the chart: *descriptive*. It is perhaps something like a still life painting which describes some layout of fruit or flowers or, more aptly, an index of 'what you are like' without any special reference to what you were like at two-and-a-half or twenty-five or fifty-one, before or after coming into your own, in a sheltered environment versus out in the world, before or after marriage, and so on. The richness of past scenarios, the range of present options, and even a constructive look ahead are blocked, clouded, rendered vague or inaccessible when the astrologer's timing tool, the natal chart, is inexact.

Each tense of time perception—past, present and future—is made more accessible, enhanced, vivified, specified, enriched when the basic timing tool is honed to exactitude. A suggested guide follows for some specialized uses and approaches in the course of one's practical work.

24.
PAST TENSE

The Astrological Biography
There are two basic ways in which a rectified chart can assist in understanding the past which an inexact chart cannot: historical, objective use, and personal, one-to-one use. The former is epitomized in *the astrological biography*.

History often gives us an incomplete understanding of the lives of the famous or infamous. Scores of fascinating lives leave vast amounts of information 'about' them, but their inner motivations, their overriding direction, and the underlying structure of their development can remain a mystery. It is a bit difficult to 'read minds' with the living, more so with those long since gone. The surface details rarely suffice to put outer events into the unique personal perspective that an accurate natal chart reveals.

However, those very surface details, such as numerous, exactly-dated events of the life, can be invaluable in *rectifying* the chart in question, from which chart a vast amount of additional information can then be gleaned. Using whatever information is available and documented, with photographs or portraits as an invaluable guide to narrowing in on the ascendant, it is a fascinating puzzle to apply the principle of 'relative determinism' to match sequences and more finely-honed astrological patterns to the given life history and, if enough biographical information is available, to locate the true time of birth. It is not as easy as having a verified and complete account of events from the native personally, but assuming your initial narrowing-down of the chart's space is accurate, the chart's timing patterns may well gel with the known information well enough and over long enough spans of time that the true birth chart may be ascertained.

An earlier book, *A Magic Moment: Bach and Beyond* (Laurie

Efrein, CAO Times, New York 1984), is a very comprehensive astrological biography, although many more incomplete examples of such are scattered throughout the astrological literature.

Understanding Motivation, Context and Effects of Past Events

In one-to-one work with the living native, a chronicling of life events is already provided to begin with, and simple verification that they are reflected in the chart is the usual starting point. However, you will also gain access to more information in the process.

Personal motivation, personal responses, and the pressures, conflicts, opportunities and even inevitabilities of circumstances are reflected in astrological configurations of the dates when major events happen in the life, even more revealing in that the natal chart—which is the permanent backdrop of experience—will now be accurate.

A real service an astrologer is in a position to perform is to simply *read what you see*—a 'playback' of what the astrology revealed happened. If the chart is truly accurate, you may find you have access to *more* information than the native provides, or clarification of the underlying context in which something came to pass. This will not only build the confidence of native in astrologer; it could clarify the meaning or purpose of life's odd or more difficult turns and, perhaps most important, it can *validate* the native's personal identity via validation of his experience—its relevance, its personal impact, and that it was indeed an integral part of a growing personal reality.

In some sense, past all the buffetings of circumstances, the greatest freedom can lie in the simple liberty to be oneself. No-one can appropriate our experience as theirs, or make it lived from another perspective on a say-so. Whatever is the personal matrix of experience, it is *valid to that person*. Sometimes life may deal us inscrutable cards, or so it seems; even for ourselves, we don't always understand why we responded as we did. But when its genuine appropriateness and personal validity shines through the chart, sometimes simply having that confirmed by someone who would 'have no way to know' is of greater assistance than any 'advice' that might be offered. Guilts may be spontaneously alleviated, or forgivenesses made. One can give oneself one's due. Burdens of the past may be re-assimilated, or accepted, even transmuted into stepping stones into the future. Our own chart, carrying the living currents of energy all the way from birth up to the present, can facilitate these internal bridges in a way that 'counsel' cannot.

The best lead-ins come directly from the astrology: 'The astrology suggests that. . .,' or 'This looks like it was notable in many ways. . .' If you think that using astrology for simple validation of what has happened in the life and its effects is not of itself 'therapeutic', you may be underestimating both your craft and your client. But without the exact timing tools of the accurate natal and progressed chart, you are severely hindered from performing this oft-times invaluable service.

There are two other tremendous advantages in being able to 'read' past events in the life with precision. One is that since you will be touching upon the actual energy patterns of what had been, the native is enabled to resynchronize with those feeling tones and swerves of circumstance, while also being eased into greater rapport with *both self and astrologer*, which will aid greatly in any continuing interchange.

The other advantage is that it sinks the astrologer into rapport with the native! The 'separation' between native's past, native and astrologer is bridged via validation of the native's own identity and the strength and worth of his experience. But to do this accurately and well, those narrow 'mathematical windows' will need to be intact; otherwise, this major tool for rapport and validation may be lost.

As a 'capper', this approach to the native's past can also enable the astrologer to open doors much more rapidly, and ground can be covered in a single session or two, rather than stringing the work out to ten or twelve. This even if one considers oneself a 'counsellor'. Psychologists are often slowed down, or thrust into a passively receptive role—not just to gain a client's trust or other purely human factors, but realistically, because *they are in the dark until the client himself reveals not only 'what happened' but also its effects*. The astrologer can constructively surface the past in ways to which the psychologist has no access.

Naturally, I would add a note of caution here. This is not a book primarily on counselling, nor should astrologers necessarily come right out with whatever they see in charts. How and when to impart information can bring many subtle skills into play which are not the subject of this book. The key, however, is having *access* to the native's past, something which an accurate chart facilitates beyond measure.

25.
PRESENT TENSE

The Function of Counselling
There are many kinds of interchange between astrologer and client that might be termed 'counselling'. Not all of them relate to the native needing 'help', in the sense of having psychological problems. The astrologer has access to special tools which are indices to the flow, currents, quality and circumstances of living, as well as a key to potentials that are uniquely one's own. Many types of 'counsel' can use an astrological basis, for practical, material, interpersonal, occupational or various other types of personal affairs—or simply for enhancement of self-understanding rooted in one's own identity, the unique natal chart.

Timing is always a key to good astrology. But psychological counselling, a major current emphasis in the astrological field, epitomizes its importance, so we will focus our attention there.

The purpose of such counselling, expressed in a simplified way, is to assist in coping with present reality. A key is frequently the integration, or access between the several time tenses since, aside from purely objective current factors, many present difficulties may stem from either difficulties in the past, patterns from the past that are inappropriate for the present, or lack of mobility in adjusting from past to present contexts, or from present contexts into the future. In regard to the present/future, there may be fear of the future as an unknown, or fear that the future might repeat the past, or fear that the future might demand resources not hitherto available, or perhaps blocked off in the past.

In any case, there is virtually no aspect of counselling which does not somehow incorporate the passage of time and how that impacts/has impacted/will impact upon the native.

Coping with Time Displacement

Many psychological problems have a basis in varying forms of time disorientation, or time displacement. This includes the phenomena of transference, projection, blocks and repressions, in that the native is 'living in the past' in some area of his mind, creating an inappropriate or ineffective present reality. Many assume that the major root of such is that the native is 'in' childhood, relating to his parents instead of relating objectively to his current circumstances and adult needs. Of itself, this approach is neither productive nor counter-productive, since even if that element is involved, using it as a primary focus may reinforce rather than alleviate underlying distress, blocking the way to other choices and options by grounding the native in past rather than present reality. It is a continuing paradox, how to enable someone to 'break out of the past' without *returning* to that past, which may involve (at least momentarily) getting into even greater distress than was posed by present-day problems.

This is where the use of the natal chart, without access to the chart's timing patterns, can be counter-productive. The underlying assumption may readily be that once the native can 'handle his Mars/Saturn square' or his Venus/Pluto conjunction, and so on, his present reality may be spontaneously altered. Without discounting the value of this common approach to astrology (since any facet of accurate analysis has its value), it limits the use of astrology to being a *diagnostic* tool, and moreover one which can easily become as static and immobile as the native's *problems* appear to be.

Much more mobile, flexible, and suggestive of productive options is the astrologer's skill in assessing not just 'the native in the past' (which for many does seem to be 'frozen into' the natal chart), but also the native in the present and the native in the future, which cannot be assessed with any sophistication or precision without an accurately-timed chart. If the native has indeed 'displaced' his present reality into the past, having the astrologer reinforce that displacement could result in many a painful—and oft-times preventable—deadlock.

Accurate timing of a chart can assist the astrologer in determining *when* certain conflicts may have been (originally) activated in the past, whether present distress is, in fact, an activation of the same or is not the current focus at all, what the future will bring into central focus for the most fruitful personal development and, especially . . . exactly *when*.

Breaking Pattern

Timing tools—*which specifically synchronize with changing and mobile perspectives*—are needed if the counsell*or* is not to remain stuck in the same static patterns as the counsell*ee*! Assisting change is difficult when one is continually staring at the natal chart, the natal chart, and the natal chart. Not only could whatever is 'wrong' be most effectively *reinforced* that way, but that much-touted 'road-map of the psyche' could easily be cast for the wrong birth time, in which case, the 'road-map' is truly for 'destination unknown'!

Shifting astrological indicators suggest both a pace and direction of growth and change. Enabling someone to know *when* it is appropriate and opportune to break pattern and *how* and, conversely, seeing ahead to where some proposed change might bring further difficulties and in what respect is extraordinarily helpful in several specific ways.

First, the native is assisted in tuning into his natural instincts, a rhythm which may have been disrupted by the propensities towards ineffective or destructive personal choices which may occur with lack of acceptance and understanding of one's true feelings and needs. Things don't happen by 'accident', but we may also suffer separation from the more constructive forms of 'design'. People with a constructive outlook towards life will tend to gravitate towards propitious timing for various types of undertakings. When that rhythm is disturbed, hence the native dissatisfied or damaged, an astrologer cannot discern the difference between 'good' and 'bad' times chosen if the timing tool, the natal chart, is not accurately-cast. Be this the case, the astrologer has no better idea whether the native is entering into something at a natural, comfortable or beneficial time than would any ordinary psychologist.

If the astrologer *can* discern the difference however, aided by precise timing tools, then the native can be assisted in learning to gauge internally what responses are the most natural, effective, harmonizing, integrating, appropriate and so on.

Opportune timing also gives a much greater probability of success in breaking through previously-blocked or difficult areas. Especially when one has had *little* success in whatever area of life, the native may gravitate towards stressful or non-productive times to try and 'break through'—perhaps a little like a woman trying to become pregnant at the wrong time of the month. A good astrologer can spare many an individual unnecessary disappointment, anxiety and stress. Success with opportune timing also assists in speeding up the process of self-knowledge, and opening up areas of the native's own perceptual processes that may have been blocked, conflicting, repressed or underactive.

Reality Orientation

Timing precision enables the astrologer to be supportive and constructive regarding *actual real circumstances*, not just constructed or fantasy circumstances, or internal complexes. This is a parameter of genuine objectivity to which the ordinary psychologist does not have ready access—even a good psychologist would not have access as *readily* as an equally-good psychologist who is also an astrologer. The psychologist will in some sense 'go blind' many times when astrological expertise could have properly identified the elements of current concern: how they may reflect the past, how they may differ, and the range of resources currently available to the native.

Neither psychologist nor astrologer has had the opportunity to live with a client through all the many experiences which may have brought him to his current juncture, which means both have to use whatever tools are at their disposal to transpose what they observe into the larger context of the native's life as a whole. Psychologists, since what *they* are exposed to directly is just what the native says and the way he acts in this current moment—and we are not discounting that here, merely broadening its context—may well tend to assume that that must contain the key to his current problems. Astrologers, since what is most readily apparent to *them* is the natal chart (many astrologers barely glance at the native himself) may readily assume that the 'cause' of current distress is one or another 'complex' which the natal chart specifies.

Having *both* vantage points, incidentally—that of the psychologist and that of the astrologer—can lead to assuming that current behaviour is essentially a direct reflection of whatever may be the astrologer's own 'internal reference guide' of the meaning of a Mars/Saturn square or a Venus/Pluto conjunction, which may also be a serious limitation of its own.

Neither of these views, of course—current/surface for the psychologist, and birth-generated/pervasive for the astrologer—are 'wrong', and both are useful. But each has static properties of its own, with liabilities of stultifying one's view of 'reality'. However, the mediation of *time linkages* inter-threading one's basic identity (the natal chart) with one's current life experience (the progressed chart and one's current behaviour) can render the native's reality more fluid and flexible, freeing the individual into new options and perspectives. Analysis alone rarely accomplishes one's purpose; it is the altered handling of *time* in which change and growth occurs. If we indeed want to help someone into a new 'space', we are best able to do it by tracking and pacing his 'time'! A timed view of reality can *incorporate* both the psychologist's and the natal astrologer's fortés and transpose them beyond their static domains into opportunities for enhanced personal freedom.

Another word might be offered regarding reality orientation. One trend of twentiety-century astrology has been to move away from specifics involving the physical native and material changes in his life, but rather to transpose our astrological information into 'symbols'. The native can change his life, some assert, if only he relates to 'symbols' and 'archetypes'. Some say that 'events' in the life, in and of themselves, have no meaning, only our response and awareness impart a meaning to them.

Somehow the chart alone 'isn't enough'. It has no 'meaning' unless it is interpreted, nor can the native grasp what astrology is or does without *our* delving into cycles and phases, mythological references or systems of symbolism. Only recently have astrologers here and there begun to question whether symbolism and archetypes are an effective way to get through to this apparently dense fellow, the native. The apparent reality that the energy currents represented in the chart are effective in life changes for everyone, even if they know no astrology at all, is somehow discounted in favour of more abstract concerns.

Without discounting the potential value of abstract thought, it is sometimes the best way to lose a handle on the timing of the chart! If one does not demand that real life circumstances match up with corresponding astrological indicators with precision, the norm can readily become wrong natal charts rather than accurate ones, and all the ensuing discrepancies of delineation, even natal delineation. For delineation of timing indicators, of course, the problems become that much more compounded.

The suggestion offered is to solidify the chart's read-out of timing indicators *vis-a-vis* the real, material changes of the life *before attempting other types of delineation at all.*

Contexts: Chart Context, Life Context
As was illustrated in Figure 6 (p. 50), two charts cast just one hour apart can contain exactly the same aspects, but in a vastly different

context. This transposes to the 'same' energies functioning in different *areas* of the life (houses), and set within a different overall approach to life (the ascendant).

This is context within the fixed natal chart. Series of changing and/or repetitive contexts are also successively created throughout the course of life, which the astrologer can effectively track as needed. For example, under what type of aspects did an 'accident-prone' native characteristically have accidents? Under what types of aspects have relationships characteristically been entered into and/or terminated? What types of configurations have characteristically produced high stress? Three different natives could have the 'same' experience with significant variations in aspecting. Seeing the exact aspecting of repetitive or problematical junctures in the life may give the best guide for constructive counsel.

Counselling Itself is a Timed Process

There will be many clients an astrologer will only see once, unless one happens to be in the counselling profession, in which case, there will be some underlying understanding that this is a process which will extend over many sessions. Even if it is a once-only situation, it is still significant that the native has come to the astrologer at some specific point in *time*; and for continuing sessions, use of the ongoing time continuum can be a most constructive therapeutic tool.

If the native has come to the astrologer specifically because of some unresolved problems, the native's perception may be that everything will hinge upon what will be happening in the life in the immediate future. It is certainly useful to assess what the native is heading *towards*, through examining the current timing indicators. Many a time, crisis, insecurity or even, in some instances, danger can either be warded off or better managed with advance preparation. Note, this does *not* mean a 'doom and gloom' approach to prognostication, especially since the words '*will* happen' (rather than 'might' or 'could') should be used extremely sparingly in regard to anything of a so-called 'negative' character in the life. But you can't rely upon the *natal* chart for a realistic assessment of the immediate future— you need timing indicators to do that. And if you are looking for constructive growth and change, and your guideposts in the chart are not at their true positioning, you could be in an unhelpful position yourself.

The astrologer can also use timing indicators to assess when the native might be best prepared to cope with specific types of suggestions or insights, or in a condition of receptivity to a new course of living. For example, if you see (transiting) Neptune exactly squaring the native's ascendant as you speak, you go right ahead and blurt out some straight-from-the-hip advice, and then wonder why the native appears disoriented and 'not taking it too well', perhaps it is the astrologer's delivery that was in error! On the other hand, if you see Mars and Jupiter gracing the ascendant harmoniously, the native's energy level and self-confidence is in a different state, and the same words might have both a very different effect upon the native personally, and a more effective implementation in his life.

Along these lines, I would repeat: don't look at just the chart; observe the *native*. Look for the responses that appropriately match up with the astrology you are looking at. That very rapport process will assist both astrologer in offering guidance and native in assimilating it.

26.
FUTURE TENSE

Timing Clusters

A great deal of predictive work is performed within routine formats such as the yearly forecast, and by 'compartmentalization', such as 'This is what the year looks like for money, this is what it looks like for romance', and so on. Without commenting on its value—since anything that is *accurate* can be of value—we might note that this is focused upon set periods of time and a set number of routine 'compartments' of life without necessarily considering what the natural organic patterning of astrology (natal, progressed, transiting) may suggest for any individual chart. One area of life or a special complex of concerns may be conspicuously dominant in the days to come, plus its timing may not conform to a yearly or monthly format at all!

I would suggest as an alternative (or supplement), the use of what I call 'timing clusters', which an exactly-accurate chart will facilitate spotting. Just as partials showed graphically the multiple convergences of different orders of aspects, such aggregates, or 'timing clusters' will periodically coalesce again and again in the shifting and changing currents of energy into the future.

First look to major progressed aspects involving the angles currently, read out the possible range of life options they suggest for confirmation from the native. Then you can assess the transits of the outer planets and the progressed Moon first, to narrow in on periods when happenings of a more specific character might be likely to happen. Give special attention to planetary stations affecting the angles. You will find that the 'shorter timers', such as Venus and Mercury will figure in once something has actually happened, but will not generally be immediately helpful in prognostication work. Do, however, keep an eye on retrograde periods for these planets, as well as for Mars, Jupiter and Saturn. Uranus, Neptune, Pluto and Chiron will spend many months over the year (cumulatively) in retrograde motion, so the effects in ordinary affairs of the life are a little more subtle, but *stations* of those planets against the chart can be very important.

When you find a 'timing cluster' involving many factors from different orders of aspects and involving angular positions then, assuming your chart is accurate, you can mark that as a period of high activity in the native's experience to come, and see what the astrology suggests about its specifics.

Specific Areas of Life

In regard to predictive work about specific areas of the life, usually some request will be made about particular areas of interest to the native currently in regard to future prospects. Since the chart's cusps are now exact—marking life's *circumstances*—these vital tools for prognostication are now precise.

Sometimes—although it is not the subject of this book—horary astrology will be the most expeditious way to cope with specific questions about the future. But a question might not be that clear-cut, and whereas horary can be extraordinary for clarification of objective factors bearing upon a current situation, the natal (and progressed) chart should not be disregarded. Moreover the question itself may well fall into some ongoing flow of trends and events which are specified by the directions coming up.

When the client poses a concern, look at the current directions to see if that is an area which the current timing of the chart highlights. If it is not, then perhaps the native's interest can either be constructively redirected or set into a more incorporative framework.

The second thing the astrologer can do is to check the natal chart to see if this might be a continuing or usual concern, and round out the perspective on the prognostication by relating it to the 'home base' of the client's orientation on the matter.

The third, sometimes most useful thing the astrologer can do is to check out 'If not now, *when*', by tracing out the areas of the life enquired about through the chart to when a breakthrough or overt concentration of interest in the requested area will be facilitated.

Rebound Predictions

This involves looking at the natal chart and the history of exact configurations of events that are in the past, to see if what is coming up relates to the same concerns and/or areas of life. If parallels, differences, repeats, new turns or new options can be relayed about what is coming up *in relation to* what happened before, new experience can be approached and assimilated within the personal context of life experience to date.

It is helpful (always!) to refer to *specifics*. A client may not be a student of astrology, but what has happened to him does have exact references to its astrological representations whether he has studied astrology or not. So instead of simply saying, for example, 'The last time you went home you felt afraid of what would happen, but now you may be able to come to grips with it and assert your own identity', it is often not 'too technical' at all, but rather helpful to point out, 'You see, the last time you went home, there was this Saturn square *here*, and its effect was that you felt constrained to express yourself and apprehensive about what might happen; but now your progressed Sun is *here*, sextile the natal ascendant and your overall confidence level is higher . . .', and so on through whatever aspects spell out the native's enhanced preparation/maturity/understanding.

Especially when situations are difficult, people often want something they can 'put their finger on'. Astrology does that literally!—and though showing an exact configuration may seem 'technical', it *is* the expression of what the native has been going through, and pointing to it and showing it affirms its 'presence' and also its meaning in the course of chart reading. Many people can cope with almost anything much better if they are clued in to its 'reality', and the astrologer has superb tools to elucidate that, the native's expertise or its lack being nearly beside the point. (Of course, if the client is of a temperament not to want such elucidations, by all means use something else! There is nothing that will work for everyone.)

There is also a subtle connection that may be drawn between the 'reality' of the past and the 'reality' of the future, which, when concretized by spoken and/or graphic focus, can assist in having the native draw inner connections independently, since just as the chart prescribes that once a ninth house matter always a ninth house matter, so is it for the *native*. You are simply surfacing the connections that are already there anyway, facilitating coming into the future out of an enhanced grounding in the past.

I call this 'rebound prediction' work, or perhaps 'cross-tense references' might say it just as well. The principle is that of relating to the future out of a context of not just the life as a whole but the backdrop of specifically relevant previous experiences.

The Solar Return Chart

There is another added bonus for predictive work using an exactly-accurate chart. The solar return chart will be an accurate index to the year ahead. That chart, bear in mind, will always be off by exactly the same measure of time as the natal chart. If the natal chart was cast for a time twenty minutes too early, for example, every solar return chart cast for that entire life will be cast twenty minutes too early!

The Responsible Astrologer

Last, but certainly not least, exactitude of working tools facilitate the astrologer assuming a responsible role in regard to any type of prognostication work. Looking into the future, with its fluid, malleable currents of change carries liabilities and responsibilities that delving into the relatively solidified past lacks. The way the native learns about 'his future', even if in suggestive or non-directive terms, may well impact upon how he thinks or acts, which could itself facilitate or detract from how an unfolding reality comes into being. This means that the astrologer's responsiblity might be said to be extended from the present time of reading into a time further ahead; and an astrologer without an accurate chart is hindered at best both in regard to the direction of prognostication and in regard to its specificity.

With many, other faculties besides technical expertise may well come into play: intuitive capacities, rapport and empathy, and various types of communication skills. There isn't any positive personal quality which cannot be a great asset in one-to-one work—in fact, counselling certainly carries many purely interpersonal, non-technical responsibilities which simply do not happen to be the subject of the present book. However, part of conveying any information responsibly involves the astrologer recognizing where his/her work has a technical back-up and where it doesn't. However effective a role intuition, empathy and communication skills may assume in conveying the native's future prospects, that is not the province of astrology *per se*, and it is responsible to clarify for the native where and/or how a statement, proposal or suggestion regarding the future life is rooted in the *astrology*—natal, progressed or transiting indicators—as distinct from what emerges on other levels of interchange.

Meanwhile, the self-evident factor astrologically is that one can unquestionably do more accurate and objective predictive work when the natal chart is cast for the true minute of birth. I close with the encouragement to find as many of those 'needles in the haystack' as possible, to achieve a level of competence and effectiveness befitting every constructive potential of modern practitioners of astrology.

INDEX